THREE PEAKS, TEN TORS

About the Author

Ronald Turnbull is based in southern Scotland, and has a particular interest in multi-day backpack trips over rough country, and in challenge walks both established and self-devised. He has achieved comfortable nights without tent on 70 UK hilltops; research for this book led to sleep-outs on Ben Nevis, Snowdon, Kinder Scout and Black Tor. He also enjoys hut-to-hut trips across hot, rocky and Spanish-speaking bits of Europe.

He has won the Outdoor Writers' Guild Award for Excellence in four separate categories: for a series of articles in *Lakeland Walker* magazine (2005); for a guidebook to the Coast to Coast Walk (1999); for two outdoor books, Cicerone's *Book of the Bivvy* (2002) and the Ben Macdui biography *Life and Times of the Black Pig* (2007); and for a words-and-pictures feature, 'Cairngorms Crag and Bag', in *TGO* magazine. In 1994 he won the Fell Running Association's Long-distance Trophy for a 10-day run over all the hills of southern Scotland.

He is seen here revisiting his first-ever hill, Pew Tor on Dartmoor, on the second day of his Ten Tors walk.

THREE PEAKS, TEN TORS

Long-distance and challenge
walks in the UK:
Tools and Techniques,
Routes and Reminiscences

by
Ronald Turnbull

CICERONE

2 POLICE SQUARE, MILNTHORPE, CUMBRIA, LA7 7PY
www.cicerone.co.uk

© Ronald Turnbull 2007
ISBN-10:   1 85284 501 5
ISBN-13:   978 1 85284 501 8
Reprinted 2010 (with updates)

A catalogue record for this book is available from the British Library.
Printed by MCC Graphics, Spain.
Photographs © Ronald Turnbull unless otherwise stated.

Section photograph captions: p17 sunrise from Snowdon summit; p74 descending
from Joppe Knowe on the Lancashire Three Peaks walk; p102 author on Pew Tor,
Dartmoor; p158 crossing the Lowther Hills on the Southern Uplands Fifty; p184
evening on the Welsh 3000s, ascending Snowdon from Llanberis Pass

Dedication

Solo walking around something you invented yourself can be very satisfying.
But so too can a route carefully worked out in advance by some kind person
who knows the country; especially when several dozen more kind people are
standing along that route with fruit cake and blister plasters. So this book is
dedicated to the organisers of the organised walks. In particular the Long Distance Walkers' Association and its local groups have lured me onto the annual
Hundred, the Hardy Annual, the Across Wales Walk, the Wellington Boot,
That's Lyth, and a dozen others not mentioned in this book.

Advice to Readers

Readers are advised that, while every effort is made by our authors to ensure the
accuracy of guidebooks as they go to print, changes can occur during the lifetime
of an edition. Please check Updates on this book's page on the Cicerone website
(**www.cicerone.co.uk**) before planning your trip. We would also advise that you
check information about such things as transport, accommodation and shops
locally. Even rights of way can be altered over time. We are always grateful for
information about any discrepancies between a guidebook and the facts on the
ground, sent by email to info@cicerone.co.uk or by post to Cicerone, 2 Police
Square, Milnthorpe LA7 7PY, UK.

Front cover: Members of the Long Distance Walkers' Association on Scout Scar,
Cumbria, at the start of a 25-mile winter challenge walk

CONTENTS

Key to route maps

■ land above 1200m		🏠	bothy or youth hostel
□ 1050 – 1200m		⌇	routes
□ 900 – 1050m		⌇	alternative routes
□ 750 – 900m		⌇	other paths
□ 600 – 750m		▬	A roads
□ 450 – 600m		▬	minor roads
□ 300 – 450m		- - -	national or county boundaries
□ 150 – 300m		🯄	start/finish point
■ land below 150m		⟶	direction of route

On summit detail maps, contour colours change at 50m intervals

Location of the walks

Tranter's Walk

Cairngorm 4000s

Lairig Ghru

△Ben Nevis

Southern Upland 50

Lakeland 3000s

Scafell Pike△

Lyke Wake Walk

Old County Tops

○ Yorkshire Three Peaks

○ Lancashire Three Peaks

The Seven Sevens

Welsh 3000s

Snowdon △○

Derwent Watershed

Across Wales Walk

Somerset Three Peaks

Ten Tors

N

Descending Snowdon towards Y Lliwedd after a night at Snowdon summit on an extended version of the Welsh 3000s walk

INTRODUCTION

Ever since man came down out of the trees, stood on two legs, and started to walk, some other fellow has been trying to walk further. The fields and fells of England, the mountains of Wales, the forests and drove roads of Scotland: these are all about healthy exercise, the loveliness of the landscape, the pleasure of good company. Except that, from time to time, they're not. They're about one (probably blistered) foot in front of the other, again and again, till you reach 30 miles or seven summits or some other arbitrary mark. That's what long-distance walking is all about.

Such self-inflicted suffering does have compensations. There's a genuine thrill in getting the view of Ingleborough from Pen-y-ghent at dawn, and 10 hours later the view of Pen-y-ghent from Ingleborough at sunset. Short walks, or even moderately long ones, can be frustrating – you have to come down just as the hills are getting interesting. Twice as far can, indeed, be twice as much fun.

Short-distance walking is a solitary, or small-group, experience. But a 'challenge walk' is often undertaken as part of an organisation or horde. The shared suffering and endeavour are more intense than life usually offers outside the field of football hooliganism. Lie down on the wooden floor of some village hall among 100 others who, tomorrow, will drip their sweat into a single furrow. As you stumble into the final checkpoint just after midnight on the following morning, be heartwarmingly applauded by the three people still awake.

What follows, then, is the 'how' of it – including, importantly, the 'how not'. Here is the 'where', with 16 routes in detail, plus the whole of the UK and the rest of your life in summary. Here is the 'why', or sometimes the 'why not', in stories of sore legs and sunrises, of Ben Nevis by bus and the underground route up Ingleborough. Here is how to minimise the suffering, to stay safe, to raise money for charity perhaps, and to find a surprising amount of enjoyment along the way.

The routes

Ultimate walks come in and out of fashion. These last few years everyone's been doing the **National Three Peaks**, meaning Snowdon, Scafell Pike and Ben Nevis (the highest mountains in Wales, England and Scotland respectively); this is described in detail in Part I. As training for the Three Peaks, try the Yorkshire version: Pen-y-ghent, Whernside and Ingleborough (Chapter 4). Meanwhile, the Lyke Wake Walk (Chapter 9), once justly famous as the most horrible 40 miles of peat in the east, is almost forgotten.

Three Peaks also means Yorkshire: Ingleborough from Whernside

The only fault of the favourites – if they have one at all – is a lack of imagination. The National Three Peaks is also environmentally dodgy as it involves driving around in cars and disturbing the folk of Borrowdale. So in the later parts of the book the thinking brain leads the legs into new and less-trampled lands. Part II introduces **Three Peaks Rather Closer Together**: the ones of Yorkshire, but also those of Somerset, South Wales, Ancient Cumbria. Use your imagination and your own local map; instead of following mindlessly in someone else's muddy footsteps, have the satisfaction of wandering into a solitary bog that's entirely of your own devising.

Fellwalking is the invention of the late 18th century: Coleridge on the Helvellyn Ridge at midnight, Wordsworth on Snowdon. Challenge walking, at about the same era, can trace its origins to the 'I bet I could do that' attitude of the Regency bucks. Would it be possible to drive a flock of geese from Norwich to London? Can I, by using the Lairig Ghru, walk to Inverness quicker than the coach road? £2500 says that I can. Part III, **Moor and More**, steps back through history into the heather, finding a taste for the waste country of Britain: the Derwent Watershed where the hard men of the Rucksack Club did their 60 or 80 miles among the peat groughs (Chapter 10), the Cold War ethos of the 40-mile Lyke Wake Walk (Chapter 9), the Lairig Ghru itself (Chapter 12).

Part IV introduces the Long Distance Walkers' Association, its annual 100-mile challenge (Chapter 15), and how to prepare the feet (and more importantly the brain) for **Survival** of this grim and glorious event.

Despite the appeal of long-distance routes, it's hard to ignore the tradition of the last two centuries: the highest form of outdoor endeavour goes over the top of the mountain. What are 50 miles of forward motion without 15,000ft of uphill along the way? 100km of 'onwards' requires at least 5000m of 'up'. So hit the big-time on Snowdon and Slieve Donard, Coniston Old Man and the Cairngorms. There's the friend you've been meaning to visit who's 20, or 30, or 50 miles away from your own front door. And finally, for those with the hill skills and the really muscly legs, there's Tranter's fabulous round of 18 mountaintops around Glen Nevis (Chapter 20).

Ridgeline east of Hare Gap, Mountains of Mourne: the Seven Sevens walk is a classic unknown to those on the UK's larger island

How to use this book

Man is an animal with two legs at one end and an overactive imagination at the other. So this book feeds the mind as well as the feet. The descriptions of specific routes can be distinguished from the stories, advice, dreadful warnings and incitements, as the route descriptions are headed by boxed data sections. The routes described are also summarised in Appendix II.

The initial part is devoted to the National Three Peaks challenge: Snowdon, Scafell Pike and Ben Nevis. It does not give instruction in map reading and navigation, but otherwise is intended to be complete, giving all the information for even an uninitiated challenge-walker.

The following two parts cover walks that, while arduous, are not among crags and crowded contours. On the moorland walks of Part III, it is likely that an inexperienced walker who is both lost and ill equipped, and who is then hit by bad weather, is getting into a serious situation. Some competence at navigation and hillcraft is assumed, and so the route descriptions become briefer and less detailed. For the mountain walks in Part V, as well as for Dartmoor and the Lairig Ghru, hillcraft including competence with maps and navigation is essential, and the route descriptions in this book are a supplement to that.

Distances have been measured with a piece of cotton on 1:25,000 scale maps, and ascents by counting contour lines. Anquet mapping software gives distances that are 5 percent to 10 percent shorter, and ascents increased by about the same. Many authors add 10 percent or more for wiggles – so that the Lyke Wake Walk and the Lakes 3000s are often quoted at 45 miles. Not here; but if you need the extra 10 percent for boasting purposes, please add it back in.

The schedules are based on Naismith's Rule, whereby 1000ft of uphill counts as an extra 1.5 miles horizontal (100m of up as 0.8km), and then a speed of 3mph, dropping after a tiring amount of walking to 2.75mph (4.8kph dropping to 4.4kph). The formula fails where ground is rocky or especially rough, and also where steep, difficult slopes occur downhill. I have adjusted the timings accordingly. The resulting pace is described as the 'standard strong walker', who can manage the National Three Peaks in 24 hours. The column headed 'Ascent' is the total amount of 'up', taking account of any undulations.

The large-scale sketch mapping of the summits of Ben Nevis, Scafell Pike and Snowdon is as accurate as I can make it, and is intended to supplement (not replace) a walkers' map of the whole mountain. The other sketch maps are not intended for navigation on the hill. At various tricky corners, 8-digit grid references are given for GPS users: provided your GPS isn't blindsided by a steep slope or obstruction, these are good within 10 metres. If your GPS requires 10

Ben Nevis at sunset, seen from the Mamores on Tranter's Walk

digits, add a 5 or any other digit to the end of each 4-digit group. To convert to normal 6-digit grid references, remove the last digit of each 4-digit group.

In this book, 100m (no 'etres') is a vertical height, while 100 metres is horizontal. A 'track' is wide enough for four wheels; a 'path' isn't.

Information on mapping, access, public transport and accommodation is concentrated in Appendix 1.

So how does it happen?

A moment of inattention – a simple 'oh I guess so' – can so easily lead into a day and a night of serious non-stop walking. The human brain is super-sensitive to the slight increase in status achieved by crossing the Yorkshire Three Peaks, while conveniently blind to the pains ahead, and afterwards equally forgetful of the agony just passed. And so, after a hot bath and a beer, you find yourself saying 'well why not' to the Dartmoor Ten Tors (Chapter 8).

For Nature didn't design the human leg just for hanging trendy kitten heels or snakeskin trainers on the end of. A convenient way to operate the brake pedal and the clutch, yes – but feet do have other functions. We humans are long-distance landscape animals. So, late on a summer's day, I found myself heading

Path above Glenuig on the Cross Ross event, second day

through long green shadows beside a sparkling river into one of the loneliest glens of Northern Scotland. There, in a small deerstalkers' lodge, were 50 or so folk enjoying a song, the sound of the bagpipes, and a very large meal, with all the satisfaction of having – after 38 miles – finally stopped walking. Self-indulgent? Not a bit of it – we were raising money for the charity Children First.

In the morning it was up and over a clouded high pass, and down another great empty glen, where the peculiar inspiration of the organisers had provided checkpoint sustenance of greasy beefburgers and neat whisky. The man in kilt and sandals showed just how sensible that outfit is for thigh-deep river cross-ings, but modestly asked me not to photograph him in revealing mid-stream. At evening, through a rocky hill-slot, we looked out over Loch Duich, golden under low sunbeams. And it was all the more beautiful for being the Atlantic end to two days that began at the North Sea.

It may or may not raise very much money for charity. It's probably going to hurt. And nobody but ourselves is really going to be impressed. So let's get into our lightweight footwear, and go out and have some fun.

PART I:
THE NATIONAL THREE PEAKS CHALLENGE

Chapter 1
Introducing the Three Big Hills

Know your enemy, and he may become your friend. This ancient Gaelic proverb (actually made up by me a moment ago) doesn't apply at all to midges or pay-and-display machines. But it does apply to mountains.

If you simply want your feet battered, Ben Nevis will do that for you. But leaping out in the dark and dashing up and down the Pony Path – what is this but a one-night stand? This hill is capable of a more fulfilling relationship. So start with some brief romanticism over a candlelit dinner. The chaps with the chat-up lines are Keats, Coleridge and Wordsworth.

BEN NEVIS

Can a man hope to be a late Romantic poet if he isn't already a hillwalker?

For Wordsworth and Coleridge, hillwalking was as important a part of their project as the poetry itself. Given such examples as Wordsworth's on Snowdon (see below) or Byron on Lochnagar, John Keats knew that if he was to rise to the heights of poetic inspiration, he had first to rise up some mountains.

He chose Ben Nevis, arriving there in August 1818 after a walk of 600 miles that had already taken in the Lake District and Loch Lomond. He was footsore, badly malnourished on a diet of eggs, oatmeal and whisky, and already ill after sleeping in wet clothes on the island of Mull. His ascent was not a success.

> *Upon the top of Nevis, blind in Mist!*
> *I look into the Chasms and a Shroud*
> *Vaprous doth hide them; just as much I wist*
> *Mankind do know of Hell...*

Ben Nevis is a hill of two halves – except that one of the halves has been carried away by a glacier, leaving a huge and extremely interesting hole on the northern side. Walkers on the normal path up the Ben see only the top edge of that hole, or even less if, like Keats, they get a day with the cloud down.

The Pony Path – the Tourist Path (or, as it's lately been renamed to make it sound more serious, the Mountain Track) – really is one of the dreariest things in hillwalking. It's stony, and relentlessly steep, and for its upper half loose and awkward as well. It takes the convex western flank of the hill, so as to look into

Ben Nevis, showing the great North Face not seen by ascenders of the Mountain Track

no hidden hollows, come among no crags (although crags do lie around and below, traps for those who stray). The view is simply Fort William, and Loch Linnhe, and the caravan site in Glen Nevis, all getting gradually further below; until you rise into the cloud and see not even them. On an urban treadmill in the gym you suffer as much, but you do at least get a television screen to look into.

At the top you have the comfort that now it's going to be downhill. Except that downhill turns out to be even worse. 'Twas the most vile descent,' says Keats, ' – shook me all to pieces.' Human legs and toes need an awful lot of walking before they can cope with 4406ft of continuous downhill on stones.

It's the other side of it – the side that isn't there – that makes Nevis into the wondrous mountain that it is: the highest in Scotland but also one of the finest. For here is the UK's largest crag, whose ridges and buttresses of grippy andesite lava give such alpine delights as the 2 miles of Tower Ridge or the 200m, mostly overhanging, of a climb called The Bat. Then winter comes. Damp Atlantic air rises against the mountainside, chills as it rises, and forms hoary crystals across the rocks. Centimetres deep, then inches, then feet; and along come the people with the bent ice-axes, to climb the frosted rocks, and the refrozen snow between, and the grey-green water-ice in the gullies. This is Scottish winter climbing, of all sports the most strange, dangerous and beautiful. Those who can climb the hard winter routes on the north face of Nevis are equipped for the Alps or the 8000m mountains of Nepal.

Here, too, at the back of the Ben, is the rock ridge that's for walkers. The Carn Mor Dearg Arête curves around the side of the great north face, with a straight-on view of it in any moments that walker can spare from surmounting the massive granite blocks. The CMD Arête is a mountain route that's higher and wilder even than Crib Goch on Snowdon. It's also slightly easier than Crib Goch, though the inspiring surroundings may distract you.

At the end of the Arête you clamber up 300m of jammed boulders or old snow. And suddenly you're on the crowded summit, where several hundred off the Tourist Route drape themselves over the ruins of an observatory, an emergency shelter in battered aluminium, or the various cairns and memorials. Since Keats, things have got yet more hellish on the sordid summit of Ben Nevis.

By Keats' time, Romanticism and hillwalking were already parting company – Shelley was a small boat man. In poetry, Romanticism was to evolve into Modernism, Post-Modernism and so on; while hillwalking strapped on its crampons to become mountaineering, and just kept going stronger and stronger. Today, for every poet still writing English Romanticism, there are roughly 100,000 hillwalkers carrying on that same tradition. And to understand why we are doing this thing up Ben Nevis, consult the *Prelude* of Wordsworth, and the mountain notebooks of S. T. Coleridge.

SCAFELL PIKE

We think of the rough, stony scenery of the Borrowdale Volcanic as the 'real' Lakeland, and shucks to you Skiddaw, worse luck Windermere. Scafell Pike is at the mid-point of that rough rock. Walk out along the ridges, and how far before you can lie down on the grass and have a nice picnic? Northwards over Gable to Brandreth – eastwards to Rossett Pike – west over Scafell to Illgill Head – you're faced with four hours of rugged walking before you get off the stones and boulders.

Naturalists have spotted, around the cairn of Scafell Pike, 5 flowering plants, 6 mosses, and 20 species of lichen. There's woolly hair moss, which looks like tufts of dead grass dropped by an eagle and too dried out to decompose. There's a lichen in the green-and-yellow colours of a Harveys map, which is called, appropriately, Map Lichen. And there's that rusty red lichen that looks like dried blood from when someone broke his leg among the boulders.

Scafell Pike, with the Wasdale ascent path (seen on the near slope), and Broad Crag behind

'Huge blocks and stones that lie in heaps on all sides to a great distance... which no human eye beholds, except the shepherd or traveller be led thither by curiosity: and how seldom this must happen!' – so Dorothy Wordsworth, after her ascent of 7 October 1818. Plenty of human eyes these days, of course. As Wainwright says: 'The summit cairn from afar looks like a hotel.'

Solitude and loneliness may have decreased since Dorothy's day; but alas, the rocks remain. Frost formed them, or more accurately frost-and-thaw, shattering the summit through the centuries after the Ice Age. But how come they're in such lumpy piles and strange upright shapes? This isn't mere frost action: this is malice. They got that way from leaping suddenly sideways under the walker's foot.

Nine times I've passed between the summit and Mickledore. Despite – or perhaps because of – the multitude of cairns I have never found more than part of the path. Always I end on the boulders, keeping one ankle out of one hole only for the other foot to slide sideways, requiring a quick leap on to a third of the boulders. The third boulder wobbles, and drops me in another hole.

Can there be a 'wrong' reason for climbing a hill? A walker on the Wasdale route was mystified when I admitted I'd been up more than 10 times. Did I try to do it a bit quicker each time? (Actually I keep trying to do it slower. My best time so far is 28 hours, starting from Coniston, with a night stop in Eskdale on the way.) To go up stony old Scafell Pike just because it's the highest in England must be better than not going up it at all. Mustn't it? Last word to a long-ago contributor to the Wasdale Head Farm Visitors' Book:

The Repentant Climber
Of Scawfell Pike I clomt the height;
And when I got upon it,
With all my soul, with all my might,
I wished I hadn't done it ...

Woe to the man on climbing bent!
He finds but falls and strains,
And mists, and much bewilderment,
And divers aches and pains ...

I scrambled down; my limbs, though sound,
Were most severly [sic] shaken;
Oft when I thought I'd reached smooth ground.
I found I was mistaken!

Let he who wills go climb the hills,
My taste with his don't tally;
Let he who wills go climb the hills,
But I'll stay in the valley!

SNOWDON

Snowdon is not only the highest in Wales – it's also the greatest, despite the mountain railway and the café. Great art – whether it's Beethoven, Breughel, or Robert Burns – is when you keep on coming back, and keep on finding something more. The same goes for great mountains.

Seen from the east, Snowdon is a perfect pointy mountain above a secret lake. Generously, Snowdon shows this profile even to motorists 8 miles away at Capel Curig. From Elidir Fawr, Snowdon is just the highest among a cluster of equally shapely summits: Moel Cynghorion and Moel Eilio and nearby

Snowdon, with Crib Goch left, as seen from Elidir Fawr on the Welsh 3000s walk

Nantlle. From the Glyders, you see Snowdon over the top of its jagged outlier Crib Goch.

The perfect mountain has various lesser but interesting outliers on the way up: and that's Snowdon. Moel Cynghorion, already mentioned, is a grass half-dome sliced off on the northern side. There's Y Lliwedd, a tall rocky edge with huge crags dropping to Llyn Llydaw; and there's Crib Goch, whose crags drop to Llyn Llydaw and also, on the other side, to the Pass of Llanberis.

The perfect mountain is rocks as well as grass and heather. Snowdon has the Lliwedd crag, main climbing ground of the 19th century; and, looking away to the west, the 20th-century Clogwyn du'r Arddu, where Joe Brown and Don Whillans hauled themselves over the overhangs and lay-backed mossy cracks high above the black tarn.

The perfect mountain descends into valleys on all sides: and that's Snowdon. You can take the Sherpa bus right around Snowdon's base, and a footpath is currently being planned as well. Thus you can go up any one of Snowdon's ridges and down whichever of the others may take your fancy.

23

And finally, the perfect mountain has ridges running all ways for walkers to walk up. Snowdon has eight. None of the eight is as dreary as the normal route up Ben Nevis, and Snowdon's own normal route is as romantic and dramatic as you could wish. The Pig Track is sometimes written as 'Pyg', by a sort of anti-acronym out of Pen y Gwryd. The path is actually named for Bwlch y Moch, the Pig Pass. And that pass takes you through to the big rocky hole in Snowdon, so that you're gazing down, suddenly and surprisingly, into the dark waters of Llyn Llydaw.

I've crossed the famous pinnacle ridge of Crib Goch in morning mist, and among the cheerful crowds of a summer afternoon. It's different again at dusk, when those pale, well-trodden holds gleam in the last of the light. Crib Goch is rocky, and there are big drops off it, but even so the main obstacles are other people. Another favourite way up Snowdon is from Nantgwynant, the one that heads into the col behind Yr Aran, to reach the summit by its sharp southern ridge. The rain flies sideways through the little rocky gaps, and the mist swirls in vertical circles behind the pinnacles, and it's all very satisfying.

But so are the other seven ways. Very satisfying is the gentle melancholy of the Miners' Track, with its abandoned buildings, and the cool air off the water, and dripping dark crags rising into dripping dark clouds – and then the path climbs into the second deep gloomy hole of Glaslyn. Very satisfying is the Ranger Path, on a day when the smooth grass is hot to lie on, and sunlight twinkles in the tarns in the bottoms of the various chasms, and there's time to stretch out that western ridge all the way to Moel Eilio.

Then there's the Snowdon Gribin, an excellent scramble as deserted as Crib Goch is busy. And again, the north flank, used on the Welsh 3000s expedition: an untrodden and intimidating way out of deepest Llanberis, by black crag and shining waterfall, onto a high green place hidden in Snowdon's steepest side. Here you can enjoy informal swimming in Llyn Glas before hitting Crib Goch's north ridge, or scrambling the Parson's Nose, or making a way onto a ridge of Carnedd Ugain.

Snowdon has always been irresistible. The Victorians found it so mountainous and exciting that they just had to build a railway up it; long before that, Welshmen and others were drawn to its lake hollows, its ridges and crags. Wordsworth climbed Snowdon in the 1780s, and wrote about his ascent in Book XIV of *The Prelude* (see below). Today's 'Centre for English Romanticism' is the Wordsworth Trust at Dove Cottage in Grasmere. Its late director Robert Woof considered that *The Prelude* is what Wordsworth's all about, and that Book XIV is the pivot of *The Prelude*. I find it slow-moving, interrupted as it is by an encounter with a hedgehog on the upward path that anticipates Mrs

Tiggywinkle on Catbells a century later. But it gets more exciting down the page, up the mountain, as he approaches at the summit still in the dark, and with the cloud down.

> When at my feet the ground appeared to brighten,
> And with a step or two seemed brighter still;
> For instantly a light upon the turf
> Fell like a flash, and lo! as I looked up,
> The Moon hung naked in a firmament
> Of azure without cloud, and at my feet
> Rested a silent sea of hoary mist.
> A hundred hills their dusky backs upheaved
> All over this still ocean; and beyond,
> Far, far beyond, the solid vapours stretched,
> In headlands, tongues, and promontory shapes ...
> In the clear presence of the full-orbed Moon,
> Who, from her sovereign elevation, gazed
> Upon the billowy ocean, as it lay
> All meek and silent, save that through a rift—
> Not distant from the shore whereon we stood,
> A fixed, abysmal, gloomy, breathing-place—
> Mounted the roar of waters, torrents, streams
> Innumerable, roaring with one voice!
> Heard over earth and sea, and, in that hour,
> For so it seemed, felt by the starry heavens.

> *The Prelude, Book XIV,* 1850 edition, line 35

Two hundred and twenty years later I was lucky enough to find myself at Snowdon's summit, at sunrise, above a cloud inversion. I'm only sorry that my pictures, done by the camera, aren't as good as Wordsworth's ones in words...

But enough of poetry. Our business on Snowdon is to touch the summit, turn round very quickly, and get down again before the clock stops.

Chapter 2

The National Three Peaks Challenge:
Ben Nevis, Scafell Pike and Snowdon within 24 hours

The hills	Ben Nevis (1344m), Scafell Pike (978m) and Snowdon (1085m)
Distance	44km (27.5 miles)
Ascent	2900m (9800ft)
Terrain	Paths, mostly reconstructed: possible navigation difficulties
Target time	14hrs (+10hrs driving)
Standard strong walker	13.5hrs

Getting up and down the highest hills of Scotland, England and Wales within a single day and night is a complicated undertaking. It involves car maintenance, comfort stops, charity fundraising, footcare, GPS programming, group dynamics, navigation, nutrition, physical training, reconnaissance, refuelling stops, route-finding, spare batteries, support driver's supper, and the phases of the moon. Really it was all so much simpler before the building of the M6, when anyone who did this did it on foot or in a small boat.

Training walks beforehand, and what to do with the rest of your life afterwards: these are dealt with in the later parts of this book. In about 30 pages from here, Chapter 3 attempts to simplify things, while at the same time introducing a whole lot of quite new complications, by doing it *without* the car. Here, I start by explaining why I think you should do Ben Nevis at the start and Snowdon at the end. After that, the book will simply begin at Ben Nevis and get going.

As you step onto the footbridge over the River Nevis, you won't be feeling intimidated by the hugeness of the hill ahead and the other two lurking down the road. You'll simply be so relieved that the organisational challenge is now, at last, almost over; all you've got to do is walk.

PLANNING

To ensure safe, legal driving, the time between the hills is fixed at 10hrs: Ben Nevis to Scafell Pike in 5.5hrs, and Scafell Pike to Snowdon in 4.5hrs. This

HOW BIG ARE THE THREE HILLS?			
	Distance mls/km	**Ascent** ft/m	**Time** hr/min
Ben Nevis (from Nevis Centre)			
UP	4.5/7.2	4400/1300	3.30
DOWN	4.5/7.2		2.00
Scafell Pike (from Borrowdale)			
UP	3.9/6.3	2900/900	2.40
DOWN	3.9/6.3		1.40
Scafell Pike (from Wasdale)			
UP	2.6/4.2	3000/900	2.30
DOWN	2.6/4.2		1.15
Snowdon			
UP from Pen-y-Pass	3.2/5.1	2400/700	2.30
DOWN to Pen-y-Pass	3.2/5.1		1.15
DOWN to Llanberis	4.3/6.9		1.30

leaves 14hrs for getting up and down the three hills themselves, with individual times as in the box above. This is not fellrunning (the fellrunning record for Ben Nevis is 1hr 25min). This is strong hillwalking, even allowing some time for putting things in the rucksack and taking them out again. The question is, will you still be a strong hillwalker by hill number 3?

Why Nevis first, and in the evening?

Every day, several dozen people make an uncomfortable discovery. Going up Ben Nevis is tough; but coming down again is worse. Cast your mind back to when you were a beginner hillwalker or, more recently, to the last time you did in your knees. And recall how that last 500ft of drop to the valley seemed like (and in terms of time and fatigue actually was) the equivalent of the lighthearted first 1500ft down from the summit.

The slowdown at the top end of a long ascent – and even more so at the bottom of a long descent – is far more marked when tired or slightly injured. When you're already tired and sore, the real pain kicks in after 2000ft of downhill. On Snowdon, that point will – with any luck – come 10 minutes *after* you finally arrive at Pen-y-Pass.

In summary: going up is tiring, but it's even more tiring when you're tired. And the same goes for going down. When you're fresh, the lower half of the huge descent of Ben Nevis may only be 10 minutes slower than the top half. When you're footsore and tired, it could be half an hour. Thus, it will save time to do the big hill at the beginning.

What also makes sense is to use the darkness for the driving. The M6 doesn't have any of those boulders to stumble over in the darkness, and it will be emptier too. Below the Half-Way Lochan (Lochan Meall an t-Suidhe) the Nevis path is wide, smooth and usually sheltered, and can comfortably be done in the fading of the day. Indeed, Nevis would be the easiest of the three to do in full darkness *provided you have the navigational skills to find your way off the summit.*

This all suggests doing Ben Nevis first, and in the evening. Consideration of the next hill confirms this.

Why Scafell Pike at dawn

Scafell Pike is best done in daylight, particularly the descent, because of the route-finding. Arriving early has the advantage of eliminating parking problems: at Seathwaite, the later you park, the further you are from the mountain. At either Seathwaite or Wasdale Head, the path starts at a campsite. The Institute of Fundraising's Charity Events Code (and common politeness) ask for no arrival before 5am.

Alternative start points on Scafell Pike and Snowdon

For Scafell Pike, the choice is between Borrowdale and Wasdale. Borrowdale is a shorter drive in, but is longer on the mountain, and with a route that's not straightforward (particularly in descent). The Charity Events Code asks large parties to use Borrowdale. Wasdale is a longer drive, but a shorter, if sharper, ascent. The time-chart above shows that attacking Scafell Pike out of Wasdale saves more than 30 minutes on the hill. However, this is mostly wiped out by the extra time required on the road. An interesting option for walkers with drivers in support is to ascend out of Borrowdale, but descend to Wasdale.

For Snowdon, Pen-y-Pass, at 300m above sea level, is the only sensible start. Parking at Pen-y-Pass is limited, and greatly in demand by ordinary hill-walkers. The Charity Code asks large parties to drop walkers off and then park at Llanberis, giving their contenders a full crossing of Snowdon and an extra 20 minutes or so of walking. Alternatively, descend to Pen-y-Pass, summon your vehicle up from Llanberis by phone, and wait for it in Gorphysfa Café; or else descend to it on the frequent Sherpa bus.

The journey plan below assumes Borrowdale, and Pen-y-Pass. Wasdale and Llanberis, and the extra-challenging Crib Goch route up Snowdon, are treated as variants and covered in the last section of this chapter (see page 51).

A NATIONAL THREE PEAKS SCHEDULE

Day 1

Glen Nevis	18:30
Ben Nevis half-way plateau	**20:00**
Ben Nevis summit	**21:30**
Ben Nevis half-way plateau	**22:30**
Ben Nevis foot	**23:30**
Glen Nevis dep	23:30

Day 2

Tyndrum	00:35
Stirling Services	01:45 first all-night fuel
Stirling Services dep	01:55
Abington Services M73	02:45
Southwaite Services M6	03:40
Southwaite dep	03:55
Seathwaite, Borrowdale	04:45
(traffic hold-ups, 15min)	05:00 travel time 5.5hrs
Sty Head	**06:20**
Scafell Pike summit	**07:40**
Sty Head	**08:30**
Scafell Pike foot	**09:20**
Seathwaite dep	09:30
Tebay services M6	10:20
Knutsford services M6	11:45
Knutsford dep	12:00
Conwy	13:05
Pen-y-Pass	13:45
(traffic hold-ups, 15min)	14:00 travel time 4.5hrs
Snowdon summit	**16:30**
Pen-y-Pass	**18:00**
(Llanberis)	**(18:15)**

Support

Thirty years ago any driver would tell you that while others might be affected by a few drinks, he drove even better after a half-bottle of good claret. Nowadays, we all know that's a load of boloney. However, the occasional driver still believes he can drive a car after staying awake all night and climbing Ben Nevis or Snowdon.

He can't. A party of three could manage an unsupported Three Peaks by starting at dawn after a good night's sleep in a hotel or hostel, and taking turns to drive and to sleep in the reclining front passenger seat. But it's simpler as well as safer to have a separate driver.

The minimum 10hrs driving time allows average speeds of 50–55mph on unstraightened trunk roads, and 65mph on motorways, as well as brief stops.

THE ROUTE: BEN NEVIS

Fort William

Food shops	Large supermarket (Morrisons), smaller Tesco Metro in High Street
Other shops	Everything including several gear shops
Eating out	At the north end of High Street, Nevisport has bar meals underneath, and a café in the shop that serves breakfast from 8am
Toilets	Cameron Square, High Street; at Nevis Centre in Glen Nevis
Accommodation	Youth hostel and Ben Nevis Inn bunkhouse, each at a start point of the Mountain Track; several other independent hostels; camping in Glen Nevis

The particular risks of Ben Nevis

Every year about 100,000 people go up Ben Nevis; no more than a handful end up falling into Five Finger Gully. This is quite surprising. The summit of Ben Nevis is in cloud most of the time. It has remarkably nasty weather, with wind, rain or (in any month) sleet. These combine to induce early-onset exposure, chilling the limbs to clumsiness and the brain to bad navigation. And bad navigation can lead you over the edge of several crag tops.

In summer, the northern plateau edge is obvious: the crags drop away sharply, and even the densest mist won't conceal them. (It's different in winter, when those crags may be corniced, so that by the time you see the edge you've already fallen through.) More sinister is Five Finger Gully, which can be reached all too easily, either by edging away from the northern brink, or else

Helicopter rescue from the Mountain Track on Ben Nevis in 2000. That year saw 36 walkers in trouble on this path (out of about 100,000 ascending it). Twelve wandered into Five Finger Gully (two parties arriving there by following another off-route party); one fell to his death over the North Face. There was one other death, from a heart attack. Nine were exhausted or lost, and the remaining 13, including the one pictured, slipped and were injured.

by ignoring a bend in one branch of the descent path. Above Five Finger the ground steepens gradually, so that going back up is first uncomfortable, then awkward, then impossible.

If the Mountain Track can be a difficult way off, it's still the easiest way. You either go down it, or stop in the summit shelter: a metal hutch, perched on a pile of stones a couple of metres above the actual summit. That height is to stop it being overwhelmed by snowdrifts, but also allows anyone inside full appreciation of the howling of the wind. Various other shelters marked on maps on the slopes of Ben Nevis have recently been removed. This one saves lives every year, and will remain.

The sketch map in this book is based on copyright Ordnance Survey mapping, so that I cannot invite you freely to photocopy it. However, shops and tourism centres in Fort William have similar maps on give-away leaflets. Every party should carry one, and GPS users should program the 8-digit grid references (see box page 39) into their gadgets.

Recce of the Ben

There is no great need to reconnoitre the *ascent* of Ben Nevis. Accordingly, you might prefer to visit the hill's spectacular side. For that route, marked in orange on the sketch map, drop past Lochan Meall an t-Suidhe (the Half-Way Lochan) on the rocky path round to the Allt a' Mhuillin, and strike up steeply left onto the north ridge of Carn Dearg Meadhonach. (An easier approach is from a car park at Torlundy NN 145 166, but you wouldn't get to do the descent recce of the straightforward lower part of the Mountain Track.)

Head up onto Carn Mor Dearg, with outstanding views of the crags opposite, and follow the Carn Mor Dearg Arête. This narrow ridge of granite boulders is easy scrambling, but becomes serious in high winds or snow. A steep boulderfield then leads up to Nevis summit.

The top of the Mountain Track is, when waymarked with ascending walkers, completely obvious. So bear in mind that those folk probably won't be there on the night of your actual attempt.

If you are overnighting in the area you could spend an hour or two the next morning walking into the Nevis Gorge from the end of the Glen Nevis road. Thus you get a glimpse of the wild beauty of Ben Nevis, so hidden from the Mountain Track.

Start points

There are three car parks and three path bottoms.

Descending the Mountain Track, just below the half-way plateau

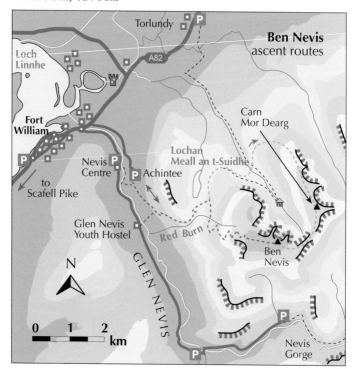

- The Charity Code asks large parties to use the **Nevis Visitor Centre** (Ionaid Nibheis). The car park is large, there are toilets, and even rowdy Triplepeakers won't greatly disturb anyone apart from other Triplepeakers attempting to sleep in their cars nearby. However, this route adds 1km, and 30m of ascent, to the return journey – at least 10 minutes.

- The **Achintee** car park is beside the Ben Nevis Inn (bunkhouse and food). The car park is not large, and fills up during the middle of the day. Note that the Ben Nevis Race, with its record time of 1hr 25min for the return journey, starts a mile back down the road from here at the sports field!

- **Glen Nevis youth hostel** is the closest start point. Parking is informal verge-side (unless you're staying at the youth hostel itself). It is often crowded.

Noisy behaviour will make enemies of up to 88 sleep-deprived hostellers. The route saves 500 metres each way against Achintee, but this is largely counteracted by the way it gives you a nasty final 150m of steep descent on jammed stones.

The route up Ben Nevis

The Mountain Track's real name is the Pony Path, or the Tourist Path; it's wide and well graded, built a century ago to serve the observatory that stood at the summit. It has been renamed to reflect the fact that, though technically easy, it is strenuous and can also be dangerous.

- From the **youth hostel** cross to a footbridge and take a built path across the valley floor then steeply up to right of a plantation.

- From the **Nevis Centre**, head downstream for 20 metres to a footbridge, cross, and turn right, upstream, for 300 metres. Turn left onto a path running up to a track, where you turn left to the Achintee car park.

- From **Achintee car park** beside Ben Nevis Inn, take a gate at the far end, and at once fork left onto the gently ascending, well-built path. After 1km it passes above a plantation, and the youth hostel path joins from down on the right. Just beyond this junction the path makes its first zigzag.

The path crosses several streams, a couple of them by little aluminium footbridges, and makes a second zigzag, then curves up into the valley of the **Red Burn**. Below the valley rim it makes a third zigzag back left; the eroded old path ahead is fenced off. The current path emerges onto the half-way plateau, wide, smooth and well built. It slants to the left across the lower face of Carn Dearg, with Lochan Meall an t-Suidhe (Lochan Melantee, the **Half-way Lochan**) below.

At NN 147 724 the path turns sharply back right: a wall-like cairn blocks the path ahead, which is the wrong one and leads round to the North Face of the mountain. After the sharp turn, the path crosses a small stream, the last healthy water source as the Red Burn above runs too closely alongside the path. The path then crosses the shallow gully of the **Red Burn**, with waterfalls just above, and zigzags in broad sweeps up the face of Carn Dearg. Up the lower part of the zigzags the path has been repaired, but above that it becomes very rough and stony. While it can be ascended in the dark fairly comfortably, coming down this upper part of the path in the dark will be slow and awkward. Gradually, the steepness abates, and you may sense the tops of great cliffs that fall away on the left.

Pride of place: resting at the summit of Ben Nevis

From this point on, glance behind you from time to time so as to recognise the path when descending. After the short rise of **MacLean's Steep**, the path has been marked by a line of larger stones on either side. It keeps to the right of, and slightly below, the plateau rim, as **Gardyloo Gully** cuts in from the left. ('Gardyloo' is a street cry of old Edinburgh: from the French, *Gardez l'eau* or 'watch out for the water', before the contents of the chamber pot came hurtling down from the top windows. The gully was where the observatory flung its garbage.)

Once past the head of the gully, the track bears left to the **summit cairn** with trig point, observatory ruins, other cairn with shelter perched on top, and third cairn with memorials.

Getting off Ben Nevis summit

If you are bewildered in darkness or bad weather, don't be embarrassed to turn back uphill – it is, in these circumstances, possible, quite literally, to die of embarrassment. Finding the summit shelter is just a matter of keeping uphill,

The day's last walker descends into Glen Nevis

and it will provide if not a comfortable then certainly a very memorable night. Also, take care when asking advice from other walkers. Even mountaineers emerging off the crags can be bad navigators (as the Mountain Rescue reports bear out). As one who can't find the way and knows you can't find the way, you are in a better position than someone who can't find the way but thinks they can. An initial question might be: 'Have you been here before?' An experienced hillwalker will not be on her first ascent of Ben Nevis.

Studying the summit enlargement map, you'll notice that there is no way down that's any easier or safer than the Mountain Track. Escape could be made southeast and then south into Coire Eoghainn, or from the start of the Carn Mor Dearg Arête: but each of these is steep, bouldery, arduous, and requires skill in navigation. So it'd be better to take refuge in the shelter.

Descending the Mountain Track, the first danger is on the right: **Gardyloo Gully**, and the top of the great North Face. The crag top is abrupt, and you're unlikely to walk over it by accident unless there's a snow cornice, which may continue into empty air beyond the crag top.

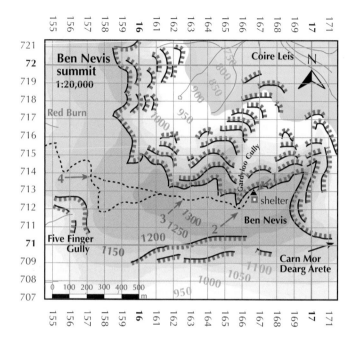

You keep edging away down to the left, away from the crag tops; and fall into the next bad place, which is **Five Finger Gully**. This is more treacherous than the North Face as the ground steepens imperceptibly, so that no sudden edge marks the danger. One branch of the Mountain Track leads directly towards its top.

Avoiding both these, in a winter white-out, is a very ticklish bit of navigation, although easier using GPS. In summer people going down simply head towards the people coming up; and the path is visible on the ground. Even so, in mist, darkness, new snow, or a combination, the path can be lost quite easily.

If firm snow is lying in the shallow hollow of the upper Red Burn, to right of the zigzags, this is a much quicker descent than the path. However, an ice-axe is needed to stop any sliding, as there's a waterfall below, dropping to where the path crosses the burn.

NAVIGATING OFF BEN NEVIS

For those using GPS, the following 8-digit grid references are accurate within 10–20 metres:

[1] Nevis summit: NN 1668 7128
   southwest 150 metres to

[2] Turning point opposite Gardyloo Gully NN 1658 7117
   285° just north of west 400 metres to

[3] Top of Maclean's Steep NN 1625 7125
   285° just north of west 500 metres to

[4] Top of zigzags NN 1572 7137
   (you have now avoided Five Finger Gully)
   down path, or
   285° just north of west, downhill, to

[5] NN 1467 7165 (on path on final zigzag)
   path, north, 200 metres to

[6] NN 1474 7186 (path crosses Red Burn)

Using compass alone, the bearings are:
From the summit to clear the head of Gardyloo Gully: pass to right of the observatory ruins, bearing 234° (roughly southwest) for 150 metres (roughly 100 double steps).

Thus having passed to left of the head of Gardyloo Gully: take bearing 285° (slightly north of west) for 400 metres to the top of Maclean's Steep, and the same bearing for another 500 metres to the top of the zigzags. If the zigzags are invisible (eg under fresh snow) the same bearing, which should be directly downhill, will eventually lead down steep soggy grass into the lower hollow of the Red Burn.

Bearings are magnetic 2006: subtract 1° for every six years after 2006.

THE ROUTE: SCAFELL PIKE

Driving from Glen Nevis to Borrowdale

Following the A82 south from Fort William is shortest, but a bad idea. The road along upper Loch Lomond is very slow, and so too can be the motorway through Glasgow. After Tyndrum (where the Green Welly Stop provides day-time fuel, toilets, and a convenient driver change-over) I prefer to continue by A85 and A84 to join the M80 at Stirling, with services just to the south; the first all-night petrol station.

The A80 past Cumbernauld has had intermittent road works throughout the present millennium. If passing at a busy time of day, check for hold-ups here in advance, and if necessary go by Loch Lomond.

At the edge of Glasgow, the turn-off of the M73 ('Carlisle') can be missed. M74 and M6 lead to the A66 turn-off at Penrith – the last motorway services are just south of Carlisle, but during the day the Rheged Centre at the first roundabout of the A66 has fuel, snacks and toilets. Don't take a slip road signed for Keswick, but at the following roundabout turn left, following signs for Borrowdale through the edge of the town. The distance has been 260 miles.

Borrowdale

Parking	Roadside parking at Seathwaite
Food shops	Small ones in Rosthwaite
Eating out	Café tearoom in Rosthwaite, also two pubs; good bar meals in the Langstrath Inn at Stone-thwaite; café at Seathwaite
Toilets	Small ones at Seathwaite, also at Rosthwaite car park
Accommodation	Youth hostel and camping barn at Ros-thwaite, camping at Grange (Hollows Farm), Stonethwaite, Seatoller and Seathwaite; all inexpensive farm sites.

Scafell Pike

Scafell Pike is often referred to as Scafell. In fact Scafell is a slightly smaller summit alongside, and fortunately the technical difficulties are on Scafell. Even so, Scafell Pike is trickier than Ben Nevis because of its confusing routes. While

Scafell Pike from Ill Crag, showing the bad ground at the back of the hill leading down to Eskdale

the way up from Wasdale is a steep slog from valley to top, the Borrowdale one takes in a lovely tarn and then the Corridor Route, which weaves among crags.

The particular risks of Scafell Pike

Getting lost! The commonest call-out for Wasdale Mountain Rescue team is people who've failed to find the path off Scafell Pike and ended up in Eskdale, south of the mountain. Eskdale is very beautiful, and very long, and – to the relief of the MR team – does not have a mobile phone signal. Keep walking – it really is lovely – to the phone box at the foot of the Hardknott Pass, just beyond Brotherilkeld.

An even easier way of getting lost is to follow cairns off the summit to Mickledore, the pass between Scafell Pike and Scafell. If aiming for Wasdale, you can now turn right, down a very steep, nasty and eroded path. If aiming for Borrowdale, hurry back to the summit. You have lost only 30 minutes; just make sure you do find your way down correctly on the second attempt.

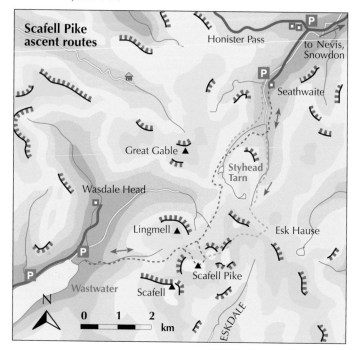

Scafell Pike ascent routes

Honister Pass

to Nevis, Snowdon

Seathwaite

Great Gable ▲

Styhead Tarn

Wasdale Head

Lingmell ▲

Esk Hause

Scafell Pike ▲

Scafell

Wastwater

N

0   1   2   km

ESKDALE

Recce of Scafell Pike

The important sections to reconnoitre are the summit itself, and (if descending to Borrowdale) the descent of the Corridor Route down as far as Styhead Tarn.

You could vary the ascent from Borrowdale by visiting Taylorgill waterfall, Lakeland's second highest. This is slightly shorter, but considerably rougher, than the route described below for use on the actual attempt. Pass through an arch opposite Seathwaite café, cross the valley floor and a footbridge, and turn left, upstream. Enter a regeneration area, where the path slants up to a ladder stile. The path passes around the base of crags, then gets slightly rocky through a gate on a ledge and up a groove with a view of Taylorgill waterfall. The path crosses scree to the top of the waterfall, and goes upstream, joining the usual route where the latter crosses a footbridge from the left.

To see more of Scafell Pike on your recce day, you could also fork off the normal route at Stockley Bridge, ascend to Esk Hause, and cross Great End, Ill Crag and Broad Crag, thus reconnoitering the Corridor in descent only.

On the plateau of Scafell Pike, with Wastwater behind

Route up Scafell Pike from Seathwaite

From the road end at **Seathwaite**, pass through the farmyard onto a wide, stone-paved path. After 1km turn right, across a handsome stone packhorse bridge (**Stockley Bridge**). The path works around a spur to join the Styhead Gill stream and, after 800 metres, crosses at a footbridge. It continues to right of the stream, and then to right of **Sty Head Tarn**, to a wooden stretcher box at **Sty Head** (marked 'Stretcher Box' on the front, reference point [4] in the GPS info box).

Turn left, dipping slightly across the col, and following a path for 200 metres up past a small pool and across a rocky little knoll. In the dip behind, the path divides at a cairn with the first little buttress of Great End's north ridge just ahead (ref point [3]). Take the smaller path on the right, the '**Corridor Route**'.

Note From this point, keep glancing behind so as to recognise the path in reverse when descending.

The path heads south, slightly downhill at first, then slants gradually uphill, to cross Skew Gill with a slightly rocky exit from the beck. Around 300 metres later it contours bare rock. Another 200 metres after that is the crossing of Greta Gill, again with a slightly rocky exit. In another 300 metres a well-built path turns up left for Scafell Pike. (The stream just below this path junction is the last water source.) If you miss the turn-off, in another 300 metres the main path crosses a stream at the top of the spectacular ravine of **Piers Gill**, a clear sign to turn back.

Having forked up left on the correct path, follow it into a wide stony gully, to reach the col between Broad Crag (left) and Scafell Pike (right) – the col is ref point [2]. The path on the right continues on bare trodden rock up the crest, or along the top of the scree slope just down to the right. Cairns mark the way to the **summit** with its huge war memorial cairn.

Getting off the summit back to Borrowdale

From the summit cairn (ref point [1]) the descent path is not obvious, even though you just came up it. It follows cairns between east and southeast for 20 metres. Just before some shelter walls it bends left, almost horizontal, before heading downhill northeast to regain the Broad Crag/Scafell Pike col (ref point [2]). Retrace steps down the gully on the left, and then turn right, back along the Corridor Route. After 400 metres cross the northern branch of Greta Gill; 200 metres later, a stretch of rocky ground is ahead. Do not slant down left, on a path appearing to bypass below the difficulty: that path is actually an unpleasant way down into Wasdale. Instead slant slightly upwards on good well-used holds across the rocks, to rediscover the path beyond.

At the foot of the Corridor Route you can fork left to short-cut direct to **Sty Head** [4].

NAVIGATING OFF SCAFELL PIKE

For those using GPS, the following 8-digit grid references are accurate within 10–20 metres.
[1] Scafell Pike summit: NY 2154 0721

Borrowdale route
[2] Top of Corridor Route, col Broad Crag/Scafell Pike NY 2173 0744
[3] Corridor Route turn-off near Sty Head NY 2217 0946
[4] Sty Head stretcher box NY 2173 0943

Wasdale route
[5] Path junction Lingmell/Mickledore NY 2146 0727
[6] Cairn at summit plateau edge NY 2136 0732

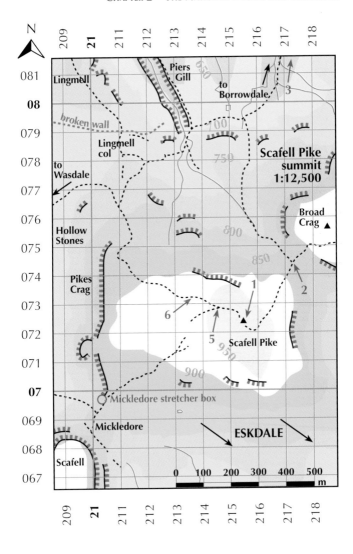

N

209 **21** 211 212 213 214 215 216 217 218

081
08
079
078
077
076
075
074
073
072
07
069
068
067

Lingmell

Piers Gill

650

to Borrowdale

3

broken wall

Lingmell col

700

750

to Wasdale

Scafell Pike summit 1:12,500

Hollow Stones

800

Broad Crag ▲

Pikes Crag

850

1

2

6

5

Scafell Pike

Mickledore stretcher box

950

900

Mickledore

ESKDALE

Scafell

0   100   200   300   400   500
m

209 **21** 211 212 213 214 215 216 217 218

45

The view you shouldn't see: Scafell Pike from Upper Eskdale

Getting off the summit via Lingmoor col

For a change, a descent route above Lingmoor col is more attractive than the ascent route but easier to get astray. It uses the Wasdale descent route (described in later in this chapter) to the 760m contour, where a 1.5m boulder with a cairn on splits the path. Around 30 metres below turn off right on a contouring path that gets clearer as it drops off the ridge face at a cairn. It passes above the top of the impressive Piers Gill ravine, to become in 200 metres the path of the upward route.

THE ROUTE: SNOWDON

Driving from Borrowdale to Pen-y-Pass

Return through Keswick, following signs 'Carlisle' as far as the roundabout on the A66. Turn right to regain the M6, and head south. About 1.5hrs later the crossing of the high bridge over the Manchester Ship Canal indicates it's time to take out the map. At the next junction, take the M56 towards Chester, and at its end the A550 coast road towards Llandudno and Bangor. At tourist times the road past Colwyn Bay gets congested, and it may be better to short-cut on the slower A548 directly to Llanrwst.

At Betwys-y-Coed turn right on A5 to Capel Curig and Pen-y-Pass. The distance has been 230 miles.

Pen-y-Pass and Llanberis

Parking: Pen-y-Pass car park is expensive and sometimes full. Having dropped off walkers, it's best to descend to the large car parks of Llanberis.

Pig Track to Snowdon

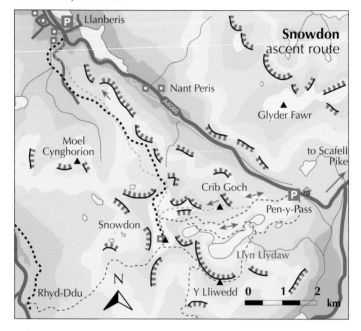

Food and sleep: Gorphwysfa Café is at Pen-y-Pass, opposite the Pen-y-Pass youth hostel. Capel Curig has two pleasant cafés, and Joe Brown's gear shop. Llanberis has Pete's Eats, nationally famous for its climber-sized portion control; another branch of Joe Brown; and plenty of places to eat and sleep. In Nant Peris and the Llanberis Pass are three farm-field campsites, inexpensive and atmospheric but low on facilities. (You'll be asleep – you won't need facilities.)

Recce of Snowdon

Snowdon is the most straightforward of the three mountains. The Pig Track is clear all the way, though it is possible to get lost under Crib y Ddysgl when coming down it in the dark. The descent to Llanberis is even clearer as it follows the railway.

If you do decide to recce Snowdon, then you may like to try, for the ascent, the spectacular Crib Goch ridge – one of the UK's classic scrambles, not difficult in dry windless conditions but with big drops under it. Given 30 minutes in hand, good conditions, and a crowd-free mountain, you might even like to

Snowdon summit, even busier than Scafell Pike

cross the pinnacles as the climax of your Three Peaks Attempt day (see Variants below).

Route up Snowdon from Pen-y-Pass

From **Pen-y-Pass** car park, head to the right behind the café, on a tarred path with waymark 'PyG Track'. It passes a helipad, then after a wall gap becomes stony underfoot with gravel. Views ahead are down Llanberis Pass, with the path rising to a slight downhill section between boulders. Then it turns more steeply up left, to pass through **Bwlch y Moch**, the 'Pig Pass', to a wonderful view of Snowdon's central hollow and the lower of its lakes, Llyn Llydaw.

Just beyond the pass, after some fencing, is a waymark post, where those aiming for Crib Goch would turn up right. The main Pig Track contours along the valley side above **Llyn Llydaw**, and then above the upper lake, **Glaslyn** – a lovely 2km of mountain walking.

Soon the steep Miners' Path joins from below, and the combined path zig-zags up to the right. Serious path restoration here is sometimes overwhelmed by

49

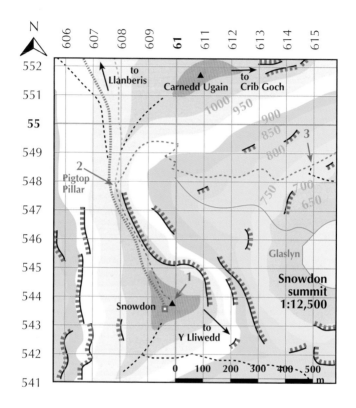

scree kicked down by unhelpful people short-cutting the zigzags. After a steep, tough climb, the path arrives suddenly at the col between Snowdon, on the left, and Carnedd Ugain (Garnedd Ugain, or Crib y Ddysgl – the name varies). A tall stone obelisk (the **Pigtop Pillar**) marks the col; just ahead and down is the Snowdon Mountain Railway.

Turn up left, with the railway on your right and big drops to Glaslyn on the left. A wide path leads to the **summit** of Snowdon.

Now all that remains is to jog back down the steep and stony path. Your feet are sore, your legs ache? Jog fast enough, and the pain will be over in only 90 minutes...

NAVIGATING OFF SNOWDON

While the railway is a very clear guide off Snowdon, it's possible to stray off the Pig Track onto the nasty slopes of Carnedd Ugain.

For those using GPS, the following 8-digit grid references are accurate within 10–20 metres.

[1] Snowdon summit SH 6098 5437
[2] Pigtop Pillar SH 6078 5479 (If you accidentally descend the southwest ridge there is another stone obelisk at SH 6088 5420 at the top of the Watkin Path.)
   On the zigzags below the Pigtop Pillar, the exact path line shifts from year to year.
[3] Top of the Miners' Track SH 6149 5485 (Carnedd Ugain blocks a lot of sky, and GPS may be unreliable. If the 5th digit of the reading is shifting, wait for another satellite.)

VARIANTS

Wasdale way up Scafell Pike

Doing Scafell Pike from Wasdale rather than Borrowdale saves about 45 minutes walking time. However, it takes longer to drive to Wasdale. The direct route south, around the edge of Carlisle, when traffic-free takes 30 minutes longer than the drive to Seathwaite in Borrowdale. During normal daylight, however, Carlisle is congested; the daytime route to Wasdale by the M6 and Keswick takes 45min longer than Borrowdale. The drive out towards Wales also adds about 20 minutes.

For large charity challenges, the National Park's code of practice prefers the use of Borrowdale, as Wasdale's road is uncomfortable even for minibuses. For the rest of us, there's not much in it in terms of time. This leaves us to choose by other criteria.

The Wasdale way up Scafell Pike is short, but steep and rather harsh. The path is clear, which will suit those who don't make a recce in advance. The scenery, under the high wall of Scafell, is impressive. But the Borrowdale way is even more beautiful: under the side of Great Gable, past a high tarn, and along the intricate Guide's Corridor. In clear weather or for good navigators, variants make it possible to change the Borrowdale route for the descent. In poor weather or for doubtful navigators, it can on the other hand be confusing.

Walkers with separate drivers in support can ascend out of Borrowdale, and descend to Wasdale. If your timings let you use the short-cut through Carlisle, this only adds 40 minutes to the driving time, while saving 30 minutes on the hill. But the situation is better than that, as if you're really efficient with your journey breaks, and don't meet any traffic jams, the safe driving time from Glen Nevis to Wasdale is still, just, within the 5.5hr allowance.

To leave Scafell Pike into a completely new valley makes it all much more interesting. It also makes it more tricky, especially the leaving of the confusing summit area.

Driving south to Wasdale

At quiet times of day, turn off at the start of the M6 into Carlisle, and take the A595 past Cockermouth, and through the edge of Workington to Gosforth. A planned northern bypass for Carlisle may make this the quicker way even during Carlisle's rush hour.

Between 7am and 6pm, avoid Carlisle and take the M6 to Penrith, then the A66 past Keswick and Bassenthwaite Lake.

For support drivers, the time from Seathwaite in Borrowdale to Wasdale Head is 1.5hrs, via Keswick and the Cockermouth bypass. Honister Pass is shorter, more scenic, but slower. Keswick and Cockermouth both have pleasant cafés.

At Wasdale Head

Parking: NT campsite, or discharge passengers and retire to a pleasant, quiet pay & display at Overbeck Bridge (NY 168 068).

Shops and pubs: Three at Gosforth; two more pubs and camping barn (Murt) in Nether Wasdale; Wasdale Head has the Wasdale Head Inn with excellent food, its own brewery, small campsite and small gear shop. At the lake head is the much larger National Trust campsite and the drop-off point for walkers.

Recce out of Wasdale

If reconnoitering out of Wasdale Head, you can vary the route by forking right on Brown Tongue and heading up by Hollow Stones to Mickledore. Thus you pass under the imposing crags of Scafell, take the very steep final ascent, and explore the wrong route that you (because of these preparations) won't be descending by mistake on the day. Then descend by the route that'll be used on the day both up and down.

To recce the Borrowdale–Wasdale crossing, start from Wasdale by Wasdale Head onto the wide path to Sty Head, then up the Corridor and down Brown

Hollow Stones, on the Wasdale way up Scafell Pike

Tongue. You won't get to previsit the clear path from Borrowdale up to Sty Head, but that shouldn't matter.

Wasdale Route up Scafell Pike

From the head of Wastwater follow the **National Trust Campsite** track, passing to right of the campsite and a pay & display parking area, to cross **Lingmell Gill**. Fork left on a white-arrowed permissive path, heading up beside the beck, to left of Brackenclose (a climbers' hut), to a footbridge. Cross it, to join a path that started in the back corner of the campsite.

Head up, now to left of the stream. After a gate the path is rebuilt in stone chunks. Ignore a path forking up left towards Lingmell but continue beside the stream. At 300m altitude (a third of the way up) the path crosses a side-stream, and continues up the spur, **Brown Tongue**, between the two streams. It's a stiff climb to **Hollow Stones**, the green place below the great Scafell Crag. At 500m (half-way up, NY 201 073) the path divides; fork left, up to **Lingmell Col**.

On the left, a broken wall runs through the col, with the minor summit Lingmell rising beyond. Turn right, away from Lingmell and the broken wall, up a wide stony path. It passes a rectangular cairned boulder, then reaches the plateau edge at a large cairn. It crosses a boulderfield, with cairns, to the summit stonepile. The **top** has a trig point and wide cylindrical cairn.

Getting off Scafell Pike to Wasdale

Note A summit sketch and (for GPS users) the grid ref box are in the Scafell Pike section above (page 45).

From the **summit** (ref point [1]), a path heads northwest (300°) for 50 metres down the first steepening, then bends left (west). After 100 metres the path forks (ref point [5]). Keep right, following cairns just north of west (the straight-ahead fork, also cairned, leads to Mickledore). After another 100 metres, a large cairn stands at the plateau rim (ref point [6]). Now the path is clear. It runs down northwest, then slants to the right down a slab strip. At the foot of this, the 830m contour, the main path turns directly downhill for 250 metres, to the 760m contour, where a 1.5m boulder with a cairn on top splits the path.

Around 30 metres below, turn off left, on the slightly larger path. This is still some 300 metres above the **Lingmell Col** which you don't actually visit. The path soon dips over the edge into Hollow Stones. The downhill path now leads inevitably to Wasdale and the **NT campsite**.

WASDALE SCHEDULE	
Day 1	
Glen Nevis dep	23:30
Day 2	
Abington Services M73	02:40
M6 top (Carlisle)	03:30
Carlisle south edge	03:45
Gosforth	04:15
Wasdale Head	04:40
(hold-ups and 2nd break 20min)	05:00 travel time 5.5hrs
Hollow Stones	**06:15**
Scafell Pike summit	**07:30**
Hollow Stones	**08:15**
Wasdale Head	**08:45**

Wasdale Head dep	09:00
A6 Milnthorpe	10:30
M6 Carnforth	10:40
Knutsford services M6	11:35
Knutsford dep	11:50
Conwy	13:05
Pen-y-Pass	13:35 travel time 4hrs 35min

Up Snowdon by Crib Goch

This is an excellent and exciting scramble to incorporate into any recce of Snowdon. On Three Peaks day – unless you're an accomplished scrambler – you'll need 45 minutes in hand, as well as dry, windless weather. But in such conditions you may be held up by other parties. In the afternoon, especially, other parties may be coming down.

From **Pen-y-Pass**, follow the Pig Track as on the standard route. It heads to the right behind the café, slanting up gently, then more steeply, to **Bwlch y Moch** (the Pig Pass).

Just beyond the crest of the pass, turn right at a waymark 'Crib Goch'. The path crosses a ladder stile then slants up the left (Glaslyn) flank, with occasional scrambly bits, where you can take the slightly more challenging lines as practice. The path regains the crest, for a steep rocky section, where a well-worn set of holds up a slightly out-of-balance 3m groove is the hardest part of the route. Above this the route heads up to the right, to the right (Llanberis Pass) flank. A couple of cairns mark the way, which heads up gently angled blocky ground, to reach the (currently uncairned) summit of **Crib Goch**.

The crest on the right continues as blocky ground consisting entirely of footholds, but exposed on the right. A loose little path runs 10 metres down the left-hand flank. At the **Pinnacles** contour left, to pass to left of the first two pinnacles around their bases; then head down left in a gully of spiky holds for 30m. Don't go too far down, as scree below the turn-off point looks walked but isn't; it has simply slid down. Look out for a well-trodden ledge heading out to the right (for someone looking downhill), across the base of the final pinnacle, then heading up to the crest behind. A steep path leads down bare rock to the levelling at **Bwlch Goch**.

A long way down to Llanberis: descending Snowdon can be harder than getting up it on the National Three Peaks

The main path leads along the crest, then just down left of it (a smaller one weaves among rocks along the crestline). After 200 metres the main path rejoins the ridge crest. Ahead, the crest is rockier and slightly steeper. Here ignore a contouring path left. The **Crib y Ddysgl** ridge starts with easy scrambling, either straight up or slightly right of the crest line. After another levelling, a steeper tower can start with a short steep wall, or easier lines slanting up the left flank. Good scrambling with large holds leads up to the crest behind the tower. This is blocky-rocky, as Crib Goch, but this time with the line on the Llanberis side. Either keep down to right of the crest by a few metres, or on a path just below.

The ridge becomes stony, with a large sprawling cairn almost filling a small col. The path continues along the crest, with some rocky obstructions scrambled or avoided on the path. A steeper step is taken by a 10m groove on the right, with the trig point on **Carnedd Ugain** not far beyond. (Carnedd Ugain is 'Garnedd' on OS maps, and 'Crib y Ddysgl' on Harveys.)

The path descends a few steps to the railway, then keeps to left of it to Snowdon's **summit**.

Down Snowdon to Llanberis

This descent is on a wide and easy path with a café half-way down. It is rather long and dull. It takes 15–20 minutes longer than the descent to Pen-y-Pass. The only difficulty (even in the dark) is being on the right path when leaving the Pigtop Pillar.

At quiet times there's roadside parking in the street at the foot of the Llanberis Path (SH 582 597). Large pay & display car parks are at the mountain railway, and beside Llyn Padarn.

From **Snowdon summit** head back down the path above and to right of the railway to the **Pigtop Pillar**, the stone obelisk where the Pig Track arrives from down right. Don't take the path forking left and crossing the railway; don't take the path forking right and uphill towards Carnedd Ugain. Take the wide path ahead, contouring and remaining above the railway. The path runs north, after 200 metres gently downhill and smooth; then it descends more steeply to join the railway and pass under it by a bridge.

Views behind are to Cloggy (the famous climbing crag Clogwyn Du'r Arddu) and across to Moel Cynghorion. Soon the descent becomes gentler. You pass the **Half Way Café**, then pass back under the railway by another bridge. At the start of enclosed ground is a ladder stile, with a last view back to Snowdon. The path runs down to a tarred lane. Follow this steeply down through a farm, and across a cattle grid, then to the left over the mountain railway into **Llanberis**. Keep ahead to join the A4086 near the bottom station of the mountain railway.

Pete's Eats in Llanberis: famous for its climber-sized portions

Chapter 3

The National Three Peaks Challenge by Public Transport

THE GOOD, THE BAD, AND THE MYSTERY SOCKS

> *Actions are right in proportion as they tend to promote happiness;*
> *wrong as they tend to produce the reverse of happiness.*
> John Stuart Mill, 1863

The business of getting ourselves up Ben Nevis, Snowdon and Scafell is complex enough, even without introducing a philosophical or ethical dimension to it all. Even so, the Three Peaks Challenge, when carried out with more enthusiasm than ethics, has made itself unpopular. We do have to think about the effect our hill fun is having on the people who live in the valleys below, and on the World as a whole.

Seathwaite: in summertime, sleeplessness is assured as hundreds of three-peakers tramp past in the dark

THE THREE PEAKS CHARITY CODE

This is a summary of the 'Outdoor Fundraising in the UK' issued by the Institute of Fundraising. That Code has a specific Three Peaks section, and follows consultation with the mountain managers. The full code is on the Institute's website (my additions are in square brackets: for contact details see Appendix I).

- Inform authorities at Ben Nevis, Scafell Pike, and Snowdon of your event's timing and numbers. [For Ben Nevis, the Nevis Partnership; for Scafell Pike and Snowdon, the relevant National Park Authority]
- Avoid bank holiday weekends, late June and early July. If feasible avoid weekends.
- Limit walkers to 200 per event.
- Stagger start times to avoid congestion on paths [as this in particular breaks down path edges].
- Check equipment and experience levels.
- No arrival or departure between 12 midnight and 5am at any settlement [campsites etc at Wasdale and Borrowdale, hostels at two of the three Nevis start points and at Pen-y-Pass].
- Do not use large coaches, only minibuses, as roads are narrow.
- Inform rescue services beforehand for larger events.
- Provide high-quality marshals with local experience. Do not expect the local Mountain Rescue Service to provide this.
- Do not rely on mobile phones – use VHF radios for communication.
- Have a plan for accidents, emergency and poor weather.
- Local amenities are limited – use motorway service areas and other facilities en route.
- Use the Glen Nevis Visitor Centre as the start point for Ben Nevis.
- If starting at Wasdale, do not use Wasdale Green as a car park. Water supplies are limited so bring your own.
- At Snowdon, parking is difficult at Pen-y-Pass. Disembark only.
- Do not race on or between mountains; agree driving times beforehand that recognise legal speed limits [10hrs minimum total driving time].

One radical solution is simply to cut out the car.

Every summer weekend, residents of Borrowdale and Wasdale have good reason to curse the Conservative Government of 1953. Why? Because they started the building of the M6, making it possible to stand on top of Ben Nevis, Scafell Pike and Snowdon within 24 hours.

The people of Borrowdale have particularly objected to coaches parked all night with their engines running to power on-board computers. But they also complain of litter, obstructed gateways, and smelly hedges were several hundred people have peed onto the roadside. Wasdale in 2004 saw approximately 14,555 Three-peakers in 125 people carriers, 864 minibuses and countless cars who between them left 76 bags of litter. On 24 June locals were woken up and asked for toilet facilities. On 29 July those caught short were more considerate, simply leaving their excrement in plastic bags on Wasdale Green. The day before, Wasdale had woken to find its walls decorated with abandoned smelly socks.

Ethics of erosion

The word 'erosion' brings visions of the American dust-bowl, where the thoughtlessness, greed or desperate poverty of farmers destroyed the soil system over thousands of square miles. What walkers do to footpaths doesn't send the ecosystem spiralling down the plughole, or turn Borrowdale into a dirty grey pile of bare pebbles. After a sudden thunderstorm, a tiny beck can rip open a hillside in much the same way as 50 years of fellwalkers – but the beck is simply an interesting natural process. However, heavy footfalls on footpaths do make Lakeland less pretty, and the paths themselves less comfortable.

Fun for us involves suffering for others. Even the harmless Sodoku craze uses up wood pulp and contributes to the grim afforestation of Glen Nevis. Is my fun appreciably more than the total discomfort inflicted on others? If, like Louis XIV, my game is shooting peasants with my gun, then the answer has to be no. However intensely enjoyable it may be to lean out of the window and pot an unsuspecting gardener, the distress of being dead outweighs it. But when it comes to footpaths, things are the other way around. It's very nice for one person to walk in Wordsworthian solitude up a small green sheep-trod. But it's better for 200 people to walk up an eroded path, even though that path is itself rather less pleasant. The footfall of a charity challenger does less damage than that of a self-directed fell wanderer, because the challenger's foot falls on a path that's already been repaired with indestructible lumps of stone. So if outdoor folk say charity challenges damage the environment, the Three-peakers can equally argue that it's independent walkers that should be banned, as by far the greater part of path erosion is caused by people who are *not* on charity challenges.

John Stuart Mill, quoted above, says that if the pleasure outweighs the pain, then the act is basically OK. But given that others must suffer to some extent for our delight, are there reasonable steps we can take to reduce their pain? On footpaths, those reasonable steps are down the middle of the path. It's tempting to short-cut the zigzags, or to take the bare ground alongside the jammed stones of the repaired walkway. But every such step does 100 times the damage of one on the path centre. The footfall of a charity challenger in a crowd is, now, disproportionately damaging, because it falls on the grass edges rather than the path. Hence the need to spread the crowd by staggering start times.

Better than that, you can take a minute somewhere in your day to clear one of the little culverts crossing the path. Water running down a path does more damage than feet. If 200 folk on a charity walk cleared 200 path drains, the National Park Authority would find, to its embarrassment, that its path rangers had suddenly become ardent supporters of the Three Peaks Challenge.

The mountains of the UK have recently become almost completely litter-free. It's not enough that people take their litter home, as there are always a few who don't. What's necessary is for a few shining moral exemplars to take a little of someone else's litter away as well. We tend to sneer at shining moral exemplars, for whatever reason – but fortunately there are now, in the UK, enough people who at the end of a long day will carry away one piece of litter that they didn't bring; thus litter leaves at the same rate as it arrives.

Orange peel, incidentally, is not biodegradable; or at least it is, but in the cold mountain environment only very slowly. A banana skin on the other hand, concealed in bracken, does rot in a few days.

Given that our fun outweighs the suffering we inflict, and that we've reasonably minimised that suffering, the third question is one of compensation. If I'm having fun, and the John Muir Trust is clearing up the mess, then what is money for if not for me to send some of it to them?

The ugliness our feet inflict on the eyes of fellow fellwalkers is balanced out by the ugliness their feet inflict on us. But when it comes to the good people of Borrowdale, they don't get the chance to visit our homes in the middle of the night, slam car doors, and piddle in our hedges. The Charity Code believes that for large numbers of folk in coaches to arrive in the night, spend 30 minutes telling each other how exciting it all is, spin their wheels in the road verge and then leave their engines running for 5 hours to warm the driver – all this is simply unacceptable. I agree and so does John Stuart Mill. Individuals who decide to do Scafell Pike by night can minimise the suffering they inflict. Urinate in advance. Know where you're going and get up on the hill without unnecessary talk. And learn not to crash car doors. Push them gently until they click half-closed: and then turn around and lean on them with your bottom. Silly and undignified? Certainly. But if you're not prepared to be silly and undignified for the sake of the good folk of Borrowdale, then sorry, but John Stuart Mill is perfectly firm. You don't deserve your status as a moral being. That's philosophy for you.

As for footpath erosion: the next Ice Age will sort that out, no problem.

Motoring and morality: the ease of cheating with the car

The Three Peaks Challenge is exhausting on the legs and lungs. But it's exhausting also in terms of the pipe out of the back of your car. When it comes to global warming, and the air pollution caused by petrol, it's not possible to determine exactly what environmental degradation is done by a day on Great Gable. In 50 years' time it may be all too evident. So, how much inconvenience do we accept to reduce our fumes? When it was proposed greatly to reduce car travel into Snowdonia and substitute buses (the 'Green Key' plan), it became clear that hillwalkers, out of our love of the mountains, were prepared to accept some personal inconvenience, to the extent of – zilch. The idea of £10 to park at Pen-y-Pass was a breach of our fundamental rights.

Whatever the correct answer may be, 'zilch' is certainly less than it.

Quite possibly the correct answer, in terms of damage and fun, would be to give up motoring, and most other activities, altogether, and spend our lives indulging in a little gentle gardening. That would be a pretty extreme reaction, so instead why not take one or two small steps in the correct direction. Sometimes use the bus, even though it's so smelly and inconvenient. If more of us use it, it'll get less inconvenient (if probably even smellier). If I've got a car I've got money: so I should spend some of it in Capel Curig.

The normal day's hillwalking consists of two comrades driving from Manchester to Langdale and walking up Bowfell. That's 12 person hours on the hill, and 200 car miles on the M6. The motorway-to-mountain ratio for the Three Peaks is even worse, with 500 miles between the hills and the same again at least at the start and end. I dislike the way that this hill challenge consists in such large part of driving around in cars.

But more: the road aspect of the challenge is fundamentally dodgy. It requires you to drive constantly at the legal speed limit, with success depending on the ability to drive fast without actually breaking the law. And quite probably, to do so while sleepy and exhausted. Hence, the 10-hour minimum road time. This is a hillwalking, not a motorway-driving, challenge. And so, if you

The Snowdon Sherpa bus at Pen-y-Pass

arrive early at Pen-y-Pass, before setting off up Snowdon you should sit in the café until the 10 hours have elapsed. To finish within the 24 hours only because of over-fast driving is not to accomplish the challenge. It is cheating, and a form of cheating that's not just unsporting but also endangers innocent road users.

By the same token, to achieve the hills in 14 hours total, but to overrun on the driving due to traffic hold-ups, is to succeed but for a technicality, and but for your responsible behaviour in not illegally speeding.

CHALLENGES AND THE IMAGINATION

The two sides of Nevis

Ben Nevis is not only the biggest hill in Britain but also one of the finest. Its tremendous North Face offers 2 miles of crag, gully and ridge, up to 2000ft in height. Here are mountain scrambles Alpine in length but darkly Scottish in character, as well as demanding rock climbs, all rising from a corrie of bare shattered rock and noisy waterfalls. On the Three Peaks Challenge, powering

The A66 seen in lyrical evening light, with Saddleback

up and down the Mountain Track, you won't see any of that – unless you're unfortunate enough to fall over the edge of it.

And when striding sweaty and energetic towards some inspiring challenge, it's easy to lose sight of the other side of your personal mountain: the side that's actually supposed to be enjoyable. The Three Peaks: it's an obvious and simple idea, and lots of people do it; even more people have heard of it and know what it is. You can boast about it afterwards without a lot of complicated explanations. However, the foot of fashion doesn't necessarily fall on the most intriguing and stimulating events. The London Marathon (35,000 people) isn't actually that much nicer than your local one (250 people). The Lyke Wake Walk, which used to draw tens of thousands annually, hasn't become horrid over the last 20 years – indeed, it's got pleasanter.

The National Three Peaks Challenge has its moments. In particular the moment at dusk descending Ben Nevis, and the moment at dawn on Scafell Pike. But with its car driving, its dull up-and-down routes, its lack of sympathy for Wasdale – it's not the most wonderful thing you can do with a summer weekend. The application of imagination can lead to a challenge that's just as challenging, but even more fun.

One inspired organisation has actually moved one of the three peaks. Events Unlimited organises an annual Four Peaks event on behalf of the British

Rugby charity 'Wooden Spoon' – the fourth peak being Carantouhill in Ireland. Several years ago, appreciating the problems for Wasdale residents, they replaced Scafell Pike with Helvellyn, ascended from Swirls. 'And we still raise just as much money,' they told *Lakeland Walker* magazine in 2004. 'Last year, our 150 walkers and 50 drivers raised £350,000.'

Standing on Carlisle station on the last weekend of the summer, I saw a trainload of tired people heading south, some of them still with wet hair. The 'Railway Children' had been attempting the Three Peaks using a special train out of Euston. 'We were very aware of the Three Peaks' bad press in the Lakes area,' said event organiser Katie Mason, 'and our aim in using the train was to make it an environmentally friendly event.'

Train travel was inconvenient at Fort William, where the station isn't exactly underneath Ben Nevis. It wouldn't work on Snowdon, where buses had to be taken to Pen-y-Pass. But Scafell Pike suddenly became even more interesting, approached from Ravenglass with the help of the Eskdale railway. This meant a preliminary crossing by Burnmoor Tarn to Brackenclose before the start of the usual route by Lingmell Col.

The charity Railway Children helps runaway and abandoned children found in the world's railway stations. Its Three Peaks by Train event of 2004, the first of its kind, had a simple itinerary: first night – Snowdon in particularly nasty weather. First day – Scafell Pike. Second night – try to sleep on the train. Second day – Ben Nevis and relax on the West Coast line back to Euston.

In the event, the combination of 100mph winds, rain and darkness meant that nobody actually made it up Snowdon (it might have been within the spirit of the day to use the mountain railway, but it wasn't running). About 180 of the 200 participants made it up Scafell Pike in surprise sunshine, with 120 also managing Ben Nevis in time for the train home. More importantly, over £105,000 was raised. Railway companies from Eurostar to Eskdale supplied train travel and teams for the event.

Trail magazine recently produced a chart to generate 8000 possible Three Peaks Challenges, derived from a dozen 3000ft summits of the southern Highlands, with the same number of 750m ones from Wales and from England. You were to choose your three with a pin: their journalists ended up on Ben Lawers, Grasmoor and Carnedd Llewelyn. All of these are slightly shorter than the 'real' Three Peaks. The tour of the second highest, however, is really tough: Carnedd Llewelyn, with Helvellyn and Ben Macdui.

I decided to take the Railway Children's idea, though, and run – or rather, walk and ride – with that one.

THE THREE PEAKS BY BUS
Snowdon, Scafell Pike and Ben Nevis – without car – in two days

Buses and trains run only during the day, and also somewhat slowly. The time limit for the 'Three Peaks by Bus' accordingly, must expand to 48 hours. Even so, it constituted a severe challenge: to the reliability and punctuality of our public transport system, but also, with its overnight crossings of Scafell Pike and Ben Nevis, to myself.

This tour can be commended to all who enjoy exploring the wide spaces and colourful scenes on the other side of the computer screen. Over the weeks of early summer I spent more time on the Internet Journey Planner than I ultimately spent on the journey planned. The Saturday timetable would let me get a slightly earlier trip on the delightful Ravenglass & Eskdale Railway, and so reach Ben Nevis at 6pm with an evening for its ascent; if that Saturday was after 20 June, the preceding evening would offer a 7pm crossing by the Derwent Water launch. Public transport doesn't just mean buses: I was aiming at the exotic.

George Borrow ascended Snowdon in 1854, quoting a Welsh couplet at the summit:

> *Easy to say 'Behold Eryri'*
> *Harder 'tis to climb his head*
> *Easy for him whose heart is cheery*
> *To bid the wretch be comforted.*

… with the second couplet being his own English addition. But Borrow was wrong. Looking out of the window at Pen-y-Pass, there's very little chance of beholding Eryri behind the raindrops and driving cloud. Ascending his head, however, is fairly straightforward: the Pig Track is even tarmacked for its first few steps alongside the helipad.

Crib Goch, the rocky ridge of Snowdon, is said to be a busy place. At 8am, in the rain, I was unsurprisingly the only person in all the 20 visible metres of the clouded ridge. The grey volcanic rock is good and grippy even when wet; the pinnacles are particularly sublime when in cloud-piercing mode; and I was quite sorry for all the crowd of ridge-scramblers not there that day on Crib Goch.

I arrived at Snowdon summit at 10am in dense cloud. No walkers were on Snowdon, but there were some railway passengers, wondering quite what they'd paid for. One of them obligingly took me my summit photograph. 'Can

Planning the public-transport Three Peaks took longer than the walk

we go down now?' asked the children, and they hurried back to the station waiting room. I could have joined them; but I was making up the rules for this myself, and one of them was: the Snowdon Mountain Railway Doesn't Count.

I descended gently to Rydd Ddu, through clear cool air and occasional shafts of sunlight, pleased to find that anyone I mentioned it to found my 48hr project thoroughly amusing. From the valley below came the echoing cry of a steam train. So much for my long hours of research; at the bottom of the path was a railway line undreamed of in the Internet Journey Planner, unmarked on my map. In the years since I'd last visited the valley, the Welsh Mountain Railway had reoccupied the old track bed, arriving at Rydd Ddu just two years before me. On the line stood an engine with steam up, and a train about to depart for Caernarfon.

I consulted my timings. Twice as expensive as the Snowdon Sherpa bus service, and at half the speed, the train would deposit me at Caernarfon too late for my bus to Bangor, thus eliminating my excursion at day's end on the Derwent Water launch. But – real steam (even if, as it appeared, generated by the combustion of oil rather than of coal or firewood). A red dragon smoking on the side of every carriage... I climbed aboard, and 90 minutes later trundled through a gap in the town walls to fetch up below the high wall of Caernarfon castle. A kindly Welsh lady guided me through the streets to Bus Stop B, unsigned in either English or Welsh for international bus travellers.

Considering it travels at 125mph, and swings sideways through angles of 15°, the Pendolino is a surprisingly unexciting form of travel. Indeed, it has less room for unpacking the backpack, finding something to eat, and going through the planning documents, than the narrow-gauge Welsh Mountain Railway.

Lunch on the Welsh Mountain Railway

'Do you understand Swahili?' For some time, I'd been realising that some of the words drifting through my carriage were ones I'd last heard, 30 years before, on not Snowdon or Scafell but the slopes of Kilimanjaro. But the young woman in the bright headscarf who came from Dar-es-Salaam – how had she known? I hadn't been sitting there laughing; my Swahili, sadly, isn't good enough for that.

However long it's going to take multiculturalism to reach Scafell Pike (and let's hope it won't be *too* long) the Pendolino gets there rather quickly. I could still get to the head of Borrowdale, by bus rather than boat, in time for an evening ascent. But as I was making the rules here, I could also change them. Real steam in Wales meant not now needing the Eskdale railway, delightful but still only diesel. Morning out of Borrowdale might offer the Derwent Water cruise; a sunlit evening cried out for a proper crossing of Scafell Pike, obtainable by an approach out of Grasmere; just so long as Oxenholme offered a connecting train to Windermere…

It did, along the railway line denigrated in two fervent sonnets by Wordsworth. A supermarket at Windermere station allowed me to buy some food, and the 555 bus took me up to Grasmere. I missed a trick, here: the Windermere Lake Cruise runs until 6.10pm, and would have taken me to Ambleside for an even longer way up Scafell Pike. However, as the sun gradually descended towards Helvellyn, I was making my way up the long ridge of the Langdale Pikes. It's a hillwalk – indeed the only specific hillwalk – recommended in Wordsworth's own *Guide to the Lakes*.

A pastel pink-and-yellow sunset saw me on Harrison Stickle. Boulders and a pale path crossed a moorland rapidly paling from grey to black. Night-walking is difficult in quite a different way from the more usual walking in the mist: a mountain shape stands against the stars, but is it Hanging Knotts of Bowfell, 1000ft above and 2 miles distant, or only a boulder? At 10.30pm I switched

Evening on Harrison Stickle

on the torch for the stepping stones at Angle Tarn; then proceeded like a tube train, a small island of light along the pre-laid way of the National Park's stone footpath. Far down on the right, an orange glow was Keswick. Far down left, another orange glow was presumably Barrow in Furness, seen along the length of Eskdale. An hour later the torch flicked over a patch of long grass that wasn't moving under the breeze, thus showing itself to be in some sheltered hollow. I unrolled the bivouac sack, lay down in it, and went to sleep.

After an hour, grass tickled my chin and I awoke. In front of me against the stars stood Esk Pike, the unfamiliar central fell that's usually obscured by others, and the last hill in Lakeland to get its own name. I went back to sleep. It's the nature of the bivvy bag to give you intimate knowledge of the night-time – an hour later, I woke again – the stars had moved round. Esk Pike was still there.

At dawn I rose, took up my bed, and walked up Great End. Since my last visit the summit had acquired a plate – quite a large one – commemorating a recently deceased fellwalker. To twist Philip Larkin: your descendents, they plaque you up. There are, according to the National Park Authority, something like 1 million of us Lakeland lovers. Supposing each of us million dies and gets a marker onto the rocks? It won't take too many generations before Scafell Pike becomes a metal mountain yellow-brown and shiny all over.

The better way down Borrowdale: Derwent Water launch

As it is, the place has a damp cairn 15ft wide and 6ft high, and a war memorial stone. After 85 years, the stone is lichening over nicely; and the monster cairn still only makes Scafell Pike the third-worst desecrated of the National Three Peaks. By the time I got down to Styhead Tarn the campers were emerging from their tents, and the day's first walkers were coming up the path.

The Borrowdale topless bus would cost a whole lot more than £1.55 if it were in a proper theme park rather than just the Lake District. And it's a genuine roller-coaster ride, over the bumps of the Borrowdale Road, with branches swishing against the screen and grabbing for the woolly hats of the upstairs passengers. The bus wiggles its hips like a Tango-dancer, and slips between the Jaws of Borrowdale.

At Lodore pier, I could dismount from the Borrowdale bus and head into Keswick across the small waves of Derwent Water. This, however, would lose me an hour, and my connection at Penrith; the final result being a delay of 3 hours at Glasgow and arrival at Ben Nevis at 9pm. Against that, the sun was breaking through, and putting a shine on the small waves of Derwent Water. I dismounted at Lodore.

Thomas West, the first guidebook writer hereabouts, wrote that the only way to see Borrowdale was from the surface of the lake. The crags could all be seen at once, unconcealed by trees; Lodore waterfall, viewed through the Claude Glass, somehow managed to appear at 10 times its present-day volume of flow; there was the thrill of bumping into the celebrated Floating Island or being surprisingly capsized by the Bottom Wind. Sadly, in the intervening two centuries Derwent Water has lost both its wandering island and its special whirlwind. The Claude Glass was a curved mirror designed to make the Lake District look properly picturesque. Seen through its modern equivalent, the camera viewfinder, no such sublime splendours or terrors appeared, but just the beautifully composed arrangement of water, the Jaws of Borrowdale, and Castle Crag rising at the entrance. On the bench beside me, a young family looked in some trepidation up at Catbells, which they were about to assault on a literary pilgrimage in the paw prints of Mrs Tiggywinkle.

If the bus out of Keswick were slightly early, and the train out of Penrith slightly delayed, I might just get to Glasgow in time for the lunchtime bus. However, market day in Keswick put paid to that idea, leaving me with 3 hours of the afternoon to spend in Glasgow. A yellow-jacketed official emerged from an office to inform me that falling asleep in Buchanan Street bus station is forbidden. However, there's grass in George Square. I shook out my sleeping bag to dry, lay down under the hot sun, and started snoozing only slightly disturbed by youths practising spectacular break-dancing moves a few metres away. I thus ran, without knowing it, a peculiar local danger. Alongside George Square is a soup kitchen for the indigent. Unkempt hillwalkers relaxing in George Square have occasionally been offered soup…

Running by the western seaboard, Breadalbane, Rannoch Moor and under Ben Nevis, the West Highland Railway is one of Britain's finest. But the Citylink coach is more frequent, faster, and considerably cheaper; and takes almost as fine a line. Through a beautiful afternoon and into a beautiful evening it carried me alongside Loch Lomond and down into the shadows of Glen Coe. I stepped down at Fort William with the last sunlight gleaming on Ben Nevis 1200m above.

Ben Nevis is a busy hill. Even at 10pm a few people were coming down the path. A blank-eyed young woman with no rucksack caused me a moment of concern, until I saw her companion, with two rucksacks, just above. Ben Nevis up-and-down the Tourist Path from Fort William is an exercise in strenuousness; Ben Nevis from the back is a mountain, and these two had just achieved one of its most magnificent routes, the 3km of Tower Ridge.

Meanwhile I was causing moments of concern to the more socially responsible of the descenders. A couple of them stopped me to make sure I'd noticed it was getting dark, and to warn of the chilliness of the summit plateau.

There was no moon; but light lingered along the northern skyline as 10.30 passed, and then 11. The half-way lochan was a pale gleam of reflected starlight. Lights came towards me down the path: a party on their way to Scafell Pike and Snowdon on the 24hr, motor-car version of my own walk. They at least didn't consider it at all strange to be wandering around on Britain's highest hill in the middle of the night.

Approaching the Red Burn, the path crosses a rocky section with dark hollows plunging towards the lamps of Glen Nevis caravan site. I paused below the waterfall to get out my torch. But the path rose a pale streak in the starlight, and while leaving the torch off did mean a bit of stumbling among the stones, it gave a much better sense of my surroundings – surroundings which, if I were to stray off the path, might even involve the 600m drop down the exciting side of Ben Nevis. Just before 1am I reached the various rubbishy structures that mark the summit.

I've been on Ben Nevis just twice in clear conditions – and both those times have been in the dark… Low-lying cloud obscured the jagged mountain horizon all around, and even the tops of the northern crags looked oddly urban against a thin mist lit orange by the street lights of Fort William. The scruffy summit structures – the monster cairn and trig point, the memorial with its brass plates dimly gleaming, the ruins of the 19th-century observatory – were like a bomb site against the stars.

> … *So many cold hundreds*
> *have pissed against the cairn,*
> *she is soiled through and wet*
> *and weary in her solitude.*

So wrote Hamish Brown in his fine poem on Ben Nevis. I was aware that the soggy state of the observatory's remaining floorboards was down to worse waters than the dews of heaven. But even so, they were more comfortable than the surrounding stones. Meanwhile, the summit hut strictly says 'emergency refuge only' and anyway one might oversleep in the dark in there.

I woke with the chill seeping up through my sleeping bag out of the half-rotten planks, and wondering if the night was almost over. My watch said I'd been asleep for just 30 minutes… Fortunately I only needed to shiver for 3 hours or so, as I had to be back at the bottom by 7.30am to hit the 48 hours. I woke for the last time at 4am, by which time a damp mist had wrapped the summit. At this point the inside of the sleeping bag suddenly became almost warm and comfortable compared with the wet grey world I had to wriggle out into. But once I was moving and off the plateau, the world warmed up. I came out of the cloud, and Fort William guided me down like an airfield's landing lights. Oddly, the rocky section after the Red Burn was by dawn's light a wide and undemanding path… Well below the Half-way Lochan, the new day's early walkers started coming up the other way. At 6.40am, 47hrs 15min after leaving Pen-y-Pass, I settled onto the wooden bench outside Glen Nevis youth hostel.

Of the 47 hours, I'd spent 11hrs 1min on 12 separate conveyances of public transport: paying £93.14 for 685km of travel at an average speed (when moving) of 62kph. No tickets were purchased in advance: however, the train

The reward for it all: Nevisport breakfast, Fort William

and coach travel was reduced by being half of a return ticket. Apart from an overcrowded train between Warrington and Oxenholme, it was pleasant or better. The two most enjoyable were also the most expensive and the slowest: the Derwent Water launch (10kph and 73p/km) and the Welsh Mountain Railway (12kph, 53p). The cheapest, as well as one of the most scenic, was the Citylink coach to Fort William (55kph, 7p). The second cheapest, as well as the fastest, was the Virgin Pendolino to Glasgow (130kph, 9p). Worst value for money was the Stagecoach bus Windermere to Grasmere, at 28p/km; buses in Wales were noticeably cheaper. Even 28p is less than the full cost of driving a car, though the car's petrol on its own would come to about 8p.

As well as 11 hours actually travelling, I spent 7hrs 42min waiting for connections. This would have been longer, but for 37 minutes cut by delayed arrivals: Keswick's market day and the Stagecoach service to Penrith.

Nowhere did the public transport system really let me down; I missed no crucial connection. Until, on my journey home, the coach was delayed 20 minutes by roadworks on the A8 and even a run under my rucksack got me across Glasgow 2 minutes too late for my southward train. The later train was 7 hours later. At least I'd had time for some shopping in Fort William. As I lay down once again in Glasgow's George Square, there was no risk of being offered indigent soup in my nice new walking boots...

PART II:
THREE PEAKS RATHER CLOSER
TOGETHER

Chapter 4

The Yorkshire Three Peaks:
Pen-y-ghent, Whernside, Ingleborough

ROUTE AND SCHEDULE

The hills	Pen-y-ghent (694m), Whernside (736m), Ingleborough (724m)
Distance	33km (23 miles)
Ascent	1400m (4600ft)
Start/finish	Horton in Ribblesdale (SD 808 725)
Terrain	Paths well made and boggy, tracks and lanes
Target time	12hrs
Standard strong walker	10.5hrs

Three notable hills stand right in the middle of England. While Whernside is a high grassy scarp, Ingleborough and Pen-y-ghent are even better, both of them abrim with Yorkshire temperament and character. The route is mostly, but not entirely, on clear paths. It's the alternation of lovely, walkable limestone and grim bogs on the grit that give this walk its particular flavour. It's not just the fact that it has the same number of peaks that makes this one such a popular practice walk for the Three Peaks (UK).

In July 1887 two masters from Giggleswick School at Settle crossed Ingleborough to Chapel-le-Dale for tea. As the weather was fine, they decided to return over Whernside and Pen-y-ghent, getting back to the school at midnight. The walk now attracts around 10,000 walkers a year, so on summer weekends is very busy indeed.

The Route
From the car park in Horton head south for 250 metres, past the Pen-y-ghent Café, to a track on the left signposted for Pen-y-ghent. In 200 metres turn right, through a farm and across a footbridge. (Large or pre-dawn groups avoid the farm, following the main road past Horton church.) A tarred lane leads up left to Brackenbottom Farm. Just before the buildings turn left on an uphill path with

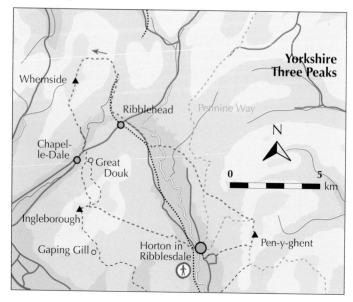

a wall on its left. After several stiles, it joins the **Pennine Way**. Turn left up the steep nose of Pen-y-ghent on a well-built path. It skirts the two steep sections on the right (east) flank but still has a slightly rocky moment. A stone shelter with seating marks the summit of **Pen-y-ghent**.

Cross a stile just to right of the shelter, and head directly away from the wall, signposted 'Horton', on a path initially unclear. As the ground steepens, the path forms, to reach the plateau edge and turn half-right (north) along it. After 400 metres (SD 838 739, ref point [1]) the path slants down the scarp side. Below a crag it reaches a signpost (ref point [2]) pointing downhill for Horton. The smooth gravel path runs down across a stile to the end of Horton Scar Lane. Turn right, away from the lane, and follow a dry valley bottom to the spectacular **Hunt Pot**.

If rivers are full, pass round to left of the Pot to avoid the river crossing ahead. Otherwise take a small path to right of the Hull Pot Beck for 400 metres. Look out for a stile over the wall on the right, as it marks the start of the path on the opposite side of the stream. Around 50 metres before the stile (ref point [3]) is a good place to cross the stream. Opposite the stile, a peaty path sets off northwest. Keep track of the boundary walls, as it's possible to lose the path by

YORKSHIRE THREE PEAKS – GRID REFERENCES

The Yorkshire Three Peaks in 8-digit grid references for GPS

[1] SD 8377 7386 Path leaves Pen-y-ghent plateau
[2] SD 8374 7422 Signpost below Pen-y-ghent plateau
[3] SD 8256 7493 Crossing of Hull Pot Beck
[4] SD 7348 8016 Path drops off Whernside plateau
[5] SD 7464 7478 Path reaches Ingleborough plateau
[6] SD 7448 7469 Path junction on Ingleborough
[7] SD 7440 7466 Ingleborough plateau northeast corner
[8] SD 7412 7460 Ingleborough summit shelter
[9] SD 7411 7457 Ingleborough trig point

diverting around swamps; the walls will then steer you back onto route. Always northwest, the path passes through two broken walls running north–south, then crosses a stream and an east–west wall simultaneously, to reach the green track of the **Pennine Way**.

Cross and continue with a wall to left, to a gap stile. Here gritstone yields to limestone, and the soggy path abruptly disappears to become a firm green field. Keep ahead and join a track that passes above the wooded valley head of Birkwith Cave. At the access track of Old Ing turn down left for 200 metres, then right, signposted for Nether Lodge. Where the track turns up right, keep ahead with wall to left, to **God's Bridge** – a natural arch at SD 798 775. Across it turn half-left, and contour on a small path that becomes a track down to **Nether Lodge**. The right-of-way bears left across a bridge, but is planned to be diverted to right of the buildings.

Follow the access track away from the farm to the B6479 and turn right to a T-junction near **Ribblehead Viaduct**. A snack-bar caravan sometimes lurks here. Cross onto a rough path that soon joins a gravel track. Where this bends left, keep ahead (not passing under the viaduct) on a well-made path to right of the railway. After 2km, ignoring a fork right for Dent, dip to cross a ford and then cross the railway on the aqueduct carrying Force Gill. The good path runs up to right of the stream with its waterfall. After 600 metres, turn off left across a stile on a path signposted 'Whernside'. It crosses streams, and joins the ridgeline fence, running between it and a steep drop on the left to the summit of **Whernside**. A walled shelter has a bench with Ingleborough view; a wall gap leads through to the trig point.

Continue south next to the steep drop. After 1km the ridge steepens, with zigzags on the path. As the ridge levels, the main path turns off left to a cairn

A hole with a river into it: Hull Pot is just one of Yorkshire's scenic surprises

(ref point [4]) where it drops steeply on rough stone steps, then runs down moorland to near Bruntscar Farm. Signs 'Hill Inn' point the way down the farm's access track. This soon becomes tarred, and leads past Philpin (summer café) to B6255.

Turn uphill, past the **Old Hill Inn**, then another 150 metres to a gate and signpost ('fp Ingleborough'). A track bends right to a gate with ladder stile. A faint green path continues across firm grass, south, for 100 metres to another gate. (Here you would turn left for Great Douk, whose treetops can be seen 300 metres up the hill.) The path ahead is now clearer, contouring green fields below the rim of limestone pavement, then turning up left. It passes between two spectacular limestone pavements, then to right of the deep **Braithwaite Wife Hole**. At a wall stile, the ground reverts to swampy gritstone, but a fine flagged path crosses this to the base of Ingleborough's steep side. Rough steps lead up this challenging 300m haul. At the top the path bears right, across a stream top, to a cairn (ref point [5]) at the plateau edge.

The path runs up the ridgeline. Just before it steepens and gets rocky, a cairn marks the turn-off left that you'll take on the descent. Ahead, the built path skirts to right (north) of the ridgeline to reach the plateau. Head west to the shelter walls and the trig point of **Ingleborough**.

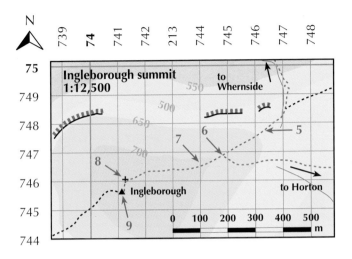

Return to the path junction mentioned (ref point [6]) and turn right. Once found, the path is wide and clear, across a ladder stile at Fell Beck Head, and down to join a wall and stream with a derelict shooting hut. Ignore a track forking right, but stay by the stream to a gate with ladder stile (NS 768 738). After another 400 metres, the path runs through a trench in limestone pavement to a wall stile.

Ahead now the path is less clear across green limestone ground. It heads gently downhill, just south of east (110° magnetic) along a green dip that runs right down across the moor. After 500 metres a steeper descent leads to a sign-post where a bridleway crosses. Continue ahead along the continuation of the green dip, **Sulber Nick**. After 1.3km, another signpost points down through a wide wall gap.

Again the path is indistinct, down limestone and grass, marked occasionally with green-top posts, yellow paint spots, and cairns but even so hard to track in darkness. Through the wall gap it bears right then turns left, then back right to a ladder stile (NS 795 730). Now it is a clay mud streak across fields, southeast across a track then up briefly to a wall gap stile. Head down to **Horton station** and follow the B6479, to a footbridge into the car park.

Descending Whernside, with Ingleborough ahead

YORKSHIRE THREE PEAKS SCHEDULE				
	Distance mls/km	Ascent ft/m	Time min	ETA
Start: Horton *				0:00
Pen-y-ghent	2.5/4.0	1550/460	85	1:25
Ribblehead viaduct	6.9/11.1		155	4:00
Whernside	4.1/6.5	1500/450	120	6:00
Hill Inn	2.7/4.3	100/30	60	7:00
Ingleborough	2.4/3.8	1400/420	100	8:40
Horton	4.6/7.3	100/30	105	10:25
TOTALS	**23/33**	**4650/1390**		

* Pen-y-ghent Café

ADVENTURES OF THE INVISIBLE WORM – A WINTER'S NIGHT ON THE YORKSHIRE THREE PEAKS

William Blake wrote about him: the invisible worm, who flies by night in the howling storm. In Blake's poem he's a bit of a villain, and we aren't invited to see things from his point of view. But on Pen-y-ghent, in the middle of the night, in the middle of winter, I knew just what the little fellow felt like.

It wasn't just the very cold wind, or the mist that threw the torchlight back into our faces. What really made us feel wormlike was the exceedingly dismal nature of the terrain – a mixture of loose stones, gravel, mud and ice. We slid about, and fell over, and hoped not to come too suddenly to the gritstone rim of Pen-y-ghent.

The path slid sideways through the gritstone: easy to follow, as its refrozen trampled slush showed dirty grey in the dark. These are sharply individual hills, showing the true Yorkshire temperament: you stand in your bit of bog and I'll stand in mine. So it's quite quickly that we drop out of the storm to find moonlight, and grey-brown curves of gritstone bog, and the bottom of Ingleborough looming across the valley, ready to pounce on us in 8 hours time, supposing we get that far. And maybe we shall; for look! Here's a useful signpost.

Scottish signposts are green and white. Lakeland signs are cheerful yellow arrows, or historic slate. Yorkshire signs are rain-stained wood, peat-blackened, aged; they resemble gibbets from which the corpse has rotted and dropped into the bog. They tell you, to the nearest eighth of a mile, just how much more bog lies in front – but happily, by torchlight, their mossed-over messages can't be read.

A bog path in the dark is full of interest – and there's 6 miles of bog path from here to Ribblehead. It's a black streak that shows up well by moonlight; and it's half-frozen, so that we hardly sink in at all except at the sudden streams. But then we climb a rickety stile – these being made of the same stained bog-wood as the signposts, and the ladder bits very handy when you need to hang up a corpse. Up the ladder and down the wall we're on limestone, and it's short easy grass and no visible path whatever.

This limestone is just as interesting as the bog was. Switch off the torch, switch off your mind, and there's a primitive linkage between eye and foot that can follow an invisible path by moonlight. Except sometimes it can't, and there's an unexpected wall. When that happens you take out the compass and find a wall on the map with the same direction, and work out which way's the next ladder. But quite often the invisible linkage does work, so that we drop down a bit of grass that could be anywhere and find exactly in front of us a handy little wooden footbridge. 'I hope you're remembering all this, Colin.'

Colin is studying the ground in case he wants to do the famous Three Peaks fell race (see Appendix I). Though perhaps it doesn't altogether make sense to show him his first ever glimpses of Yorkshire in the dark...

Six miles of stumbling about is about right. At Ribblehead Viaduct we're ready to enjoy the arches in the dark and stride away on the wide paths up Whernside. The cloud's lifted away; the moon, one day past the full, is pouring its radiance into the bogs of Yorkshire. Down on the left in Ribblesdale one or two dim lights show, and there's a car over by Pen-y-ghent. On the right – civilisation! Orange lights of Lancaster flicker in the distance, and Heysham power station is a black block against Morecambe Bay. On the rocky edge of Whernside the moon doth shine as bright as day, except when a cloud rushes by and it goes suddenly dark just as you're stepping off a boulder.

One thing William Blake didn't tell us about the Invisible Worm was what it did in its time off. But clearly, the place for an invisible worm is an invisible wormhole. And if you're doing the Yorkshire Three Peaks in the dark, you might as well do them underground. Great Douk Cave makes a logical route up Ingleborough: it eliminates nearly a kilometre of path, and a stile.

Logical isn't the same as sensible. Great Douk Cave is, in fact, a stream. It's a cavers' Grade 1 (the least difficult grading), and some of the richly varied dangers of caving do not apply – no unexpected holes in the floor, no wrong turnings to take. 'But if I get claustrophobia we come out,' says Colin. This will be his first go at underground mountaineering.

Great Douk is strange. Walking across an empty moonlit meadow you hear trees in the breeze, and there they are, down in a hole, with their top twigs at the level of your toes. Stretch a green cloth over the branches and make a cunning trap for dinosaurs. A little path leads down, and you're in a different place altogether, with stony ground and cliffs. A place that's not so much Douk, as Dante: the first canto of the *Inferno*. The entrance to the underworld is always through a darksome wood. Moonlight seeps between the branches, and a sprinkling of silvery lights is the stream that runs from nowhere to nowhere across the bottom of the hole.

But in fact the stream does run from somewhere. Follow it up through the trees to where it emerges under a pale brow of limestone. 'We're going in there?' Colin doesn't trust an entrance that's so obviously going to lead to a magical other world of trolls, and green-eyed persons offering poisoned cream cakes.

'Let's have a look, anyway.' Colin's not a climber, and so he doesn't recognise this one – it actually means: 'We'll go on till we get scared, by which time it'll be too late to go back.' We scramble up the little splashy waterfall, enter

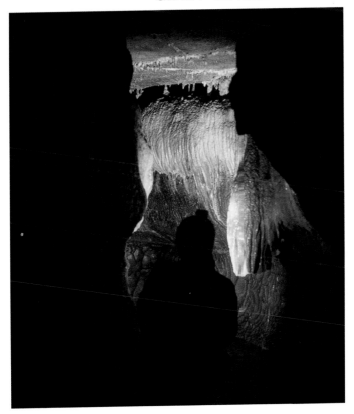

In Great Douk Cave at 4am

the hole under the crag. The wrong turning on the left is reassuringly where the guidebook said it would be, while on the right the stream runs up into the mountain. The hole is two people wide, about four people high, and rounded shapes like intestines seen from inside.

There's no getting away from the fact that the bottom nine inches of this passage are full of running water: our peaty feet are getting extremely clean. The passage sides are lumps of calcite, and stratified cracks, and glittery crystal. The top, miraculously, opens into a starry hole fringed with fern. We're passing under Little Douk Pot, and above is most of the Big Dipper so we can tell where north is and verify the direction of our wormhole.

The hole continues to wiggle into the hill. It begins to seem almost natural to walk in water by torchlight in a slot of dripping rock. If this isn't the afterlife, then it certainly isn't the before-life either: rather, some sort of in-between. There are two little underground waterfalls – or rather, cataracts; like the ones the sun-boat of Ra steers underneath Egypt between dusk and dawn. But then come side-passages, and part of the stream runs away into the wall, and we have to stop and read the guidebook.

The guidebook has various junctions, and a hole in the roof leading to a low place, and a wet exit and a dry one. It doesn't say anything about crawling around in nine inches of water. Maybe caving books take it for granted you crawl in water and only bother to mention when you don't. We crawl in water down one passage, we crawl in water up another; maybe we're just about to get to the hole in the roof and maybe we aren't. (Proper cavers go in the cave with someone who's been in the cave before.) After a while it gets tiresome, so we go back down the stream and out by the hole we came in by. The cave hasn't been any logical route up Ingleborough, but a mere excursion. Shucks!

So we're back walking up Ingleborough, and what with one thing and another the night is now ending and it's getting light. At 8am we reach the summit, just as a rather bent-looking orange sun creeps up behind a cloud bank. 'Yorkshire, how interesting,' says Colin. 'So this is what we've been walking about on all night.'

Let nobody say that Three Peaks in the Dark is an isolated or eccentric endeavour. The first record I find is of the fairly famous mountaineer Frank Smythe. (Nanga Parbat? Route Major on Mont Blanc? Well, I did only say fairly famous.) He made a night attempt in the 1920s, at the age of 19. Too young, really, to appreciate the subtle joys of night Yorkshire. He got sleepy and didn't do Whernside – perhaps the bike ride in from Bradford hadn't been such a great idea. Fifty years later, Duncan Kyle celebrated those joys in a book called *Green River High*. What do you do when you're being chased round Pen-y-ghent, Whernside and Ingleborough by two unattractive characters with shotguns? The answer, if you can't work it out for yourself, is at the end.

And this very night, under this very moon, three walkers from Liverpool are in front of us on the Yorkshire Peaks. We were going to go together, but they didn't want to wait for us and anyway the bit in the cave really was too silly. But they have left, on the cairn of Ingleborough, two boiled sweeties. We stop for a moment to enjoy the sweeties and the sunrise, then make our way down to Horton and the Pen-y-ghent Café. (I phoned Liverpool later and they hadn't

Ingleborough at sunrise

left any sweeties. Poisoned bait from the trolls? Or were there even more of us sightseeing Yorkshire in the dark?)

At the café they give you orange juice in pints to turn your fry-up breakfast into something healthy. 'Going out on the hills are you, lads?'

'Well, actually,' I admit, 'we've already been.'

The shotgun villains? You hide up until night among the clints and grikes of the limestone; and then you head round the south side of Ingleborough, and at a crucial point you go 'Oh, oh! We can't take any more, just shoot us straight away or else leave us alone with our sore legs'; and they rush towards you with their shotguns and fall into Gaping Gill. Clever, eh? Colin looks from the Pen-y-ghent Café up at Pen-y-ghent. He wonders if anyone's ever done the double circuit, dark then daylight. But I go 'Oh, oh! Can't take any more!'

Never one to miss a literary reference, me.

Up Ingleborough underground

As caving routes go, this is less dangerous than most, as it's always possible to turn and retrace steps downstream. Do not attempt it if the stream is in spate, or if heavy rain is forecast.

A stile leads to a rough path down into Great Douk hollow (SD 747 770). At its head, the stream emerges as a waterfall. Scramble up the waterfall. If the stream above is too full to stand in without hanging on to the rock walls – retreat advised.

Immediately inside is an inconspicuous wrong turning on the left. The right way runs upstream, knee-deep, in a comfortable passage with many bends. After 100 metres you pass briefly back into daylight (or starlight) as the stream passes along the bottom of Little Douk. The passage continues for 800 metres (0.5 mile). Calcite bulges in from either side: eventually you have to crouch to get past one bulge. About 100 metres after this, the passage divides. The stream emerges from a low arch on the left, but take the higher and drier passage on the right.

This passage is already too low to stand upright, and over the next 100 metres gets lower, to crouch height. Now it divides, both branches being crawl-high.

Take the left-hand one, sometimes holding about 10cm of water. Crawl for about 50 metres in shallow water. Around 5 metres before the end of the passage, there's a hole in the roof.

Go up into a passage that's an even lower crawl, a knee-elbow squirm (but at least it's dry) for 5 metres. Now the cave divides. Turn left into what looks like a wide, low, dead-end. A narrow passage leads after one bend to daylight. Squirm up through the clints of limestone pavement into open air.

Ingleborough from underneath

Chapter 5

The Lancashire Three Peaks:
Longridge Fell, Easington Fell, Pendle

PEN-Y-GHENT – OR PENDLE?

At 9am we climbed out of the Ribble Valley and looked back across it from the slope of Longridge Fell. 'It's the southernmost fell in England, you know,' said my Lancastrian companion. I raised some eyebrows: for isn't there the Peak District, and even a place called Dartmoor?

'The southernmost *fell*,' he repeats. 'All the others are hills, or beacons, or Pen-y-something. Also, it's the Centre of the Kingdom, according the Ordnance Survey. At least, it is if you count the UK's six main islands but ignore all the smaller ones.'

For a place with such a weight of geography, and etymology, Longridge is a surprisingly small fell. This despite the way that embarrassed Lancastrians have attempted to enlarge it, raising the trig point so that its base stands a metre above its 350m ground level. The ground it stands above is a pleasingly rugged mix of gritstone and heather, dropping suddenly to the north for a view of the Bowland Fells, and the West Pennine Moors, with three grey humps in the horizon being the Three Peaks of Yorkshire.

An old ramped path leads down off Longridge; but it was quicker, as well as more authentically hilly, to take the steep bilberry and bracken direct. At the fell wall, I paused and scanned the map in my left hand for the right-of-way line. The map in my left hand wasn't there. It was lying idly on the trig point, 2m above the top of Longridge Fell.

The hills of Lancashire are less small when you get to do them twice over.

Richard of York Gave Battle In Vain. The initial letters of this useful slogan help us remember the colours of the rainbow from red to indigo and violet. But the phrase also reminds that the Wars of the Roses ended with a win for Lancashire. (Richard Crouchback; Battle of Bosworth; 'My kingdom for a horse' – and if you saw it with Laurence Olivier, that scene where in every direction a line of dark warriors rises from behind the near horizon.)

Lancashire won – with the final score in killed kings standing at 2–1. But you wouldn't know it. Yorkshire has crept outwards from its famous Three Peaks, colonising even the hills of Bowland and reaching within 9 miles of Lancaster town hall. And even as they got Bowland back, the Lancastrians lost (to Cumbria) proud Coniston Old Man across the sands of Morecambe Bay.

Today's walk was a continuation of the Wars of the Roses by hillwalking means. Yorkshire has Wensleydale cheese, parkin, and *Dalesman* magazine: Lancashire has Lancashire hotpot. Yorkshire has Fountains Abbey and York Minster: Lancashire has *The Liver Birds*. Yorkshire has *Emmerdale* and *Heartbeat*: Lancashire has *Coronation Street*. Yorkshire has the Brontës: Lancashire has the Beatles. Yorkshire has Whernside, Ingleborough and Pen-y-ghent. Lancashire has... Well, what?

Bowland is quite high, but exceeding heathery. The West Pennines are a lot like the East Pennines. But 8 miles away, Easington Fell rose out of a sea of green fields like a dead whale. After 489 years of uneasy peace, the Wars of the Roses broke out again in 1974 when Lancashire suddenly took over most of Bowland and the town of Barnoldswick. The purpose of this invasion was now apparent. Seized-back Easington, formerly in Yorkshire, could now be nominated as the second of our newly-invented Lancashire Three Peaks. While the third peak just had to be Pendle.

Having descended for the second time Longridge Fell, the Lancastrian led me northwards. Not the quickest way to Easington Fell; but a diversion to take in the second of three river features. Already we'd visited an abbey at Whalley, where we'd crosssed under a viaduct perhaps not quite so impressive as Ribblehead. As an off-beat feature, the Whalley viaduct has two of its brick arches in Early English Gothic, to conform to Whalley Abbey. We'd also walked the banks of Calder and Ribble (the Yorkshire Three Peaks has only a much-reduced version of the Ribble) before crossing what calls itself the 'Philosophers' Golf Course' at Stonyhurst. These diversions, scenic in themselves, would also take this small hill walk well beyond the 35-mile mark (the Yorkshire Three Peaks is only 25 miles).

The Hodder Valley, says Wainwright in his *Bowland Sketchbook*, used to be considered, controversially, as the prettiest river in Yorkshire; it is now, much less arguably, the prettiest river of Lancashire. The locals haven't noticed, and still take the *Yorkshire Post*. We passed the ancient coaching inn at Whitewell too early for a Lancs lunch. Below the church, rights of way from both sides arrive at the Hodder, presumably so that Yorkshiremen and Lancastrians could shout at each other across the water. Secure in possession of both banks, Lancs Council has now built some handsome 'hipping stones' for us to hop across.

'When we get up onto Easington, I'll introduce you to some friends of mine: Old Ned and his Wife.' I somehow suspected that they would not stand smiling offering hot pots of tea and Eccles cakes. Eccles cakes come from Lancashire, and Ned and Wife are piles of stones. Ned comes first; with age he's let himself

Approaching Easington Fell, the second of the Lancashire Three Peaks

go to pieces. The Wife, 200 metres on, has kept herself in rather better shape. They stand in low, springy grassland; Easington Fell lives up to its name, being after a lie-down lunch rather difficult to get up out of. Around Easington's edge the Three Peaks of Yorks rise exactly like those dark warriors when Laurence Oliver started on about his kingdom for a horse. Still, seen from here the Yorkshire Three are clearly smaller and a lot further away than Pendle.

We passed down Easington by bracken and a tree gap romantically named as Shivery Ginnel, and crossed the Ribble again to get into Sawley. Longridge had been fairly long, Easington had been quite easy, but now a nice drink was Sawley needed. I didn't dare ask for Lancs hotpot and black pudden' as Sawley is a mile and more inside the conquered territories (you can paint a white rose red but that doesn't get rid of the prickles...)

Sawley offers the walk's second Cistercian abbey – although there's not much left of it as the monks found it too damp and decamped to Whalley 800 years ago. Not having had any hotpot we were flagging slightly; and Pendle was just getting bigger and bigger. A handsome packhorse bridge led over Ings Beck. We had now crossed back into undisputed Lancashire. Perhaps because of this, my Lancastrian friend became noticeably more confident. 'Don't worry

Descending from Pendle

about Pendle,' he reassured, 'once we're down in Downham, can hire ourselves broomsticks to get up Pendle. Can't possibly be classed as mechanical
assistance.'

Downham is an excessively pretty village haunted by non-existent witches
and impended over by Pendle. Hanging baskets of satanic size drool with
genetically modified geraniums in strident orange. The scarlet salvias are almost
subtle by comparison. Downham's public toilets have authentic urinal stalls,
these being in an old shippen for cows and other livestock. Downham has a little stream through, and no TV aerials; don't bother to want to buy a house here
because you can't. Downham's main entertainment is attempting to feed the
ducks . Even the ducks are gentrified, and don't eat white sliced. Black pudden',
perhaps? Certainly not parkin.

Above Downham, Lancs man pointed out the knoll called Worsaw Hill,
with white fissured rock and smooth greensward: 'It's the very last of the mountain limestone.'

'You mean, we're looking at the final foothill of the Yorkshire Three Peaks?'

It may just have been the steep side of Pendle that caused the lack of reply
to that. Still, a clear grass path zigzags in a kindly way up steepest Pendle. It
bends into a little mossy hollow, splendidly situated just below the slope top

and with a view across several hundred square miles of Lancashire. Behind the boulders, an iron plate covers Fox's Well.

'I was moved of the Lord to go up the top of it [Pendle Hill], which I did with much ado, as it was so very steep and high.' George Fox drank from this well in 1652 and was inspired to found the Quaker movement. It's an excellent legend, though in cold fact Fox seems to have gone up Pendle, like so many of us since, for the sake of the view. He needed to work out where the big villages were so as to go and preach in them. 'And the Lord let me see in what places He had a great people to be gathered. And I went.'

The pewter cup is chained to the underside of the iron plate. There's a technique: drop the cup in sideways so that it sinks, then lift it out smartly, causing the black flies on the surface to flow out and away for a fly-free drink. It's the usual sacred-well story, drink from the waters and descend the hill either inspired or insane. Or in the case of Lancs Three Peaks pursuers, both.

The former Yorkshire border runs across the flank of Pendle. Lancastrians may laugh, but some Yorkshiremen, ignoring the result of the Battle of Bosworth, claim Pendle as a Yorkshire hill 'really', pending reconquest.

A well-trampled path leads to Pendle Hill's summit trig. Because of its witch legend, Pendle is a popular ascent in the dark at Hallowe'en. And sinister statistics do show that of all those that go up, slightly fewer come down – but the discrepant ones, snatched off the slopes at midnight, are not on broomsticks but in helicopters and stretchers of Rossendale Mountain Rescue.

So how does Pendle compare with Pen-y-ghent? Both are splendidly steep around the sides. Pendle scores by its long level plateau, 3 miles and more, suspended (broomstick-rider style) above the fields and towns of Lancashire and former Yorkshire. Sun emerged for us at this point, making the fields go golden and lying across the concrete towers of Clitheroe's cement works. After passing the surprising ski resort at Pendleton Moor, we reached Nick of Pendle, then crossed a lower moor where a hollow in the ridge has strange fallen stones, one of them helpfully labelled 'Joppe Knave Grave' just like on the map. Except that the carver didn't realise he was living in Ancient Times so didn't use the proper OS ancient writing. A robber was beheaded and buried under it in the Middle Ages, but dug up again and relocated in 1608.

Fourteen hours after leaving it, we dropped into Whalley. The sunset lit up its chimney pots; and the monks had built a mill pool for the comfort of ducks and as a last lingering-spot for Lancashire-bagging walkers.

Should Yorkshire worry? Pendle against Pen-y-ghent, Ingleborough against Easington Fell. The Lancashire Three Peaks are more scenic than the Yorkshire ones; they offer three big rivers, half a dozen woodlands, and two Cistercian abbeys. The Lancashire Three Peaks may not be as high – but they're a long way further apart.

The Lancashire Three Peaks – or as a Yorkshireman might say, the Lancashire One Peak, plus one from oughter-be Yorkshire and one former Yorks that we'll reconquer by and by.

To which the Lancastrian replies: our 36-mile Three Peaks is too long for your legs – no wonder you wanted to swap your kingdom for a horse.

ROUTE AND SCHEDULE

The hills	Longridge Fell (350m), Easington Fell (396m), Pendle Hill (557m)
Concept	A rival to the Yorkshire Three Peaks
Distance	58km (36 miles)
Ascent	1600m (5400ft)
Start/finish	Whalley (SD 733 362)
Terrain	Field paths, tracks and lanes, open hilltops
Target time	18hrs
Standard strong walker	15.5hrs

Lancashire, too, has Three Peaks: the proposition has now been proved. Though smaller than the Yorkshire ones, they're further apart. The walk around them is as much countryside as hill, and rather more strenuous than its Yorkshire rival.

The long walk in brief

From **Whalley** Abbey head west under rail arches, then cross the Ribble on a footbridge below them. Field paths lead roughly west, over the A59, then to the Ribble again at Hacking Hall. Keep west past Aspinalls and Moorgate Farm, then turn north to a suspension footbridge (SD 686 365) across the Ribble for lanes to **Hurst Green**.

Head out on lane towards **Stoneyhurst**; before ornamental lakes, turn left on a lane, then cross the golf course due west to Higher Deer House. Turn down left across Dean Brook to join track past Greengore. Where the track exits into open field, bear half-left up field to ladder stile on skyline (SD 665 390), and cross fields northwest to a lane. Turn left for 300 metres to Low Hill Wood,

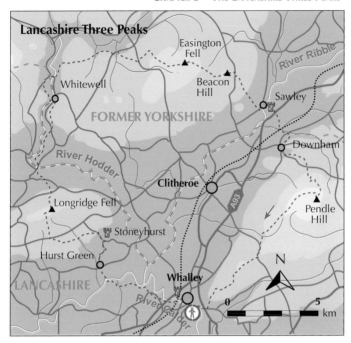

then up wood edge, roughly north, to hill crest, turning right for 400 metres to the summit of **Longridge Fell** (SD 658 410).

Head straight down north, and take field paths past Weed Acre to cross **Doeford Bridge**. Field paths near the river lead to a lane crossing (SD 658 452) and **Whitewell** inn. Cross the Hodder on stepping stones west of the church. Head up to New Laund, then recross the Hodder by **Burholme Bridge**.

From Burholme Farm, head northeast up Fielding Clough on a path to **Giddy Bridge** (SD 682 494) then east by Foolscales and Smelfthwaites. Pass Old Ned and Wife to the 396m summit of **Easington Fell** (SD 730 486).

Head down east along plantation edge, then into trees (SD 746 482) to join the Shivering Ginnel path to the trig point on **Beacon Hill**. From Scriddles Farm descend east past Till House, then southeast down field paths to **Sawley** with its Spread Eagle inn.

From the abbey ruins head southeast, across fields and A59, to an arched packhorse bridge (SD 785 453). Path leads up Downham Green to **Downham**.

Streamside and field paths lead southeast to Lane Head at the base of Pendle. A clear grass path climbs steepest Pendle to a ladder stile (where you can turn back left for Fox's Well at SD 806 420, not on the main path.) Cross the ladder stile to **Pendle Hill's** summit trig.

Return to the ladder stile, cross and bear left on a fairly small path around the plateau's northern rim and down a southwest spur, to cross Ashendean Clough to the road just below Pendle Ski Centre. Follow the road to its top at **Nick of Pendle**.

Follow an indistinct quad bike track along the ridgeline, to trig point 315m. Ahead is a wall corner, with ladder stile and stile to a rock slab at the slope top. Around 200 metres down, a hollow in the ridge crest has fallen stones, labelled **'Joppe Knave Grave'**. Drop south to join a bridleway track past Wiswell Moor Farm, then take a track on the right curving right on Clerk Hill. Take a field path downhill, to **Spring Wood** car park.

Cross at traffic lights onto a path to right of the B6246. After 300 metres cross to a riverside path and follow it into **Whalley**.

LANCASHIRE THREE PEAKS – SCHEDULE				
	Distance mls/km	**Ascent** ft/m	**Time** min	**ETA**
Start: Whalley				0:00
Hurst Green	5.2/8.3	250/70	110	1:50
Longridge Fell	4.4/7.1	1050/300	125	3:55
Whitewell	4.4/7.1	350/100	100	5:35
Giddy Bridge	3.1/5.0	450/140	75	6:50
Easington Fell	3.8/6,0	950/280	110	8:40
Sawley Bridge	3.6/5.8	150/40	85	10:05
Downham	2.1/3.3	450/130	60	11:05
Pendle	2.5/4.0	1400/420	100	12:45
Nick of Pendle	3.5/5.6	250/70	85	14:10
Whalley	3.5/5.6	150/50	85	15:35
TOTALS	**36/58**	**5400/1600**		

Chapter 6
Everywhere has Three Peaks in it

Peaks in Threes

> *I the Trinity illustrate,*
> *Drinking watered orange pulp –*
> *In three sips the Arian frustrate;*
> *While he drains his at one gulp.*
> Robert Browning *Solioquy of the Spanish Cloister*
> 1842

My eduction involved compulsory church. Every year, a certain number of weeks after Ascension Day, would come Trinity Sunday. Every year, I'd wait for the Chaplain to explain this great Mystery of the Christian Religion. And every year, he never would.

The reverend chaplain wouldn't. But when it comes to hills, I will. Three in one walk: why?

A walk is like a story. Any author will tell you, get a good title and you're half-way there. A challenge is a way of advertising your personal splendours to the world at large. Any advertising copyrighter knows all about the poetic effect called 'assonance'. 'Three Peaks' is simple and vivid; but it also has that repeated 'ee' sound. Compelling.

However, every bit as compelling is the alliteration (shared first sound) in the 'Two Tops'. That's a mock-modest name I gave to a 280-mile walk linking Scotland's easternmost hill with its westernmost one. In literary terms such understatement is called 'Litotes', and can be overdone: names such as 'Dorset Doddle' (32 miles) and the 'Wilmot Wander' (Derbyshire, 36 miles) may appear to sneer at perfectly normal humans who find such distances a drag.

Then there's straightforward rhyme, as in the 'Ten Bens', or the 'Six Trigs'. Always fun is the pun, as in 'That's Lyth' (24 miles of the Lyth Valley near Kendal) or the 'Wellington Boot' (62 miles out of Wellington, Somerset). Add to this the echo, exploited by the Seven Sevens of Mourne (though it doesn't actually help you decide which peaks the 'Peaks of the White Peak' ought to be).

Poetic effects, then, lead not just to the Three Peaks but also to such compelling events as the 'Four Tors', the 'Five Pikes Hike', the 'Seven Summits' and

On the Dorset Doddle, a 32-mile coastal walk with more uphill than Ben Nevis

so on. While this technique might help you avoid calling your new challenge 'The four quite well-known hills near Wooler' or 'The Happy Toes Sponsored Walk', it doesn't explain why the summits crossed should be specifically three in number.

One summit is what people do in the Lake District. Two summits make a walk that boringly doubles back on itself. But Three Peaks make a triangle. You come down each peak by a way that isn't how you went up it; you walk around a fair area of countryside. As you stand on Peak Two, you look back with pride at Peak One already achieved, and forward with forboding towards Peak Three. Thus the emotional ups and downs correspond with the ups and downs of the itinerary.

So, in South Wales, we get Skirrid, Sugar Loaf and Blorenge: as names alone, even more compelling than Ingleborough, Whernside and Pen-y-ghent. The walk is 20 miles, with 5000ft of uphill (32km/1500m); it's organised as the 'South Wales Three Peaks Challenge' by the Cardiff Outdoor YHA Group every March. Start and finish are at Abergavenny; the time limit is 10.5 hours; you can chose your own direction.

The Roaches, on a self-invented 'Peaks of the White Peak': the way to make this one work was to go after the 12 summits of 500m or more

Three Peaks in Cumbria give the 'Old County Tops' – 36 miles (57km) around Helvellyn, Scafell Pike and Coniston Old Man (see Chapter 17). In fact, every county (even Essex) has at least three peaks in it. Save petrol by choosing the Three Peaks of Wherever It Is You Live.

The peaks need to lie in a triangle rather than a line. Six miles crow-flight between summits makes the other two seem pretty distant from the one you're standing on; those miles expand to 8 or 10 as you walk them. Valley ground between should be tracks and footpaths, by riversides, non-boggy moorland, interesting villages, but not too many fields. Look in particular for paths contouring across some steep slope, as these are especially enjoyable. Sometimes a choice of start point can drag the lowland crossing into a better line; Whalley on the Lancashire Three Peaks worked that way.

Two are too few; four is more than enough. Three Peaks make one long walk. For your starter, here's Somerset.

THE THREE PEAKS OF SOMERSET:
DUNKERY BEACON, PERITON HILL, SELWORTHY BEACON

The hills	Dunkery Beacon (591m), Periton Hill (297m), Selworthy Beacon (308m)
Distance	25km (15.5 miles)
Ascent	900m/3000ft
Start/finish	Porlock (SS 886 466)
Terrain	Field paths, tracks and lanes, open hilltops
Standard stong walker	7hrs

The Exmoor coast has been a place to walk over for at least 200 years. Romantic poets Coleridge and Wordsworth may very well have done the three peaks here in a one-er; if they didn't, it'd be because they were on a longer day out aiming for the Quantocks or the Devon border. It's not just the sea views: the steep wooded valleys behind Horner, and the coastal peak of Selworthy Beacon, are the highlights here. These small hills may surprise by their steepness; the descent to Hurlstone Point (avoidable) is really rugged. If training for the National Three Peaks, start at Wootton Courtenay so as to get the longest climb when already tired. Otherwise, walk them from Porlock purely for pleasure.

The route

Leave **Porlock** on a lane southwards, at the village edge turning southeast (signed for West Luccombe) then taking a bridleway on the right to **Horner**. A track runs south into Horner Woods. After 1.5km a sign left is for 'Dunkery Beacon'. It takes a footbridge (the second footbridge) over Horner Water, for a path running up the valley of **East Water**. After 600 metres, and 20 metres after the second crossing of the stream, a bridleway path forks up right in zigzags, and then more gently to a cross-track and bench.

Turn right for a few steps, to a field gate. Follow the left edge of a field to a short track leading to **Cloutsham Farm**. Short-cut the road's downhill zigzag and turn back uphill for 200 metres (SS 893 430). Across the East Water stream, a path runs up south onto **Dunkery Beacon**.

From the cairn follow the main ridge, east then north of east, to cross a road and descend to Brockwell. A lane leads down to **Wootton Courtenay**. Turn left

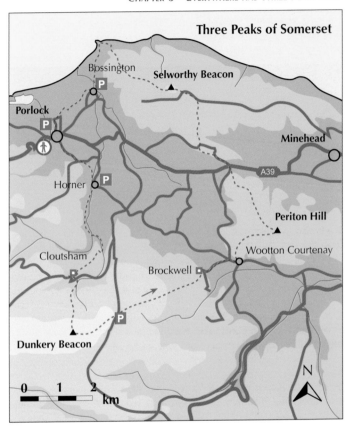

Three Peaks of Somerset

on Roadway Lane (a track) up past the village hall. Above the steep climb in woodland, bear right and seek out the trig point on **Wootton Common** under the trees. (The summit is also referred to as Periton Hill.)

Turn sharp left and follow the main ridgeline, signed for Selworthy, on what becomes a leafy path down to the A39 at **Headon Cross** (SS 935 459). Cross to East Lynch and the green track of Dean's Lane to **Selworthy Beacon**.

Head down northwest, to the top of steep Hurlestone Combe. The Southwest Coast Path heads straight down the grassy dip, or you can turn right for an even steeper descent of rugged ground to **Hurlstone Point**. Turn inland

99

along the slope foot to **Bossington.** A street northwest for 150 metres leads to a field path southwest into Porlock.

SOMERSET THREE PEAKS – SCHEDULE				
	Distance mls/km	Ascent ft/m	Time min	ETA
Start: Porlock				0:00
Cloutsham	3.3/5.2	800/240	90	1:30
Dunkery Beacon	1.0/1.6	1000/300	50	2:20
Wootton Courtenay	3.1/5.0		60	3:20
Periton Hill	1.0/1.6	550/170	40	4.00
A39 Headon Cross	1.4/2.3		30	4:30
Selworthy Beacon	2.0/3.2	650/190	60	5:30
Hurlstone Point	1.5/2.4		45	6:15
Porlock	2.1/3.4		45	7:00
TOTALS	**15.5/25**	**3000/900**		

THE MARILYNS: 1554 HILLS YOU PROBABLY HAVEN'T HEARD OF

The 3000ft summits of Scotland are named Munros after Sir Hugh Munro, baronet, who listed them. Once the foot has followed the questing brain over the 284 Munros, and perhaps the English 2000ers, it naturally stretches forward towards a list with 1554 hills on it... surely five and a half times as exciting as 284?

Not so. A Marilyn is a hill, however low, that has 150m (492ft) of clear drop all around it before the ground rises to any higher point. Thus Ben Nevis is a Marilyn, but so too is Arthur's Seat in the middle of Edinburgh. On the other hand, neither Cairngorm nor Derry Cairngorm is a Marilyn: in each case the ground drops only 140m before rising towards the summit of Ben Macdui. The drop requirement means that a Marilyn itself must be no less than 150m high. The lowest is in fact 152m, the summit of an island in the Outer Hebrides. The lowest mainland Marilyn is Arnside Knott, just south of the Lake District. At 158m it's separated from the rest of England by Silverdale Moss at 7m altitude. The Marilyns are named for Miss Munroe, for two obvious reasons.

Many fine hills fail to make the listing: notably Scafell, Clach Glas on Skye, Glastonbury Tor and Carnedd Dafydd. On all Dartmoor, only High Willhays

Notable prominence: Arthur's Seat is a Marilyn, but at 251m features on no other hill list

gets in there, but Shropshire emerges as one of England's main Marilyn-walking areas. The list also includes someone's front garden in the town of Crowborough, Sussex.

When seeking the Three Peaks of Somewhere, I refer first to the Marilyn listing in *Relative Hills of Britain* by Alan Dawson. The 150m of drop means any Marilyn will give at least some uphill, and a view; there will usually be low ground to cover in between them. The Yorkshire Three Peaks are all Marilyns, as are the ones chosen here for Lancashire and for Somerset. But the White Peak Three Marilyns would be Shining Tor, Cloud, and something called Gun – not a stimulating walk at all. Over there, the criterion to make a good walk turned out to be: Everything Over 500m.

PART III: MORE AND MOOR

Chapter 7

A Weakness for Bleakness

Two Voices are there: one is of the sea
One of the mountains; each a mighty Voice...

So wrote Wordsworth in 1807, reflecting on the fact that Napoleon had just conquered free Switzerland. Mountain ground has obvious appeal in its interplay of crag and valley, its sheltered waterfall hollows and its sudden views across the cultivated plains. The sea is in a sense its opposite. Ever-changing, and yet never particularly different; random, disorienting, and dangerous.

Moorland is the dry land equivalent of the ocean. It's as bleak and featureless as the sea, as challenging to the endurance. When Wordsworth was helping his friend Coleridge rough out his great ocean poem *The Ancient Mariner*, they did it over a four-day walk on Exmoor. Such unmountainous upland is seafaring without the boat. And it shares the subtle appeal of the sea.

Heather drags our boots back, and slows us to 2kph; we wish it wasn't there and try to avoid it. But in world terms, our heather moorland is as special, and rare, as the laurel cloud-forest of the Canary Islands, or the cactus badlands of Arizona. In the uniquely UK wilderness of Yorkshire, or Dartmoor, or the Grampians, the ubitquous *Gramineae*, the grasses and bamboos, are replaced by a sort of knee-high tree. Here are special heather beetles, and caterpillars of a pecular hairiness. Ruling it all, the winged equivalent of the heather plant, the heather-brown red grouse. It lives in tall heather, and eats short heather. Its fluffy chicks are coloured like dead heather heads, and its double-squawk is the sound that heather itself would make if it only had a voice.

And then, in August, the whole affair bursts into flower.

But after 6 or 8 miles, we come into a damper dip, and there's the cotton grass, for you can't keep family *Gramineae* at bay, not even in the Forest of Bowland. The seed heads lie white across the ground below the early morning mist. The general nothingness of everything brings dreams of huge hounds with phosphorescent jaws, or of death by ecological absorption in Wizard's Slough. Four walkers in North Yorkshire spontaneously broke into a folklore dirge, thus founding the Lyke Wake Walk (see Chapter 9). That's the romantic, noisy way to do it. But there's also a fundamental emptying of the mind in a place that's a step away from being nowhere at all. Mist, and a few metres of heather... 'The higher part of contemplation, as it may be had here, hangeth all wholly in

Dove Crag, on the sandstone Simonside ridge of Northumberland

this darkness and in this cloud of unknowing; with a loving stirring and a blind beholding of the naked being of God Himself only.' So wrote the anonymous author of the *Cloud of Unknowing*, a mediaeval handbook for mystics. 'Of God himself can no man think. And therefore I would leave all that thing that I can think, and choose to my love that thing that I cannot think.'

Finding God is one thing: finding Dartmoor's Great Mis Tor may be quite another. The process of getting there is addressed as 'navigation', just as if you were doing it by boat. The business with the map and compass, steering through the mist by the direction of the slope, and finally finding the small stream leading down to Slaidburn off the Bowland Hills (supposing that's where you were). It's useful, indeed essential, if you don't want a damp night among the heather. But it's also a fundamental form of fun.

I'm convinced that we humans have maps in our minds, long before they were ever on paper. My evidence is from a first ascent of Great Gable at the age of 7, and my recalling it aged 47 as having been straight up the spur above

Wasdale Head. Aged 48, I revisited what is a rather unlikely route for taking a youngster up; and found that Little Hell Gate was, indeed, familiar, as well as slightly less hellish when walked up with longer legs.

Once we've found food and a girlfriend or boy, our next urge is to understand the country. No matter how broad-shouldered or large-breasted, bad mental mapping will leave our primitive ancestor as a very hungry hunter, a gatherer with an empty basket. The wrong side of the hill could even mean attending the spring sacrifice of the incorrect clan, and becoming the one under the altar stone in the crouching position.

Maps matter. There is even some evidence, albeit not very convincing, that the mental maps are different between the sexes. Women go all the way back by that roundabout with the flowerbeds: men plunge bravely into the side streets hoping for a short cut. So it's a shame in a way that, 2000 years after the lodestone, 200 years after Bonnie Prince Charlie carried his ivory compass across the Scottish Highlands, technology is about to render this particular form of fun redundant. The gramophone meant no more family evenings around the piano. The camera killed off the lady watercolourist on holiday. The coming of the crampon put an end to the noble art of step-cutting. And the mindless accuracy of the GPS device will, in a decade or two, finish off the cunning craft of map-and-compass.

It's all very well to confront mythical monsters, actual icefalls, and sharp little hailstorms, all of them trying to make your game harder and nastier. But what about the technological advances that make the game easier and less dangerous? Rock climbers and mountaineers have always had to face up to these counter-monsters. A slab climb on granite is no more subtle than the conflicting ethics of climb-on-sight or red-pointing, the piton for aid, the sling left by a previous party; the oxygen-free ascent, the lightweight Alpine style. Walking, so far, has not suffered such ethical conundrums. But while the tendency to add waymarks for safety has mostly been resisted, even the mobile phone has compromised the remoteness of the moors.

Let's not complain. Technology has given us rucksacks that are almost bearable to lug about, and aluminium tentpoles. Technology has given us the warm waterproof jacket, not to mention the warm motor car to drive home in afterwards. Most of all, it's given us the leisure to be out there in the first place. Walkers' paths criss-cross the high mountains; but most of us, still, don't choose to do it on the moors. The Forest of Bowland, the northern Pennines, Scotland's Southern Uplands: these are still bewildering and wild. Once walked by thousands, the Lyke Wake Walk is empty – along its first 25 miles, to where it joins the popular Coast-to-Coast, I didn't meet anyone at all.

Tibet has forests of rhododendron; the southern USA has sagebrush. Heather, seen here in the Manor Hills of Peeblesshire, is the uniquely UK wilderness.

The walkers are all in Lakeland, or Scotland, or Snowdonia. But me, I've got a weakness for the bleakness.

Chapter 8

The Dartmoor Ten Tors:
50 Miles of Moorland over Two Days

The hills	Ten tors chosen from a list of 18
Distance	58km (35–55 miles)
Ascent	About 2000m (6000–7000ft)
Start/finish	Okehampton Camp (SX 587 925)
Maximum altitude	584m Kitty Tor (highest official Ten Tors tor)
Terrain	Open moorland, largely pathless
Target time	34hrs including night stop

HISTORY AND GEOGRAPHY

The army-organised Ten Tors event has been run with little change in format since 1960, with one break for foot-and-mouth disease in 2001. It is for teams of six teenagers, now limited to 400 teams a year. From the army's point of view, it's a way of exposing 2400 young people to the sort of fun they could continue to enjoy by joining up later on – but leaving out the gunmanship and killing people. It's also a valuable exercise in logistics; especially in 1996, when the moor threw a blizzard at them and they had to evacuate the teams with helicopters very quickly. In 1998, scarcely less dangerous temperatures of 25°C caused heatstroke and exhaustion.

The young people learn about small teams and long distances, and the fun to be achieved through suffering. The army's 43 (Wessex) Brigade is an effective protector: they (aided by the other armed services) helicoptered everyone safely out of the blizzard in 1996. At the same time soldiers do understand about self-reliance, and how getting it wrong does have to involve some discomfort and danger.

To ensure properly heavy rucksacks, the event is over a full weekend, with an overnight camp on the moors. There are three levels:

* Bronze: 35 miles –14–15 year olds
* Silver: 45 miles – 16–17 year olds

Ten Tors trainees among the Beardown Tors

- Gold: 55 miles – 17–20 year olds (who have already achieved a Silver route)

Each team gets a different selection of 10 tors from the 18 marked with black triangles on my sketch map (page 110). All routes start through the shaggy country of the northern moor, but by the first evening even the Bronze routes will reach the pathed ground just north of the Princetown road. Gold teams will cross further rough ground to reach Puper's Hill, Trowlesworthy Tor, or both.

Training walks take place during the bleak months of winter, officially starting in February. The three firing ranges of the northern moor are active on 5–10 days a month, with Willsworthy the busiest. Given the red flags, the boundary marker poles, and the advance information on the Internet, it's easy enough to plan a route that won't get shot at. The range boundaries on the Ordnance map don't correspond with the red-and-white poles on the ground; my sketch map shows which of the crucial tors is inside each range.

The event itself is on the second weekend in May. The start is at 7am on Saturday, at Anthony Stile at the edge of Okehampton Camp (SX 587 925, informal parking). Teams of six must stay together, and finish together. Bronze teams must overnight at one of the manned checkpoint tors, no further along their route

Pupers Hill, just before sunset on Day 1

than number eight. Silver and Gold teams may camp anywhere. Checkpoints are all manned, and supply clean drinking water; Dartmoor's streams are infected with *cryptosporidium*, a protozoan causing a fortnight of diahorrea. (On my unsupported walk I used a spring, marked on the map, high on Ryder's Hill. It would also be possible to cache water along the Princetown road.) The checkpoints also offer emergency evacuation, but not food or anything else. They close at 8pm and open again at 6am. The last finishing time is 5pm.

It's about endurance, obviously, and the satisfaction in suffering but overcoming it. But it's also about mental toughness, when that ninth tor up in Okehampton Range is reached through 3 miles of knee-high tussocks. It's about self-reliance, but even more about teamwork, and whether to give the slow bloke at the back a kicking or a sweetie. It's about seeing the night sky, and finding out about the way the moon moves across it. It's about starting to feel at home in the wild world that humankind evolved to be rambling about in.

And sometimes, it's about, quite simply, survival. The bogs may not suck you down but the rivers could perhaps drown you, and the blizzard is not a play of virtual-reality electrons across a plasma screen. 'Parents would ask us: "Can you guarantee the safety of our Johnny?" And our response would usually be, "No, we certainly can't, Ma'am. Fact is, we go the other way and guarantee

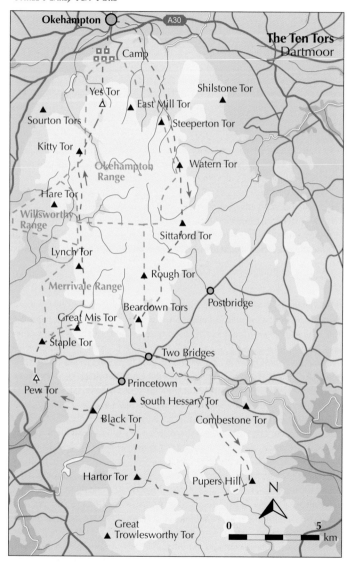

Okehampton

A30

Camp

The Ten Tors
Dartmoor

Yes Tor

Shilstone Tor

East Mill Tor

Sourton Tors

Steeperton Tor

Kitty Tor

Okehampton Range

Watern Tor

Hare Tor

Willsworthy Range

Sittaford Tor

Lynch Tor

Merrivale Range

Rough Tor

Beardown Tors

Postbridge

Great Mis Tor

Staple Tor

Two Bridges

Pew Tor

Princetown

South Hessary Tor

Black Tor

Combestone Tor

Hartor Tor

Pupers Hill

N

Great
Trowlesworthy Tor

0   5
          km

you the genuine possibility of his death."' So wrote Everest-climber and guide Willi Unsoeld. The army wouldn't put it like that. So far, and unlike Unsoeld, they have not lost anyone under their protection across the Ten Tors. But in a world of invisible cancer-pollutants, and car accidents, and heart attacks caused by overeating, on the one hand, and of pricey fake adventure from commercial companies on the other, there ought surely to be a Campaign for Real Risk.

Some of the young people may enjoy the exercise of these soldier-like qualities so much that they go on to join the armed forces. Others may merely be nudged into a lifetime of hills. Others again, whose parents may have told them 100 times that they'd have more fun if they got up onto their legs and switched off the TV – they may simply have confirmed that as usual the parents were completely wrong, and sink with relief back onto the sofa.

For those between 14 and 18 years old based in the Westcountry, your college or school probably already organises a Ten Tors team. If it doesn't, pester the gym teacher; the contact details are at the back of this book.

Disco dancing, binge drinking, and exposing one's tummy button in public: these are reserved for the under-20s. But there seems no reason for the Ten Tors to be purely a teenage treat. Accordingly, I decided to work out my own version: the Ten Tors for grown-ups.

TEN TORS FOR GROWN-UPS

For the Victorians, it was the night-time howl of the monstrous Hound of the Baskervilles, echoing across Grimpen Mire. For my father's generation it was the Hairy Hands, on the clouded, lonely road between Two Bridges and Postbridge, seizing the steering wheel and hurtling you into the heather. For others it might be the sudden mists, or the unexploded ordnance.

For me, growing up in Horrabridge in the decade or two after the war, the bogs of Pew Tor were simply good fun to pick up and throw at one's little sister. The escaped convict out of Princetown, found in the French master's wardrobe just getting into a pair of the French master's trousers – he was a sporting fellow, and left some prison-issue bog paper for the pupils. None of these held any terrors. No – the dread rumour of Dartmoor was called the Ten Tors. On the edge of the football pitch the gym teacher and the headmaster discussed it in lowered voices. Occasionally it captured and took away someone's big brother, returning him a week later limping and white faced. Where were these tors, and what were their names? Nobody knew. What we did know was that they were 50 and more miles apart...

But by secondary school I'd moved to another county. And so it was not in Dartmoor but the Black Mountains and Brecon Beacons of South Wales that I

Black Tor, at dawn

learnt to misread the landscape, not look at the compass, disbelieve the compass, and the various other techniques for coming down into the incorrect valley. By the time fate brought me back to the moors, I was too old by a quarter-century for the Ten Tors. To confront the missed challenge of my teenage years, I would have to make up my own version: the Ten Tors for Grown-ups.

First, for distance. Silver (for 16–17 year olds) is 45 miles, Gold (17 and up) is 55 miles. I decided to count myself as about 17 years old, so that the distance should be a sort of 'Silver Threads among the Gold' – roughly 50 miles. The official Ten-Tors tors actually number 18; I selected eight, well spread, then added Yes Tor as the moor's high point, plus Pew Tor for personal reasons. It would be impossible to recreate teenage ignorance of maps and compasses; I substituted several decades' worth of ignorance of the moor. Did those wide-spaced contours mean pleasant grassland, arduous heather, or the horrors of Grimpen Mire? I would allow myself no recce to find out.

I would be doing without the friendly squaddies in tents below each tor. But if older means anything, it ought to mean more money, so I'd also do without the heavy rucksack, and carry good, light, gear and no damned tent at all.

With all these technical and ethical details settled, a February dawn saw me heading out of Okehampton, along the green and deep East Okement Valley. The viaduct stood high against the grey light of dawn. A half hour later, grey wrinkled shale gave way to rounded granite, bright ferns to yellow grasses and pincushions of pony-nibbled gorse. Ahead, a succession of beige curves shaped the day ahead, each curve topped with a splinter of tor. The only bright note was the red flags flying on the tors of Okehampton Range on my right.

Elsewhere in the UK, hills attract, or intimidate, by their shapes: the perfect pyramids of Lakeland's Wasdale or the Cuillin of Skye, the towers and pinnacles of Ben Nevis. But Dartmoor is a place of textures. There's the granite itself, smooth rainwashed grey interrupted by white chunks of quartz. There's the slope of yellow grass, perhaps smooth underfoot but actually not, as its tufty tussocks are thrown into relief by the low sun. There's the different sort of slope made up of little gorse knobs like the stitches of a needlepoint tapestry. Then there's the slope sprinkled with boulders, offering the pleasantest of going on the well-drained grassland between. All these textures are mimicked in the map, speckled as it is with grey loops or little brown squiggles. But above all there are the tors, the essential sprinkling of salt over Dartmoor's plain porridge.

And most important among them, Pew Tor. Recorded in my logbook as my first ever ascent – but recorded not in my own handwriting, as I hadn't learnt to do logbook entries at 1 year 11 months. Pew Tor has shrunk: I glanced back from the summit block and realised that in stepping there I'd crossed, but not even spotted, the fearsome once-intimidating chasm that splits it. At the same time, the scamper along the bottom of that chasm, sandy floor between rock walls, was something I no longer had nearly enough smallness for…

The tor was smaller but just as scrambly, the summit hollow as useful as ever to hold the rucksack as I rummaged after my marmalade sandwiches. And, failing 43 Wessex in support, I had a breakfast rendezvous with an outdoor-writer colleague, one I'd only met over the phone but who lived up the road from my childhood home. Over fresh-from-thermos tea and the so-appropriate rock bun, he regaled me with Horrabridge gossip of my missing 45 years. The smithy where I peered over the half-door to hear the red-hot horseshoe sizzle on the hoof amid clouds of horse-scented smoke – it has just been restored as the Smithy Cottages. A tractor driver out of control bashed in the parapets of the ancient bridge – a lady tractor driver, confirming traditional prejudice. One village ancient had claimed, when quizzed, to remember the infant me.

Meanwhile the sun slowly warmed the summit of Pew Tor, and the sunbeams reached down into the valley of the River Walkham to colour in the view.

Looking back across Dartmoor from Yes Tor

'I counsel you by way of caution, to forbear from crossing the moor in those dark hours when the powers of evil are exalted.' So reads the ancient manuscript that conveys the Curse of the Baskervilles. As evening faded into dusk, listening out for the cry of a spectral Hound of monstrous size, I followed the Abbot's Way – until I mislaid it among the tussocks. Ahead, the lower ground containing Hartor Tor was lost under the last glare of day and the just-switched-on street lights of Tavistock. By torchlight I headed hopefully west. Clear winter air had so far offered little opportunity for getting lost; now darkness would serve instead of the famous Dartmoor mist. I fell into a small stream, a stream sheltered and with tempting long grass to unroll the bivvy bag. But I took a compass bearing along its line to identify it, and decided I'd found Deadman's Bottom. Ancient burial cists spotted the map all the way from here to Evil Combe. However little the spectral Hound might be howling, I was not going to sleep in Deadman's Bottom.

Anyway, the moon was high and bright, and it wasn't even 7 o' clock. So I followed the stream to its intersection with the infant Plym, and took another, fairly careful, compass bearing. Ten minutes later the low bouldery wall of Higher Hartor Tor rose out of the rushes.

I walked northwards, finding black shadowed holes of the old tin mine at Eylesbarrow, and an earth path shining under the moon. Something tapped my leg – it was my own trouser bottom, frozen hard in the night air. Ahead, in case I didn't know about the Pole Star, the red lights on Hessary Tor gave me my line. Then a leat, chuckling in the darkness, led me around the slope. By River Meavy I found an overhanging gorse bush to snuggle under. Any time I cared to open my eyes, moonlight was sparkling in the frost a few inches away. But all night long, shucks, not even the briefest little howl from the spectral Hound. Apparently, under the Countryside & Rights of Way Act, Dartmoor National Park has banned Hounds of any size unless on a 2-metre lead.

So no, the Ten Tors is not just for the teens. Adults, and even oldies, can enjoy it equally. Choose 10 tors to make up 50 miles, or 55 if you see yourself as an 18-to-21-year-old, or 40 if your years weigh heavy on your legs. But don't let the tors be too familiar – the official 18, many of them intriguingly obscure, are on the Dartmoor Ranges website, where you also discover when you're not going to get shot. The north is where it's tough, and on the second afternoon you may be ploughing through rushes knee-deep, with the gentle ridge cut by a sudden valley, green and bouldery, and a little rocky river that's still not quite little enough to cross in comfort. And at its head, the hollow with the two standing stones where Hugo Baskerville lay with his throat torn out, and above him the great black beast with its blazing eyes.

Such fun should not be reserved for the army, and the under 21s.

The author's tors:
Watern Tor, Sittaford Tor, Beardown Tors, Pupers Hill, Higher Hartor Tor, Black Tor (Walkhampton Common), Pew Tor, Great Mis Tor, Kitty Tor, Yes Tor; 83km/52 miles, 2000m/6500ft.

Chapter 9

Mastery of Misery:
The Lyke Wake Walk

THE EASIEST WALK IN ENGLAND?

Certain sorts of landscape infect the mind. The open skies and wide spaces of the Netherlands created the cool rationality of the 18th-century enlightenment. The clarity and olive groves of Tuscany infuse the poems of Dante, while the cosy slopes of the Quantocks and Lakeland inspired Wordsworth and his pals.

The bleak moorlands of North Yorkshire gave us the Lyke Wake Walk. Right the way across, from Ravenscar above the North Sea to Osmotherley in the west – brown gritstone, prehistoric hummocks, and acres of blackish heather make a day that's not just gloomy, but one that actually revels in its gloom. You know the way a tune gets into your head and sticks there all the way to the end? When Bill Cowley walked these 40-odd miles for the first time back in 1955, the music going through his head was an ancient dirge: one that details the journey of the soul through an Afterlife of prickles and purgatorial fire.

> *When thou away from here hast passed*
> *Every neet and a'*
> *To Whinny Moor thou com'st at last*
> *And Christ receive thy soul.*

This is the unique ambiance of the Lyke Wake Walk. Complete it, and you'll be issued a black-edged Card of Condolence and a badge with the emblem of a coffin. The club holds 'wakes', with ceremonial intonings of the Lyke Wake Dirge's 13 verses. Those whose sufferings on the walk are too mild are urged into double or even triple crossings of the hills, bogs and heather.

Whitby makes its living marketing the memory of Dracula; and the folk of North Yorkshire have some remnant of Gothic romance in their souls. For in their hundreds and thousands they have embarked on this long, long day of dismalness and gloom. In 33 years an astonishing 135,000 completed this trial. Six-year-olds have been urged along it by parents who presumably spent their own childhoods walking 20 miles to school in clogs two sizes too small and don't see why the modern young 'uns should have it any easier.

What all this shows is the triumph of idea over actuality. For this is, out on the real landscape, England's easiest walk. It starts, uniquely, with 5km gently

Lilla Cross on Fylingdales Moor: the first of the evocative structures that punctuate the Lyke Wake Walk

and continuously downhill. Then there's a good, clear path all the way. For the eastern half that path is on soft but firm clay ground, or yielding peat. There follow a few miles along the gravel of an old railway, and all the western end is the paved way over the Cleveland Hills. Consider further: the amount of uphill per mile is a mere 110ft (20m of up per km). Ever-improving views encourage you forward; and there's a café, just where you need it, 6 miles before the end point on The Beacon.

Just one contrary fact, though; that café is also 31 miles after the beginning. The walk may be fast, but it is also rather long. For my own attempt, I was particularly unlucky with the weather. Late spring, and several weeks of rainlessness, had left the peat pale brown and lightly dusty, while imparting an uncanny firmness to the yellow clay. Wearing lightweight trail shoes, absolutely porous, I finished the walk with dry feet, as well as slightly sunburnt knees. I imagine they'll refuse me my Card of Condolence, and make me go back and do the walk properly.

It was different in the old days. There was none of this paths nonsense; just miles and miles of knee-deep heather, with careful route choice turning up easy bits in the form of bog. None of this namby-pamby Right to Roam: half the walk was trespass and the miles past Fylingdales were military zone complete with unexploded bombs. The walk is a victim of its own success, with thousands of walkers creating the wide pathway, thus eliminating the navigational interest as well as the heather-scratched kneecaps. Fortunately the human imagination can overcome this intrusion of easiness, simply by striking up an appropriate dirge.

> *Hosen and shoon thou ne'er gav'st nane*
> *Every neet and a'*
> *The whins shall prick thee to the bare bane*
> *And Christ receive thy soul…*

A quarter moon was fading, and skylarks were gradually replacing stars in the grey sky. At ankle-level, cotton grass shook in the breeze, so dense as to resemble plastic sheeting laid across the grey moorland. Here and there, a small gorse or goat-willow humped out of the black heather.

White blocks of camper vans marked the parking area on the silent A171. I crossed onto a concrete track, soon petering into path among the heather stalks. Ahead rose several skylines of moorland, lightening now from black to grey. And then, behind a hump of heather, the ground opened suddenly in a canyon that the surprised eye reads as being several hundred metres deep.

The shadows and the steepness contribute to the trick. The trees opposite are actually birches, and small specimens of birch at that. But also, it's the detailing: where a real canyon is great expanses of orange and ochre, little Jugger Clough is patterned with bright bilberry, and dark heather, and dun-coloured gritstone. In the event, the baked-clay path down took just five minutes, and not much more than that out again opposite. A sudden harsh bark, and a roe deer bounded across the horizon in black silhouette.

After the sudden incursion of prettiness came some more moor. And as low light sneaked in from the east, it made the near heather lumpy, like waves of the sea. Overhead, lapwings flapping like sailcloth. At sea, you go on and on and nothing much happens; and this heather moorland is much the same. After 17 days of nothing much, a piece of driftwood with weed and a small crab. After two hours of moor and more moor, a tumulus hump and a standing stone with a primitive face shape. And then, when you thought the grey would undulate for ever, a green island (as it were) in the sudden dip to Wheelbeck. Water sparkles between blocky beige stepping-stones, and willows spring green from either bank, with sunlight glowing on toad-shaped boulders. Wheeldale now is someone's second home, with people-crusher cars parked on the gravel. But this was once a lonesome hostel, where Lyke Wake walkers could stop and sleep, and still, after an early breakfast, finish the walk within the 24hr limit.

They've taken the tops off the Fylingdales radar domes, to leave a pyramid of stark grey concrete. What was a monster fantasy is now, simply, a strikingly

Bilberry and heather, Wheeldale

ugly structure. And strikingly large. I noted with amusement that the thing is so secret that it didn't even appear on the map, and pencilled in its rectangular block on its empty patch of moor. And then realised that it was marked indeed, just five times as far away as I realised. Here is where eastbound walkers with shins already snapped by the boulders of Hasty Bank, thighs lacerated by heather and whin of Wheeldale Moor, and half-drowned by the bogs of Loose Howe, would traditionally stumble over a strange steely object down among the heather stalks and get exploded. Sadly, it's folk memory only. Nobody's come across a bomb since the early 1960s, and the ghostly presence that once roamed here has been absent for almost as long.

Even without its white balls on top, the concrete ziggurat dominates 10 miles of moorland. It's not as big as an Egyptian pyramid; but with a similar message of death. Signs and white poles mark off the Prohibited Place alongside, and a notice warns of non-ionising radiation, though without suggesting what precautions one might take. Non-ionising radar rays are zipping through my innocent limbs, mementos from the cold war era when the Lyke Wake Walk came into being. They say the Americans want us to build new domes: apparently us and NATO still need protecting against the Reds.

But my non-ionised limbs are now turning pink under the moorland sun. And in the context of this walk, Uncle Joe Stalin joins the bogeymen out of the ancient tumuli, and the strange Blue Man i' th' Moss, and the bog of Rosedale Moor, the boggiest bog so far, which seems the place to pull out the Lyke Wake Dirge:

> *From Brig o' Dread when thou hast passed*
> *Every neet and a'*
> *To Purgatory Fire thou com'st at last*
> *And Christ receive thy soul...*

From the bog I emerge with all 13 verses downloaded from the computer printout into my own memory, and feet as ochre lumps of clay mud. And just beyond the bog is squatting Fat Betty, the white-headed hunk of gritstone.

At Fat Betty, England's easiest walk suddenly makes itself easier yet. Under warm breezes the clay dries off my feet and flakes away. After a short road, it's the ironstone railway, and I put away the compass, switch off the brain, and point the eyes outwards. On either side, green Cleveland dales creep into the moor. And after the railway, it's Cleveland Way all the way, with Cleveland Way's path paving, and Cleveland Way's waymarks and signs. Memory also aids, if you've ever done Wainwright's coast-to-coast: these Cleveland Hills are Wainwright's second best section, taken backwards. Just don't remember how, in Wainwright's walk, Sutton to Clay Bank was a day, and today it's to be just half an afternoon.

People on Wainwright's walk are coming the other way now. Encouragingly they tell me how fine is the food at Osmotherley's youth hostel. Food that, to encourage myself onward, I've paid for in advance and am now walking rather quickly to arrive at before 7pm, when they serve it. But the other-way folk, who (confusingly) have left Osmotherley not this morning but the morning of yesterday, inform that I have to arrive for my food not at 7, in order to eat it, but at 6, to choose what it's going to be. Accordingly, from walking fairly fast, I now have to switch into walking rather faster.

And while it's naturally disappointing to be doing the Lyke Wake in quite the wrong sort of weather, there are compensations. The western edge of the Clevelands drops like a shoreline into a sea of green, squared up with blazing fields of yellow rape, fading into blue distant haze. Sitting on Wain Stones, the rock heat comforts tired thighs while the cooler breeze dries sweat off the shirt. And at Lord Stones, a squat aluminium box is excreting a continuous twirl of non-milk fats into inverted cones of biscuit. Just remember to put your rucksack

Beginning of the hills: Hasty Bank from Carr Ridge

back on before accepting your ice cream. Passing cone between sweat-damp hands while threading into the straps can result in tragedy, followed by the resigned expenditure of a further 75p.

After the teatime crowds around the ice cream machine, the afternoon hill is empty; just me, and the wide yellow Vale of York, and a crow floating in the thermals. The long, gentle edge of Gold Hill leads down to the valley floor, and then for the first time the walk is under branches, oaks and pines, with tatty late-season bluebells below. But inside the wood comes the longest climb of the entire route, 200m of ascent and pretty steep between the bluebells. With 3 miles to go, and menu moment only an hour away, I still must linger at a carved stone at the pathside. For the stone commemorates Bill Cowley, who walked this way in 1955 in a party of (of course) 13, humming the ancient dirge. Not to mention that 200m of ascent do rather need to be paused in.

But now the signpost says Osmotherley; and the path emerges at the top of the wood, and passes the final trig point. It's unreachable over barbed wire, and as end point of the walk is mostly symbolic as there's no handy helipad to lift you off. But the path slants gently down the wood, and around the edge of the Cleveland scarp; and if that scarp edge is symbolically speaking the sea, then the A19(T) supplies the roar of the waves. The track reaches road, the YHA's green triangle beckons, and by not slowing down at all I get in with five minutes to spare for filling in my menu. Kindly, they offer me extra chips.

ROUTE AND SCHEDULE

Concept	A full crossing of the North York Moors
Distance	62km (39 miles) to Osmotherley
Ascent	1500m (5000ft)
Start	Ravenscar Beacon (NZ 970 012)
Finish	Osmotherley (SE 461 981)
Maximum altitude	454m Round Hill
Terrain	Paths, often boggy in eastern half, rebuilt and smooth in west
Target time	24hrs
Standard strong walker	16hrs

For much of the last century, this end-it-all expedition was a must-do, walked by thousands every year. In the wimpish 21st century it's fallen out of favour. This despite the fact that it's got a whole lot easier. Those thousands have trodden a path across the moors, and in the west the well-made Cleveland Way is almost a pavement. While the dedicated would often turn around at Osmotherley and do the dreadful thing again in the opposite direction, a usable bus service now means you can eat and sleep at Osmotherley youth hostel and head back on four wheels.

The time limit is 24 hours, if you're to attain membership of the Lyke Wake Association with its coffin emblem and dirge-singing dinner. A dawn start from Ravenscar Beacon and a brisk pace can get you to Osmotherley by suppertime at 7pm. Alternatively, if you can find it, there's a fairly handy bothy at Pinkneys, half-way across. However, lost at night among the heather is an essential part of the walk's special atmosphere. 'And Christ receive your soul.'

Wain Stones, with the Vale of York behind

The route

Around 100 metres north from the car park, a path on the right leads to Ron's Seat, and a sea view to start you off on.

From the car park's back corner a track leads to **Beacon Howe's** trig point. A rutted track now leads south-southwest down the moor. A diversion track left avoids a wet bit; at its end, 1km from the trig point, an X-junction has a waymark arrow pointing right, but keep ahead on the main track. As it bends left, keep ahead on a path. The same direction, ignoring a tempting fork-off left, leads to the **A171** (NZ 945 002, parking).

Cross into a concrete track. It shrinks to path down to Jugger Howe Beck then climbs out again, west across High Moor, to a cairned tumulus at Burn Howe. Beyond the howe, the path widens to a clay track. It bends left, and as it bends back right, take a cairned path directly ahead to the first of the walk's standing stones, **Lilla Cross** (SE 889 987). Head down across a bridleway path and cross a track to a gate onto a clear track ahead. After 200 metres, ignore the walk's only 'LWW' waymark forking right, but stay on the track for another 200 metres to a small cairn (opposite a sign warning of non-ionising radiation). Turn off right for 20 metres then left, onto a small path. Follow it to right of a line

123

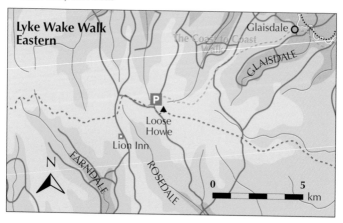

Lyke Wake Walk
Eastern

Glaisdale ○

The Coast to Coast Walk

GLAISDALE

P ▲

Loose
Howe

□ Lion Inn

N

FARNDALE

ROSEDALE

0   5
        km

of white marker posts, then beside Little Eller Beck *(water here)*, to **Eller Beck Bridge** (SE 858 983, parking).

Cross A169 leftwards onto a track, tarred at first, keeping ahead onto a path down to Fen Bogs. Cross the railway, and head west on a clear path across moor. Keep 200 metres left of the white trig point, to a small stone circle on **Simon Howe**. The path continues down west, after 1.5km dropping steeply into Wheeldale. Pass to left of buildings to stepping-stones across Wheeldale Beck.

Head straight uphill, with a wall on your right, until a fence crosses. Follow this left, to cross **Wheeldale Road** onto a wide earth path. After 25 metres, at a path junction easily missed, fork off right. The small path contours just north of east, and after 500 metres you see ahead the plantations along Wheeldale Gill. The path heads towards the far top edge of these. After crossing a small stream by a line of grouse butts, the ground becomes sandy with stones. Where the heather has been burnt, the path line is not obvious, so look out for small cairns. These lead past **Raven Stones**, a couple of glacial erratics. After them, the path's line keeps 50 metres up from the plantation edge, and is narrow through deep heather. The marking cairns just emerge from the heather. At a forest corner (SE 780 990) the plantation edge bends away. The path keeps on the same line as before, still with cairns; then, as it levels on the plateau above, bends slightly left (west). As it starts to descend it passes the **Blue Man i' th' Moss**. The standing stone has had blue paint applied. A wide eroded path continues down to cross a minor road (SE 744 995, small parking area).

Continue on a path marked with stone boundary markers. It becomes boggy before reaching **Loose Howe** and dropping to a minor road. Turn right

124

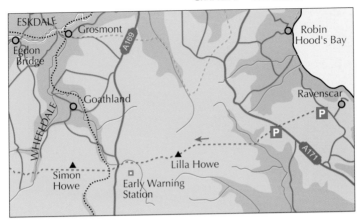

to a junction with a standing stone and parking (NZ 697 013). Fork left on road for 300 metres, then bear right on a moorland path to rejoin the road near Fat Betty stone (NZ 682 020). From the stone, cross the road onto a path that heads southwest, climbing to recross the road at Margery Stone (NZ 674 013).

The left-hand track continues southwest across moorland to the old iron-stone railway. Turn right. After 4km (NZ 631 020) the embankment crosses *reasonably drinkable water*. After 5km of old railway you reach **Bloworth Crossing** to join the Cleveland Way. The rest of the route follows this well-signed and heavily repaired trail.

After 400 metres turn down left, climb to a new track, and follow it over **Round Hill**. Follow the Cleveland Way's track then path down to **Clay Bank Top** (NZ 573 033, parking 200 metres down right).

Cringle Moor, in authentic Lyke Wake weather

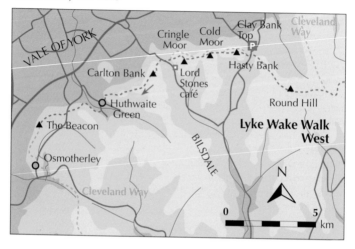

Around 200 metres up the opposite slope, the wide path ahead is the bypass route north of Hasty Bank. But Hasty Bank you really shouldn't miss. So take the stile on the left for the steep climb onto **Hasty Bank** and along its north-facing brink. On the descent, you thread through the spectacular Wain Stones (the reason for not missing Hasty Bank).

Around 150 metres up from Garfit Gap the path goes through a small gate. Cleveland Way ahead crosses **Cold Moor**; or, more relaxingly, take the miners' path by turning right immediately above the gate, and taking a path above the top of woods. At the foot of the steep slope of **Cringle Moor**, a bridleway finger-post indicates a path to the right, running past a dome of brown scree spoil – this is the old alum miners' contouring path, which is wide and clear with views. However, in clear weather, the path up and over is even finer.

At the car park beyond Cringle Moor is **Lord Stones café** (NZ 523 030) with a useful *fountain* for filling waterbottles.

Around 100 metres up the road, the Cleveland Way leads up the left flank of **Carlton Bank** and down the ridge crest to **Huthwaite Green** (phone box, parking). Road ahead, then track across a stream, lead to a gate into a field. Here you can short-cut half-right on a footpath (yellow arrow), to left of a wood corner, to a stile onto a wide made path. Turn right along the wood foot for 1km, to a gate on the right that would lead out of the wood. Turn left, and in a few steps bear right on a path with Cleveland Way sign. It climbs steeply to a forest track; just before joining this, it passes the memorial stone to Mr Cowley, the man who first sang the Lyke Wake Dirge on Wheeldale Moor. Keep ahead at the same level to reach a minor road (NZ 473 003; parking for one car).

Cross a cattle grid, and turn right up a path signposted for Osmotherley, with a wall to its right. At a signpost, keep ahead ('Cleveland Way, Osmotherley') on a wide earth track. It rejoins a corner of the wood on the right, passes through two bridleway gates to run along the slope top next to the wood, and in 200 metres reaches the trig point at the top of **Beacon Hill** and the end of the Lyke Wake walk. The trig is not accessible due to barbed wire.

For the official end point of the Lyke Wake Walk you'll need to backtrack 200 metres, then down to the Lyke Wake Stone at Cod Beck car park (SE 469 994). Otherwise follow the Cleveland Way along the scarp edge then slanting down to a gate at the edge of woods. Take the field track ahead out of the woods, after 600 metres forking left at Chapel Wood Farm, to **Osmotherley**; turn left for the youth hostel.

LYKE WAKE WALK – SCHEDULE

	Distance mls/km	Ascent ft/m	Time min	ETA
Start: Ravenscar Beacon				0:00
A171	1.7/2.7		35	0:35
Lilla Cross	3.8/6.1	550/160	90	2:05
Eller Beck Bridge	2.0/3.2		40	2:45
Wheeldale Beck	3.0/4.8	350/100	70	3:55
Road nr Blue Man in the Moor	4.5/7.1	550/170	120	5:55
P near Loose Howe	3.2/5.1	450/140	85	7:20
Ironstone railway	2.9/4.7	150/50	65	8:25
Bloworth Crossing	3.3/5.2	150/50	75	9:40
Clay Bank Top	3.3/5.2	150/50	80	11:00
Lord Stones café	3.4/5.5	1800/5500	135	13:15
Huthwaite Green	3.1/4.9	400/120	80	14:35
The Beacon	2.8/4.5	550/160	80	15:55
TOTALS	**37/59**	**5000/1500**		
to Osmotherley	1.9/3.0	100/30	40	0:40

Note Times to ironstone railway will be slower if the ground is soft. Taking contouring paths around Hasty Bank, Cold Moor and Cringle Moor saves about 30 minutes and is a lot less tiring.

Chapter 10

The Derwent Watershed:
39 Miles in the Dark Peak

FOR PEAT'S SAKE

The Dark Peak is a land disclaimed by either Staffordshire, Cheshire or Yorks. It's the place at the back of the Black Country where they eat black pudding and black peas. But most notably it's the place of black peat. One fifth of the world's fossil carbon is in the form not of oil, coal or rain forests, but of peat. Peat was formed in cold, damp centuries after the Ice Age by the partial decomposition of sphagnum mosses, trees, pollen, and Bronze Age victims of ritual sacrifice. Of the particularly swampy sort of peat known as blanket mire, some 13 percent is here in the UK. Peat, in fact, is so fascinating that I just had to go and walk around in it. All day long.

From its reputation, the Derwent Watershed is a walk requiring real strength of leg and of mind. It's a little more than Kinder Scout (some 20 miles more) but less than kind. The Kinder bit is a rock-rimmed plateau, 16 miles in circumference, dropping to green valleys of Edale and Woodlands and Goyt. The unkinder bit is the deep peat, the confusion of the groughs, and the boots weighted with lumps of partially decomposed organic matter.

In the event I found much that was enjoyable – perhaps it hadn't been raining enough. I emerged out of night-time Edale onto the Win–Lose ridgeline. The ridge appears by a paradox narrower than the 2-metre path along its crest. By night the 2-metre path was empty and untrodden, but still useful as it meant not having to spoil the night vision by switching on any torch.

Below the ridgeline, the limestone mill at Castleton was a cathedral of ugliness, its windows black in yellow walls, its chimney neon-lit from underneath. Even peaceful Edale had seven sodium lamps in a line, and halogen flaring at every farm gate.

I took the road to the bottom of Stanage; the direct route over Bamford just looked like hard work and wet legs. (And if you're being picky, the Win–Lose ridge isn't on the Derwent Watershed either, is it?) Below the crags, I filled up with the last of the pale-beige water. From here on, there'd be water in the socks but not a lot in the bottle; and what there was would be dark brown.

On the Stanage boulders, I revisited the classic holdlessness of the gritstone that I remembered from rock-climbing days. For mountain chronicler Walt Unsworth, Stanage is the Throne of the Gritstone Gods – but from the path, you

Wheel Stones, on the Derwent Moors

see only its well-trodden top, and climbers looking down lengths of rope into the small abyss underfoot. However, the Wheel Stones rise above the moor, and on their balanced boulders I rediscovered even more feelingly the lack of handholds on Peakland grit.

Some criticise the overbuilt flagstone paths, because of the way they lift you 6 inches above the wilderness and keep your feet dry. They're a strip of city: look at the rough and heathery landscape, but don't actually tread in it. But I thought they were just great, and followed them past the Wheel Stones, and was quite inclined to keep following them after Back Tor. But Back Tor is where the Watershed Walk veers off into the authentic bog – I'd have been disappointed if it didn't.

The trouble with the Derwent Watershed is that it doesn't actually shed water. Instead the stuff runs round in the same place, passing from time to time through a pair of walkers' socks. Very quickly I discovered how the area got its name. 'Peak District' is obviously incorrect: the place is flat fields and moorland cut about by some steep little limestone valleys. The original name has to have

Anvil Stone on Bleaklow

been the 'Peat District'. Footprints plod round and round black conical piles of the stuff. Rain (rain is quite common here) washes it smooth again, and next week the path will plod around the other side of the pile. You divert past a green-scummed drainage channel, and backtrack around a side-channel, and within minutes you have to scramble up black crumble onto wobbly grass, and hope that at the top you'll see somewhere to go to next.

The stuff resembles a glacier, but in black. Instead of crevasses, its cracks contain cold water. Crampons wouldn't help, but at one point I found myself kicking steps up a semi-compacted slope and wanting to stab in an ice-axe if I'd only had one with me. Ravens, rather than choughs, wait above to pick clean the travellers' bones. And never mind the glacier-cauldron and the ice-table, here ever-weirder rock features supply waking hallucination. At Featherbed Moss, a wrinkle-sided stone stuck up out of a pool, the leg of some primordial elephant dead underground since the end of the Ice Age.

Still stranger are the stones of Bleaklow. A clump of them rise out of the peat in shapes that would win the Turner Prize if they were only a bit more cutting edge and less obviously influenced by Henry Moore.

The deep peat groughland, wandering below the moor, is only a couple of shortish sections, Stainery Clough Head and Bleaklow, but it makes an impression out of proportion to its mere mileage. After Bleaklow, paved Pennine Way ran through evening sunlight; I dodged motorbikes across the Snake road, then trod some more slabs into the sunset.

At Kinder Downfall the water wasn't blowing back into the sky like it does in all the descriptions. I found a sheltered peat hollow and lay down in it. I ate the rest of my sandwiches, and watched the arrival of the night.

The colour orange

By day, the Derwent Watershed is black peat and grey grassland, the faded colours of the wilderness. But by night, you see more clearly. The place is nothing but a suburb; and the colour of the suburb is sodium orange. To the west, the lights of Glossop and behind that Manchester shine into the sky, and bounce down off the cloudbase onto the rocks and hags. To the east, it's the streetlights of Sheffield that shine wastefully into the lower atmosphere; making streets safer for motors, but hideous for human beings.

Orange is the most horrible of colours; that's why they wear it in American prisons. Of our 1000 English wildflowers, just two are in orange. Orange was the last of the nine main colours to be named. The fruit it came in on was originally a norange, rather than an orange. Spanish *naranjo* means orange tree, with the Naranjo de Bulnes being a magnificent (and in some lights norange-coloured) rock in the Picos de Europa.

An over-zealous chemist, Friedrich Runge, in the 1830s analysed the fish-smelling black sludge from a failed experiment with coal tar, and came up with the Aniline dyes, thus allowing strident orange as a clothing colour for humans. But it's fluorescent orange, as seen in street lamps, roadside safety tape and fake suntans, that is the distinguishing colour of the unnatural 21st century. The fake suntan is bad enough: but most odious is the sodium. The quantum nature of energy means that an electron collapsing towards a sodium nucleus releases a particle of light at a single, orange, wavelength. Under sodium streetlights, no tones of colour are possible. Your lips are blackish-orange; so are your teeth; so are the flowers you bring in your blackish-orange hands.

Someone down in Glossop has left an orange safety flasher flashing, two times every second, all night long. And every few minutes an airliner drones over low, and sinks like an aluminium vulture onto its reeking orange nest.

By 6am the jumbo jets had settled into their airport, leaving the sky uncluttered for the day's first sunbeams. The peat was velvetty, the green blobs of grassland glowed. By careful compass-work I found Kinder top, a little cairn with old stakes in, standing on a low peat island amidst a silvery puddle.

Edale from the Woolpacks, Kinder Scout

Kinder edge, overlooking Edale, has a dry and stony path, above the green shadows of Edale and below a succession of rockpiles. One of them is named the Mushroom Garden, and make no mistake, these mushrooms are the hallucinogenic sort. Once off Kinder, the well-named Brown Knoll supplies a final few miles of peaty gloop, just to remind what this walk is all about. But then the grit gives way to limestone and narrows into Lord's Seat and the beginning again of the Win–Lose ridgeline.

Castleton mill is no longer an orange cathedral, but diminished by daylight into an ordinary eyesore. The ridge path's width is no longer a night-time guide, but still necessary by daylight for the crowds of walkers walking along it (and even the occasional paraglider preparing to leap off).

I dropped back into Edale, retrieved my dry socks from under a thorn bush, and went off to test the breakfast at the Nag's Head, official start point of the Pennine Way. Outside the window, the really long peaty path of the Pennine Way set off for Yorkshire, Hadrian's Wall and Scotland.

ROUTE AND SCHEDULE

Concept	Around the Derwent Reservoirs
Distance	63km (39 miles)
Ascent	1700m (5600ft)
Start/finish	Car park near Edale station (SK 124 853) or other points on the circuit
Maximum altitude	636m Kinder Scout
Terrain	Two thirds on good paths, one third on swampy bog
Target time	24hrs
Standard strong walker	18hrs

This walk dates from 1918, when men were men and mostly came from Manchester. Members of the Rucksack Club and the Sheffield Clarions found escape on the nearby peat moors from their working weekdays: escape also from pursuing gamekeepers, a process that made them extremely fit and fast. The Derwent Watershed route was devised by Eustace Thomas of the Rucksack Club, who took up serious walking at the age of 50 and outdistanced his younger companions not just here (his time, 11hrs 39min) but over the Welsh 3000s and Lakeland.

Tamed today with built-up paths and flagstones, this isn't quite the grim, mud-spattered walk those early grough-hounds favoured. To recapture the 1920s flavour, the fellrunners hold their High Peak Marathon, which follows this route, in early March and overnight (see Appendix I – if you're brave enough!)

While large parts of this are now paved path or otherwise easy, there remain 15 miles or so of the authentic swamp. Bog-hopping being a declining industry, the bog paths are little used and even quite grassy. Even so, the groughs, with head at the level of the moorland grasses and feet 2 metres below in black peat, make an impression out of all proportion to their mere mileage.

Putting aside the peat, the walk also includes the rocky edge of Kinder Scout, the elegant ridge of Lose Hill, and a selection of rocky tors east of the reservoirs. It's a lot less grim than its reputation, and a lot more varied as well.

You can enter the circuit anywhere: this description starts just off the route at Edale.

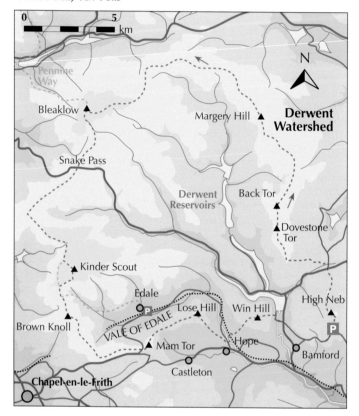

The route

From the car park near **Edale station**, follow the road east, across a stream and ignoring a first track on the right. Around 400 metres after the bridge is a second track on the right; before it is the signed path, which joins the track at once. The track crosses the River Noe, and bends left past a muddy shed. Just through a former hedgeline now grown out, fork up right to a gate up steps. An eroded path runs uphill, then slants up left, to reach the ridgeline at **Hollins Cross**.

Turn left along the ridge top, on a broad firm path. At the col before Back Tor, the main path contours along above woods, but head up left to follow the crest over Back Tor. The path continues to **Lose Hill**.

134

Head down right (southeast), on the main path, to the sign at the foot of National Trust land. Here fork right, onto a green path with a fence above on its left, to pass a tree clump. Turn left to contour above Losehill Farm, then after a stile turn down right 'Hope'. Go down the right edge of the field, then slant slightly left to pass a barn. Go straight down the next field, then slant to the back left corner of a field, to find a stile between paint-marked posts. The footpath is now clearer, with field edges on its right, to a bridge over a light railway where no more than 20 persons may cross at a time. Cross it (in groups of less than 21). Follow waymarks between the first buildings of **Hope**, then turn down left, signed 'Edale Road'.

Cross the main Edale Road into the cul-de-sac Bowden Lane. Keep ahead to pass under a railway bridge, then turn sharp right, on the track up to Twitchill Farm. Go through the farmyard onto a grass path. It runs steeply uphill, crossing a bridleway, to a stile and open access sign. After the next stile, emerge onto heathery open hill. At the top of the steeper slope the path bends right, to the rocky top of **Win Hill**.

The path ahead (east) runs down into trees. Keep straight downhill, with a stream (Parkin Clough) to the right, on path quite rocky, rooty and awkward. At its foot, cross a former railbed to a tarred track, and turn right for 100 metres to **Yorkshire Bridge** over the River Derwent. Look at the water flowing underneath, and realise you must walk all the way around the top of it!

There is some informal roadside parking as you ascend near houses. At the lane top, cross the A6013 leftwards, and turn right up a lane with views (New Road). A path on the right short-cuts the crossing of Hurst Clough, then rejoins. After a cattle grid, with a parking area on the right, take the track ahead. Cross a watercourse, which runs below rock climbs, so delay filling the drinking bottle. At the plantation end, ignore a stile on the left, but in 20 metres turn left over a ladder stile. A path runs up through bracken to the crag foot, where turn right over boulders and up between crags. Turn left along the crag top, on the well-used path to **High Neb**'s trig point.

The path continues along the top of Stanage Edge to Stanage End, where it drops left through the remnant of crag beside piled blocks of a former quarry. The path continues north, wide, green and gently downhill. Stay with it as long as possible, then slant down northwest, on a slope becoming bracken as it steepens, then rough grass again, out to a road junction (357m spot height, SK 225 877).

Cross into the side road ahead and follow it north for 200 metres, then turn left down a track. Just before a stream runnel, turn left at a signpost, on a grass path to left of the stream. Cross the stream to a wall corner, where the swampy path has the wall on its right. Cross a stile to a track, which turns left, with a wall on its left, to a gate onto open moor (SK 217 879).

A good path continues ahead, due west. At grouse butts keep ahead at the same level, with a waymarker post. Cross a stream, with *drinkable water*. Continue west to a col overlooking the Derwent reservoirs. Here turn right, on a good path becoming flagstones, to pass to left of **Wheel Stones**. The scramble to their top is Grade 2, lacking handholds above a gap step.

The flagged path continues north, to **Back Tor** with its trig point on bare rock. Here ignore the flagstones continuing northwest to left of the tor, but follow the line of rocks right, then head down northeast on a peaty path. After 2.5km, at the second wide shallow col, a post marks the turn-off of a peaty path on the left. This joins the Cartledge Brook *(drinkable but brown)* and runs up to right of it, before petering out near some grouse butts. Tramp heathery moorland northwest, to reach Howdon Edge overlooking the reservoir. Turn right along a path following the rim, then fork off right on a path to the trig point of **Margery Hill**.

A wet peaty path continues northwest, along **Outer Edge** (another trig point), and down to Stainery Clough Head. Here the path wanders through groughy ground of peat hags and bare peat moor. Then a path still wet but not groughy runs slightly north of west along the flat rounded crests of Howden Edge and the walk's second bog called Featherbed Moss. At the end of this the path bends slightly right (south of west) and descends past a **toadstool stone** standing in standing water. It's a useful 'how far have we got?' marker (SK 138 985). In the col beyond, the path crosses streams running down to the right, then rises to a stile in a temporary fence of DEFRA for regeneration of peatland.

About 1km after the fence, the path turns left, now climbing southwards. A few isolated stakes mark the way. Various paths run up slightly below moor level, along the base of grough runnels, finding running water but also a firmer stony surface.

At the top you reach **Bleaklow Stones.** The stones are shapely, including the striking Anvil Stone. Head west, without path, weaving among conical peat heaps to **Bleaklow Head**. It's marked by a large sprawling cairn with a post in it. The Wain Stones are 300 metres southwest. Return for 100 metres and head down east of south to find the **Pennine Way** (which is easy to follow for most of the rest of the walk). It runs down to a small stream and follows it down into little Hern Clough. It crosses the stream, turns left beside it briefly, then slants up right, out of the clough. The path continues clear to the flat top of **Alport Low**. This is bare gravel, and you might miss where the path changes direction to the

Mam Tor from the west

right. It continues as laid gravel in the groughs, stone slab on the wet moor top, to cross the A57 at **Snake Pass**.

The path continues as laid slabs to Mill Hill summit. Here it turns left, downhill, across a col, and up onto the pleateau of Kinder Scout. It leads to the right, round the pleateau edge, over rocky blocks to **Kinder Downfall**. *Drinkable water here.* Cross the stream above the fall and continue along the edge for 1km to the next stream (Red Brook). Here leave the path to turn in away from the plateau edge by one of the branches of the stream on a compass bearing (133° magnetic). After 15 minutes, if the bearing was sufficiently careful, is a cairn with old stakes in, on a peat island with moat. At 636m it's the summit of **Kinder Scout** (rather than the 632m point with 'Kinder Scout' beside it on the OS map). Kinder Low's white cairn is in view on the right for taking back bearings.

Also visible from the summit is the rock tor Pym Chair to the southeast. Just below it is the good path around the southern rim of Kinder plateau. It runs behind a rock tower Noe Stool, then contours below the corner plateau called Swine's Back. Here it turns downhill to a col with a Pennine Way signpost. Down left would be the Jacob's Ladder path down to Edale. However, keep ahead, with a wall on your left, on a path that's slabbed at first. As it bears right, away from the ridge boundary, it becomes a peaty trod with frequent wet slops to cross, to the trig point on **Brown Knoll**.

The path continues peaty, southeast along the plateau. It dips at last to the col at Chapel Gate top, where it meets a track at a tall marker post (SK 098 832). Turn right along the rutted track for 300 metres, then left at a T-junction, now on a stony wide path along the crest line, with a rebuilt wall on the right. The wide path passes to right of the grassy summit of **Lord's Seat**, then follows the crest of the attractively narrow ridge. At the ridge end, drop right to join a bridleway track just below, to emerge on the road at a point where you can cross directly to a path opposite. That path climbs on stone-mortar steps to **Mam Tor**.

The slabbed path descends beyond, to close the circuit at **Hollins Cross**.

DERWENT WATERSHED – SCHEDULE				
	Distance mls/km	Ascent ft/m	Time min	ETA
Start: Mam Tor				0:00
Hope (north edge)	3.6/5.8	400/120	85	1:25
Yorkshire Bridge	2.2/3.5	1000/300	85	2:50
High Neb (Stanage Edge)	3.0/4.8	1000/300	90	4:20
Dovestone Tor	4.4/7.1	750/220	135	6:35
Margery Hill	4.4/7.1	450/140	130*	8:45
toadstool stone	4.1/6.6	250/70	110*	10:35
Bleaklow Hill	2.9/4.7	450/130	80*	11:55
Snake Pass	3.1/4.9	70/20	70	13:05
Kinder Downfall	4.6/7.3	650/200	125	15:10
Brown Knoll	3.1/4.9	200/60	80*	16:30
Mam Tor	3.6/5.7	350/110	100*	18:10
TOTALS	**39/62.5**	**5600/1700**		

Note* The schedule allows for some slowdown in the boggy bits, but after really rainy weather they'll be a lot slower than the schedule.

Much of the route is on grouse moor, on access land opened under the Countryside & Rights of Way Act. However, there are widespread restrictions on dogs, and some on humans too during grouse shooting from 12 August–12 December. The Pennine Way is a right of way.

Chapter 11

The Across Wales Walk:
From the English Border to the Sea over Plynlimon

WALKING ACROSS WALES

The walk from Anchor, in southwest Shropshire, to Cladach Bay near Aberystwyth, covers 45 miles (72km) and goes over the top of Pumlumon Fawr (Plynlimon in English). It's a group effort, organised within the calendar of the Long Distance Walkers' Association. It was in 1964 that 12 members of the West Birmingham Hostelling Group first walked from the English border to the sea. The walk has been repeated every year since, although adjusted when a windfarm was built on its route at Pengwyn Mawr. Entries are limited to two coach-loads (about 100), and it is always over-subscribed.

The event begins in England. Indeed, to make this absolutely obvious, the event begins at Clun. For Clun embodies Englishness taken well over the top. A village green is surrounded by ice cream shops and car parks, all overhung by ancient horse chestnut trees. Ducks paddle in the village stream. Overhead, a castle helpfully wrecked by the Welsh provides a decorative ruin against the sunny English sky, as well as somewhere to walk to (supposing you don't fancy Aberystwyth).

We spend our Clun night lying on our backs, in our lightweight walking gear, on the wooden floor of the village hall. But not going to sleep doesn't matter, as we're getting up again at 4 o'clock. With last-minute checking of gear, a cold and indigestible breakfast, and another last-minute gear check, we pass our final half hour of stationary existence.

At the same time, an event organiser has taken a flask of hot tea down to the start point at Anchor, and is walking along the hedge bottom with a torch. Here and there something stirs and groans, and a torch shines back. For, having imagined the possibility of crossing Wales all the way in a day, the human mind cannot stop but must at once imagine the possibility of crossing Wales in the other direction as a warm-up the day before. And where the human mind can go, the human foot is eventually sure to follow...

A dozen stiff figures emerge from the hedge, dump their sleeping bags into the event minibus, and prepare for the pleasure of returning all the way across Wales with slightly less load on their backs, albeit with considerably sorer feet. Away over England the edge of the sky is going grey. And down the road on rubber feet pads a monster with the bright eyes of 100 head torches. It stops at

First checkpoint on the Across Wales Walk

the small bridge at the edge of Wales, stamps its toes, and mutters quietly to itself in the half-darkness.

Dawn comes along the Kerry Ridgeway, and the lumpy bumpy green borderlands glow with the enamelled colours of an illuminated manuscript. Such landscape in this polluted age we see only at dawn, before the chimneys and car exhausts start to smoke. For comfort against the many miles ahead, I'm keeping company with a friend called Alan whose pace is slightly less than my own natural one; and this allows me to enjoy the emerald and golden tones of the dawn fields laid out below. Then the sun rises to show, ahead of us, the splendid Welsh Marches; small hills crammed together like a tightly penned flock of giant green sheep. As this is the Welsh Marches, the sheep in question will be stolen ones from the English.

No country is the same all the way across, and Wales is particularly varied. Accordingly, after crossing several of the small sheep hills, we climb a wooded lane into a pass to reach the green/brown boundary. Over the top are fewer fields, but dead bracken, and moorland rising into cloud. We come down to the Severn, to find the small town of Llandinam still enjoying its Saturday-morning slumbers.

The sun, at least, is up, and coming through between the branches, and a path leads ahead through the Waste Wood. Being lost, do we press on and hope for a way through, or lose time to retrace our steps? I elect to turn back and hunt about for the footbridge made of discarded crash barrier mentioned in the route description supplied by the organisers. And from the fields beyond that bridge, I hear the emotional voices of walkers who decided to press onward, in hope, into an entanglement of brushwood.

As I've been travelling slightly slower than my natural speed, I have an illusion of extra energy. The route between the checkpoints being suggested but not stipulated, I divert in pursuit of a small adjacent hill that happens to be a Marilyn. (What are Marilyns? See Chapter 6. I quietly grab these small hills so as to impress three people I know who are impressed by such things because they too are bagging Marilyns. Otherwise, I just say 'because it's there' or 'I haven't ever been on it.' And sidle away before you see the lack of logic.) The small and very green Bryn y Fan (Van Hill) rises behind the village of Fan. Its top is an enclave of bilberry and black heather high above the agriculture. But at the back a bracken slope leads down to a lonely reservoir, and suddenly it's the mountain ground.

By this personal quest I've placed myself half an hour behind: it's noticeable that the folk I'm now among are easier to overtake. Overtaking is encouraging; so much so that I break into a jog along the tracks in the early afternoon, with the result that I catch up at the checkpoint with my slightly slower pal Alan, just about to depart.

But I can't leave alongside; for the checkpoint offers a special orange-beige nectar. The gourmet subtlety of the carrot and caraway soup means that, despite my overtaking-inspired enthusiasm, I linger for a second plastic beaker of the stuff. And even ask for the recipe.

The checkpoint cook looks politely surprised. 'Well, you get a whole lot of hot water,' she explains, 'and then you pour it on the powder.' The nectar effect is caused by salt depletion, starch depletion, and the special ambience of spruce trees and sweating walkers. You could reproduce it in a restaurant (remove roof and doors, invite in all the homeless) but it might not work unless you also made the customers walk 25 miles to get there.

Knowing I'll be reverting to pal pace lets me keenly jog out of the checkpoint until I catch him. He has made friends with a couple from Somerset who are charming in their personalities but, much more importantly, are going at a pace that exactly suits Alan.

On a brisk summer afternoon, or in the clarity of autumn, Plynlimon feels slightly like being in a helicopter, the way it hangs in the sky with a view end-to-end of Cardigan Bay. That was how Plynlimon was last year. This year, Plynlimon is beige and nondescript grass, and fences fading into the mist.

Climbing to Bryn Gwyn on the Across Wales Walk

At Nant-y-Moch reservoir checkpoint, sitting in drizzle at grey day end, 'Oh dear,' said the English, 'the midges.' There were two of them. Midges, not English, I mean. It seemed odd to a Scot, to be sitting in such conditions with only two midges. From the checkpoint I could reach another Marilyn, Drosgl, if just prepared to swim across the reservoir. But I got enough funny looks by departing the checkpoint south instead of northwest, to do Disgwylfa Fawr. (Disgwylfa Fawr is not listed in the official Marilyn list. But a confession. There is a special newsletter for Marilyn-baggers, full of fascinating facts, such as that a railway has been carved through a crucial col in Dorset, creating the needed 150m drop behind Nine Barrow Down. And, in a recent revision, the col behind Disgwylfa Fawr has also been deemed to just satisfy the criterion. It is a *newly discovered* Marilyn.)

Thus I exercised my mind with some mapreading, and visited a pleasant grassy summit well below the cloud base. At its back were two cyclists, lost on the cycle trails: 'Oh look, here's a man with a map.' It was hard not to feel smug when the 12 miles they'd have to do if they continued around their wrong route was really too much for them – and them on wheels!

Slow-fast-slow can be a good way to go. I rejoined the main walk beside a small moorland lake, and again encouraged myself by overtaking the slightly slower walkers I'd fallen back among. But after 20 minutes a sudden access of energy had me swooping down the Craigypistyll ravine at 7mph with shrieks of glee. Sore legs, sore feet, and scree: Craig y Pistyll can be completely unpleasant to pick down, and the heather, yellow gorse and so on are an irrelevance. But not with feet and knees miraculously still working, and the descent steep but not too steep, loose enough to add some slide to the swoop, and the bright waterfall far below, the yellow gorsebush flashing past at ankle level, the green fields unfolding ahead.

At the end of the lovely green valley, we emerged to evening sunshine, sticky cake, and some folding chairs where we could change into our comfy trainers. The last stretch is along country lanes, and it doesn't matter if it gets dark. For the last mile there are even streetlights.

Clarach Bay is an entertainment resort in brash but faded plastic. Hot soup was served: there would be a minibus by and by. In the meantime, we could walk out past the flashy lights, onto the night-time beach, and listen to the ripples arriving off the Atlantic.

Then we clambered stiffly into the minibus, slipped into a dream behind the misted windows, before arriving at Aberystwyth's halls of residence for supper and sleep. The usual signs in the bathrooms warned of the danger of slipping – except that, in the Welsh-language version underneath, the fresh-washed floors had become, more romantically, a 'Peril'. Even more perilousness was implied in the appeal not to swim off Aberystwyth beach in the dark, in midwinter, while drunk.

The students wouldn't need such odd adventures – not if they tuned in to Marilyn-bagging, and the Across Wales Walk.

BRIEF ROUTE AND SCHEDULE

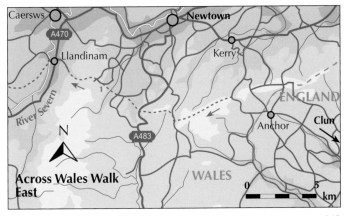

Concept	English border to the sea over Plynlimon
Distance	72km (46 miles)
Ascent	1700m (5600ft)
Start	Anchor, Shropshire (SO 174 855)
Finish	Clarach Bay (SN 585 841) near Aberystwyth
Maximum altitude	752m Plynlimon
Terrain	Quiet roads, field paths, and a crossing of Plynlimon
Target time	18hrs
Standard strong walker	18.75hrs

While 30km of the route is on roads, it doesn't feel like it – apart from the 11km to finish. The roads are small and quiet, and come in short sections. The route is varied, with rolling lumpy countryside becoming gradually rougher and bleaker, to the rough and grassy crossing of Plynlimon. The descent to Bont-goch is in a very picturesque ravine. The final lanes are an opportunity to socialise.

Route choice is free between the checkpoints, but a recommended route is published on the event website. As well as food and drink, checkpoints offer a baggage service: so you can send dry socks and shoes ahead to Bont-goch.

Note The path to right of the Craig y Pistyll ravine (SN 713 856) is not as awkward as the official description suggests, and is very beautiful.

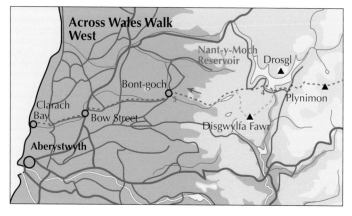

ACROSS WALES – SCHEDULE

	Distance mls/km	Ascent ft/m	Time min	ETA
Start: Anchor bridge				5:00
Two Tumps (Kerry Ridgeway)	4.4/7.1	500/150	95	6:35
CP1 (SO077861 nr Pentre)	3.0/4.8	350/100	65	7:40
Llanidlam	4.2/6.7	750/230	95	9:15
CP2 (SN975868 nr Oakley Park)	4.0/6.4	650/200	90	10:45
Afon Clywedog	4.6/7.3	600/180	100	12:25
CP3 Hafren Forest	4.3/6.9	750/230	110	14:15
Plynlimon	4.8/7.7	1600/470	140	16:35
CP4 Nant-y-Moch dam	3.2/5.1	150/40	75	17:50
CP5 Bont-goch	5.5/8.8		110	19:40
Bow Street	4.3/6.9	267/80	95	21:15
Clarach Bay	2.4/3.8		50	22:05
TOTALS	**45/71.5**	**5600/1700**		

Note My 'standard strong walker' is going to get minibussed to the finish, as he doesn't quite make the checkpoint closing times. So this schedule is 10 percent faster than him. Encouragement of fellow-walkers, light pack, and in particular lightweight trail shoes should achieve the necessary speed.

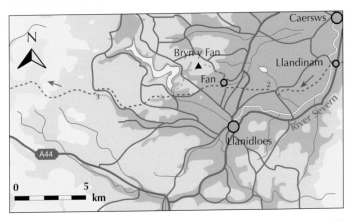

Chapter 12
The Lairig Ghru:
The Great Through-route of the Cairngorms

Through the Ghru

The Cairngorms are Scotland's largest mountain range. Right through the middle of them runs a 500m-deep valley that still, at its highest point, is higher than most hills of England. From the end of the Ice Age to the coming of the car, the Lairig Ghru, 28 miles from Braemar on Deeside to Aviemore on the Spey, has been Scotland's highest and finest through-route.

The walk through the Lairig Ghru is long; but even longer is the getting back again afterwards. The only bus back to Braemar runs from Aberdeen. From Aviemore you can get round to Aberdeen by way of Perth, but it's slightly less slow via Inverness. Once you've made it to Braemar, there's a daily postbus to Linn of Dee, not at a convenient time. The walk, from B to A through the Lairig, takes between 9 and 12 hours. The return from A to B takes roughly twice as long, provided you get your buses right.

I got my buses wrong.

Specifically, my birthday party the night before meant that I was still asleep as the crucial 7.45am bus pulled out of Aberdeen. The next bus was 2 hours later, and 2 hours later than that I arrived at Braemar. Noon, in mid-March, meant just 7 hours left to get through the rugged high ground before nightfall. My plan accordingly was to stop and sleep somewhere near the Pools of Dee, just before the pass top. At least, that had been the plan until the chap on the bus told me just how nasty the weather was going to get. Sunshine was to turn to cloud, and wind, and wet snow; followed for the second half of the night by a hard frost. 'Take a wee walk along the Dee,' he suggested sympathetically, 'then stop in Braemar, the B&Bs are cheap in March; and start through the Ghru nice and early tomorrow.'

The Met Office, on the other hand, had suggested only a little light drizzle, with pressure remaining high. Temperatures, too, were high. In the sunshine outside the bus, the snowfall of the previous weeks was rushing as green water down the Dee. Cloud was gathering, but not any high cirrus suggesting a front coming along. And half-way through the long through-route would be the squalid shelter of Corrour, if things really did turn untempting.

Besides, I did that wee walk along the Dee last summer.

The full Lairig Ghru, for the drovers who developed the route, meant going with the cows all the way to Falkirk market. No worrying about that Braemar

The northern edge of the Cairngorm plateau, split by the Lairig Ghru

bus, either, for the Chevalier de Johnstone, fleeing after Culloden. He kept at it as far as the Fife coast before taking ship for France. But a century ago the full route meant merely Aviemore to Braemar, A to B; or back again, B to A. Thus it was for the farmwives of Glen More, carrying their eggs through the high mountains to the markets of the Dee. Thus, too, for the three tailors aiming to dance their New Year's reel at the Dells of Abernethy and of Rothiemurchus, and at Dalmore on Deeside – though they scored only two dells out of three and died in the drifts under Ben Macdui. It was A to B, too, for the hobnailed walkers, before tarmac and the car shrunk the hills of Scotland into daywalks from Edinburgh.

Accordingly, having reached Braemar I rejected the idea of waiting a further 90 minutes for the postbus to Linn of Dee. It wouldn't save me time, only legwork. And legwork is what the Lairig's all about.

The walk out of Braemar starts through Morrone Birkwood. The birches are beautiful even with the leaves off. And leaves-off lets you see the snows-lopes of Beinn a' Bhuird across the valley. I held the birchwood in my memory, for later comparison with the pines of Rothiemurchus on the other side; and crossed the flooding Dee by the white-railed Victoria Bridge. A forest road leads through more woodland to the Lui river, and a wide and boringly smooth dirt road runs up to Derry Lodge. One way to make the Lairig walk even more interesting is to do this Derry track fast and in the dark, and have the sun come up behind Ben Macdui to strike an evil gleam off the dewy slabs of the Devil's Point.

Beyond Derry Lodge, the path stays smooth and easy to the ford of the Luibeg Burn. Grey waves of meltwater were plunging almost head-high, so that I was glad of the footbridge flung across the flood by the Cairngorm Club 50 years ago. And the quarter-mile of boulder and mud non-path to reach that footbridge made me think more kindly of the smooth flat walkways constructed by Mar Lodge Estate, and even of the dull Derry track.

Around the shoulder of Carn a' Mhaim came the expected light drizzle. Unfortunately, it was coming at about 50kph on a nasty wind. Sleeping out seemed unlikely to be fun under such vigorous drizzle, and on top of an inch or two of flowing meltwater. However, over across the Dee, the wet slates of Corrour bothy gleamed invitingly.

But... it was only 4.30. And since the man on the bus and his confident weather forecast, I'd shifted my grand plan; away from the dramatic sunset-to-sunrise sleepout, in favour of crossing right through the pass in the dark, aided by my new torch whose light-emitting diodes wouldn't run out for another 99 hours. Even though drizzly and grey, it was not particularly cold. Quite the contrary: it was particularly warm. My feet sank deep into the snow patches, and meltwater streamed down a dozen brown waterfalls and ran ankle-deep over the path. The Tailor Burn splashed wide and bouldery across several metres of hillside.

A mile past the bothy I saw a spark of life: three Irish walkers coming down the pass, even their bright jackets turned to grey by the day's dark and the great snow-streaky mountains on either flank.

'Is the bothy really there?' they asked.

I pointed out its roof gleaming in the distance, and the most emotional of the Irishmen – the one who'd been lagging behind a bit – bowed down towards its wet welcome and raised his hands in the air. I added that the bridge they saw on their map had been existing in the real world for 50 years now, and had been continuing to exist as I passed it 20 minutes ago – and took a quick step backwards in fear of getting kissed.

The March Burn was as wide as the earlier one of the Tailors, and the infant Dee ran brown and lumpy between banks of dirty snow, like something coming out of a glacier in Switzerland. The footsteps of the Irishmen wandered deep and black across the soggy snow, occasionally bottoming out into running water. Among the boulders the Pools of Dee showed greeny-grey, with floating snow

Corrour bothy, a sometimes squalid shelter at the half-way point

islands. Irish footholes led me across steep snow-banks above the water. The top of the pass was a narrow stonefield between steep slopes that rose, grey snow and black boulders, into the dark cloud not far above. A solitary ptarmigan in winter white wandered across the stones, sampling the newly-exposed damp moss. Behind the bird, a streak of neon orange was the lights of Aviemore, 10 miles away and 2000 feet below.

The chill of the oncoming night was making some of the snow almost OK to walk on. But between the snow patches were darkening boulderfields, interrupted by the youthful and boisterous Allt Druidh. The path appeared briefly, then vanished into a temporary Pool of Druidh – there aren't usually pools on the Aviemore side of the pass. I hurried downhill. There's a point where the path crosses a mighty pile of boulders with the Allt Druidh flowing through just below. I wanted to get to that point before it got dark: especially if, in the snowmelt, the Druidh should be flowing not underneath but over the top of the boulders.

The boulders were still managing to be bigger than the river. In half-darkness I clambered from rock to rock, with river noise coming out of the black spaces between. On the path below, I hunted out my new torch and switched it on. And, as happens when you switch on a torch, the darkness rushed in, and the world shrank from massive dim hills to one pale patch of path. A metaphor, of course, for modern civilisation, its technology eliminating the wilderness. And good for modern civilisation, I say, when it means hardly at all falling into smelly peat holes on the way down the Lairig Ghru.

In the Lairig Ghru, below the Devil's Point

After half an hour, the edge of the torchlight showed heather stalks rather than stones. Pine-tree shapes stood black against the orange glow of Aviemore. Wind in the branches paradoxically made the weather sound worse even as I entered the shelter. I reached the path junction Piccadilly, so named because of being so busy, but while nightfall brings drug dealers and girls in tight trousers to the one in London, in Rothiemurchus Forset it's only the wind, and the river half a mile away, and an owl.

A windswept empty car park, and the sudden transition from bare Cairn Gorm to the cramped tin interior with its lamps and dials and vinyl upholstery: that's the modern way to end the Lairig Ghru walk. But the old way is with 6 miles of pines. The miles are smooth, and would be easy enough if not for the 23 or so of them already behind. By daytime the wide paths are slightly boring unless on a bike. At night, though, you switch off the torch (despite that its civilised diodes still have 98 hours of life) and follow the pale sandy streak below the trees, and listen to the river and the owl. And think about thieves in the night, passing silently between the trees two centuries ago on their way to Ryvoan Pass and the fat cows of Aberdeen. A quietly splashing blackness by the path is Loch an Eilein, and it's worth the extra half-mile to see the castle standing dark in the starlight, under snow-streaked rounded mountains and jaggy pines.

A pheasant shrieks. Braeriach's northern corries gleam between the tree trunks. A scrap of pathside litter catches the light of the moon. The Spey has flooded out into the forest, a black shadow below the birches, and runs strong and almost silent a metre below the old railway bridge.

Lights shine on the other side. 'You must be joking,' says the SYHA warden. My 'Not full up then?' had indeed been with humorous intent; for what has Aviemore to offer, in wet March, as the Spey carries the last of Cairn Gorm's ski season away into the North Sea? What but 28 miles of forest and mountain, and two great rivers – the ptarmigan and the owl – and the island castle under the moon.

Lacking the sudden pheasant, the hostel was even quieter than Rothiemurchus Forest. I had just half an hour to make up a meal in the empty, echoing, members' kitchen, before they locked it against me and made me go to bed.

ROUTE AND SCHEDULE

Distance	45km/28 miles (full version)
Ascent	700m/2400ft
Start	Braemar (NO 151 914)
Finish	Aviemore (NH 896 123)
Maximum altitude	835m
Terrain	Paths, mostly good, through very remote country
Target time	1 day
Standard stong walker	11.25hrs

There are various ways for the car-borne to shorten the walk. They can start at Linn of Dee rather than Braemar. They can finish at the Sugar Bowl car park under Cairngorm, though this is to miss out the rather nice Rothiemurchus Forest and replace it with the Chalamain Gap (rather nasty, especially in the dark).

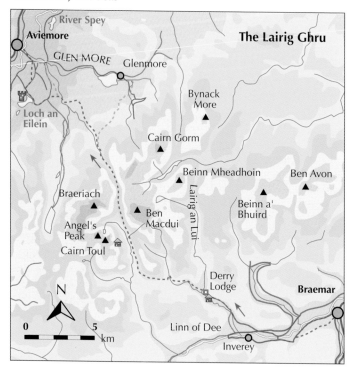

Best, though, is to arrive at Braemar by bus and spend the night there ready for an early start. The opening wander through the beautiful Morrone Birkwood can be replaced by an early morning road walk. The road will be peaceful; but there won't be any dawn deer herds browsing below its branches.

Note At half-way, the journey can be broken at Corrour bothy. Despite its remoteness, this gets crowded at summer weekends.

The route

At the west end of **Braemar**, fork left up Chapel Brae. At its top, a car park and duck pond are on the left. Keep ahead on a track through a deer fence, then at once fork off right on a path. This crosses another track and enters **Morrone Birkwood** nature reserve, contouring alongside a deer fence.

After a gate through the deer fence, the ground is more open, with only scattered trees. After crossing two streams, the main path forks up left. It passes above a heathery hump, and joins a track above. Just ahead, the track leaves the reserve at a gate and stile. Follow it into a plantation, ignoring a side-track down right, and in another 20 metres crossing a ford. Now turn down right, on a sketchy path to left of this stream, but in 50 metres fork left into a tree gap with a rough wet track. Follow it down for 100 metres to cross the dam of a small reservoir and bend left onto a well-made track. This slants down west, to join the Deeside road near a car park (NO 118 897).

Turn left along the road, over the bridge at Corriemulzie (with a waterfall below), to white-railed **Victoria Bridge**. Cross it, then turn left down a bank to the riverside. Head upstream, ignoring gates in the fence on the right. After a corner under fir trees, follow the flood embankment, then cross a ladder stile on the right (NO 092 898). With Mar Lodge nearby on the right, turn left up a tarred driveway to road. Keep ahead for 200 metres and fork right, up a rough track, soon passing through a vehicle barrier.

The track runs straight across an X-junction into open forest, then down to join Lui Water. Here a major track arrives across a bridge from the left. Follow this track ahead, through a meadow past township remains. Approaching Derry Lodge, at the first scattered pines to left of the track, turn off left on a small path, to pass the newly rebuilt Bob Scott's bothy at the riverside, cross a track end, and follow the tree edge on the right to a wooden shed with an emergency phone mounted on its end. Turn left, away from **Derry Lodge**, to cross a footbridge over Derry Burn, and turn left signed 'Lairig Ghru'.

The path is wide and grassy across floodable grassland, past Luibeg Cottage opposite, then becomes gravelly and clear at the corner of a plantation. Rebuilt path runs upstream beside Luibeg Burn. Where a smaller path forks right (for Glen Luibeg) keep to the main path, down slightly left through a staggered fence gap into an enclosed plantation, to reach the ford of Luibeg Burn.

This ford is often impassible, in which case head upstream on a selection of small rough paths for 400 metres to the **Cairngorm Club footbridge** (NO 013 942). It has a plate saying how far from Braemar (12.5 miles) and how far still to go (quite a distance). From the bridge, a boggy path runs left, rising gently away from the river, to rejoin the main path just before a gate in a deer fence.

The path remains fairly good around the base of Carn a' Mhaim and into the Lairig Ghru. An obvious path forking left runs down to an aluminium footbridge over the Dee and **Corrour bothy** opposite on its patch of green; but the main Lairig Ghru path keeps up-valley, to right of the river. The path gets gradually rougher, and slants away from the river as it passes the entrance to

Heading into the Lairig Ghru from the north

the Garbh Choire opposite. Then it rejoins the now-smaller stream of the upper Dee. The stream rather surprisingly stops in the rocky ground entering the narrows at the pass top, and so does the path. The best way may be found passing to left of the **Pools of Dee**, which have no inlets or outflows and never freeze (so that must have been congealed peat froth I saw lying across their surfaces).

After two large pools and a small one, you pass the top of the pass. The path gradually gets clearer, with the new stream of the Allt Druidh sometimes on the surface and sometimes out of sight under the boulders. The path keeps to the left side of the valley, until it is joined from the left by a rebuilt path descending off the end of Sron na Lairige. Here it turns down a steep slope into the stream slot. The path crosses boulders, from below which the Allt Druidh flows out as a small river (NH 958 037).

The path runs down now to right of the stream. In 100 metres, the pitched path for the Chalamain Gap forks up right. (It climbs for 100m to pass through the uncomfortable, bouldery canyon and continue easily to the Sugar Bowl car park.) For Aviemore, though, a reduced path runs alongside the stream, rising

Loch an Eilein castle

gradually above it. After a stream crossing, a very slight rise takes it through a small col (NH 956 048) to join a stream trickling down beyond. The path leaves this stream, to follow the top edge of the banking that falls left to Allt Druidh. After the signed path for Rothiemurchus Lodge forks off right, the main path runs ahead into trees, where its sandy line between heather clumps can be followed by torchlight or moonlight. After 1.5km under the trees, it reaches the major junction **Piccadilly** (NH 938 075).

Here turn left on a wide path signed as a cycle route to Loch an Eilein. This soon runs close to Allt Druidh. A side-track forks left to a ford, and 50 metres later the main path crosses the **Cairngorm Club footbridge**. A sign indicates how far you've come from Braemar (24 miles) and how far it still is to Aviemore (not that far at all; and all easy going).

Across the footbridge turn right on a track, in 200 metres reaching a fork. The track ahead runs to Coylumbridge for Aviemore. But if it's still light, you have time to divert 800 metres for Loch an Eilein. And if it's already dark, Loch an Eilein by moonlight is magic!

Walkers in Rothiemurchus Forest

So fork left, signed for Loch an Eilein. After passing **Lochan Deo** on your left, cross a track junction, still on the cycle path for Loch an Eilein. At a second track junction in 50 metres, you can keep ahead on the cycle path, but it's rather wide and dull. The walkers' way turns right on a track that bends left to Achnagoichan. Turn right before the house, and left onto a small, signed path around its fenced enclosure. Behind the house you join a wider path. Follow it through open pinewood with heather understory: again, followable by moonlight. After 800 metres the path widens, and forks; the smaller path ahead is slightly shorter than the wider path left, but both lead to **Loch an Eilein**.

Follow the wide path to the right, along the northeast side of the loch. Around 400 metres after a fence gate, take a smaller path on the left across tree roots to the loch foot, turn left across its low earth dam, and follow the track left for 500 metres to view the island castle under the moon. Or don't take the smaller path on the left, and miss out the moonlit castle.

At the lane end below Loch an Eilein, bear right onto a track marked 'Estate Vehicles Only'. After 1km it reaches scattered houses at **Croft**. After the houses,

LAIRIG GHRU – SCHEDULE

	Distance mls/km	Ascent ft/m	Time min	ETA
Start: Braemar				0:00
Victoria Bridge	3.6/5.7	450/150	85	1:25
Derry Lodge	4.9/7.8	350/100	110	3:15
Luibeg: Cairngorm Club footbridge	2.1/3.3	300/90	50	4:05
Path junction Corrour bothy	2.5/4.0	400/120	65	5:10
Lairig Ghru top	3.8/6.1	900/250	115	7:05
Path junction for Chalamain Gap	1.8/2.8		45	7:50
Piccadilly	2.8/4.5		60	8:50
Loch an Eilein dam	2.9/4.6		65	9:55
To castle shore and back	0.6/1.0		15	10:10
Aviemore	2.9/4.7		65	11:15
TOTALS	**28/44.5**	**2400/720**		
Start: Linn of Dee				0:00
Derry Lodge	3.1/4.9	100/30	65	1:05
Path junction for Chalamain Gap				7:50
Sugar Bowl: end	3.1/5.0	400/120	75	9:05

bear left on a driveway track, and keep ahead, to right of a garage, onto a small path running due north through woodland. After 400 metres it crosses a larger path, and in another 50 metres joins a second large path. Follow this ahead, still north, to emerge through a green gate onto the road triangle at **Inverdruie**.

Pass around the road triangle, to the Glenmore road at the Rothiemurchus Information Centre. Cross and turn left on pavement, and at the first bend keep ahead onto a cycle path along a former railway. A walkers' path is in woods alongside. Cross the old railway bridge into **Aviemore**, and turn right along the riverside. For the youth hostel and information centre take the first bridge under the railway on the left; for the village centre take the second one.

PART IV: SURVIVAL

Chapter 13

Time and Space:
The Fundamentals

'Distance equals speed times time' – so we were taught at school. If only it were so simple! In the event, slower is often faster, while faster often means not getting to the end at all. The state of mind is crucial, as is the state of the feet. The same distance can feel different on different days, and certainly in different shoes.

As an experiment, I once went for a walk across South Wales without a wristwatch. It was strangely liberating, like walking with no clothes on. Watchlessness rather than nakedness had the extra advantage that I didn't have to worry whether that speck along the ridge was another person coming towards me.

Not that it ever was. The Black Mountains in those days were pretty well empty. I crossed Lord Hereford's Knob, and Waun Fach, without once worrying that I should really have been on them a half hour before. As I'd been indoors taking exams the previous week, I wasn't clued up on what time the sun would be going down. But when it did, on a high bluff overlooking the Usk Valley, I unrolled my orange polythene, laid my sleeping bag on top, and went to sleep.

When the sun got up again, so did I, and wandered down into Crickhowell for milk to go on my muesli. Down in Crickhowell, it turned out to be 5 in the morning. I had to sit in a bus shelter for 2 hours before I got any breakfast.

You can allow so much extra for height gain: 1000ft counts as 1.5 miles. If you're using modern units, then 100m counts as 1km if you're doing it in your head, or 0.8km if you're doing it in your computer. But 1000ft of up at the start of the day is much less of an obstacle than it is at the end. By evening, it might count as 2 miles, and 2 miles of the slow evening sort at that. And 1000ft of up at the beginning is always quicker than the calculation. Thus, in the next section of this book, I arrived at Ballencleuch Law 30 minutes earlier than expected.

The first function of a schedule is to warn when you're too fast. The quick-step, any ballroom dancer will tell you, actually goes slow – slow – quick quick – slow. Too fast means getting tired; real speed lies in slowness.

The second function of the schedule is the exact opposite. Being in front of it gives a sense of relaxation, as having just sneaked out of the great Mall of Time with some of the stuff hidden up your jumper.

Dawn above Nithsdale, on the Southern Uplands Fifty: the first hill is always faster than the schedule suggests

Thus, when it comes to scheduling, the mind and the legs are at cross purposes. As they are in the game of long-distance walking as a whole: the legs always failing to persuade the brain that this is in fact *pain*, and the thing about pain is that it is *not enjoyable*. Wha'd'ya mean, says the mind: we just gained 2 whole minutes between Ballencleuch Law and the motorway. That's pleasure for you!

So if you're being sensible, slow down and go with the schedule. If you feel like fun, speed up and get ahead – and then get tired. Even more pleasant, if also less sensible, is no schedule at all, and no wristwatch to time it by. Time, says Immanuel Kant, is a fundamental given, obliged to exist if there's to be a Universe at all. How fine an achievement, then, to pretend that Fundamental Given into non-existence even for a brief 50 miles.

And then, just when you didn't want it to, it gets dark. Instead of a time-piece you could carry a torch, and a sleeping bag, and not worry about the coming of the night. But then you'd have to worry about the weight of the sleeping bag...

The final hill is more tiring than the equivalent distance on the flat: walker approaches Coledale Hause at mile 70 of the Lakeland Hundred

Choose shoes

I would never have achieved in a comfortable day the Across Wales Walk, or the Lyke Wake Walk, wearing walking boots. I, like almost every other member of the Long Distance Walkers' Association, wear trail shoes. In a walking shop, rather than a running shop, these may be referred to as 'approach shoes'. They look like trainers, with fabric uppers and padded soles. The difference is the footprint: where trainers have flat bottoms, trail shoes are deeply incised. They grip well on grass slopes, fairly well on rocks and mud, while still being comfortable on hard paths and roads.

Trail shoes have two disadvantages:

- They don't provide ankle support, and when you first start wearing them you suffer some twisted ankles. After a couple of hundred miles, your ankles strengthen, and you learn not to put them down crooked, or to tumble over quickly when you do.

A well-worn pair of trail shoes

- While some shoes claim to be waterproof, mine aren't. Wet feet mean, eventually, blisters. I use Vaseline, others use cocoa butter or lanolin, to keep the water out of the feet for the first 20 miles. Then there are blister plasters, Spenco and Moleskin, that I carry always, as well as wisps of sheeps' wool gathered from fences to twist around the toes. If your feet are well used they will last longer.

There is one advantage:

- You go 20 percent, and one and a half times, as far. At least until those blisters…

Specialised fellrunning shoes have no internal padding, and studs underneath. They grip like Velcro on steep grass, and are good in mud, and not bad on bare rock and firm snow. But after 20 miles they become very uncomfortable, especially as they're normally worn tight on the foot. Running roads in fell shoes gives you blisters very quickly.

Chapter 14

Fifty from your Front Door:
A Southern Upland Story

Concept	Visit a friend 50 miles away
Distance	80km/50 miles (or your usual maximum + 50 percent)
Ascent	1500m/5000ft if you live somewhere hilly
Start	Your front door at dawn
Finish	A suitably distant friend
Terrain	Off-road
Target time	1 day
Standard stong walker	20hrs

Suffering from stiffness and too much staring into the computer screen? Draw a circle that's slightly more than you can do in a day – 20 miles, 30 miles, 50 miles – find a friend on the circumference, and go. But it helps if you live in the Southern Uplands. Fifty miles, my personal not-quite-in-a-day distance, can take you over 20 hills, and only three tarred roads.

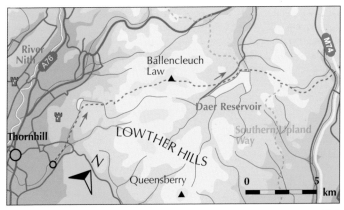

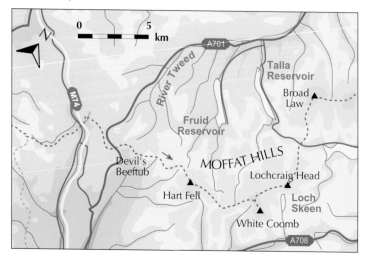

Home, says T.S. Eliot, is where one starts from. Starting from home means a good night's sleep, and no driving around in the pre-dawn dark. Just up, into a big bowl of muesli, and off out the door.

The plan was simple. The Lowther Hills; the Moffat Hills; and then the Manor Hills. I remembered some paths across the Manor Hills, and the Harvey map shows fences to follow. But being Southern Upland hills they are, here and there, a bit boring. Doing the Manors in darkness would add excitement. And then, at the end, there was the Tweed. Into Innerleithen the choice was a bridge a mile south or a bridge 2 miles west. But on the map a farm track ran down to the bank and stopped; and the name of the farm was Howford.

I asked my friend at the end, and her *History of Peeblesshire* knew all about it. She sent me a picture of 18th-century commuters crossing the How Ford on stilts. Rivers shift over the centuries. But in the slightly featureless Uplands, a possibly impassible ford generates exciting suspense.

As I rose out of Nithsdale up a handy Landrover track, the sun was already well above the grassy Lowthers. Straw-coloured light gleamed between bars of cloud. The day was basically grey, but far-seeing. From Ballencleuch Law, distinguished as the second highest of the Southern Lowthers, I saw across the sea to Skiddaw. Behind me, green Nithsdale ran southwards to the Solway; ahead, the Clyde headed north for Glasgow. Further east the Moffat Hills spread along the horizon, and a wide black hump beyond was Broad Law.

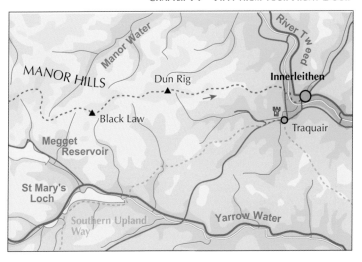

The going across the Lowthers is fast and grassy. Quite quickly I was across them and down at the Daer Reservoir. Daer is pronounced Dar. Its hills lie back slackly, its waters spread colourless between bare stone banks. The dam is wide concrete; the houses are concrete too but more cheaply constructed.

Down at Daer, the end of summer was dribbling away in grey haze. I crossed the dam, and below me half a hundred swallows were swooping after midges and dipping their beaks in the reservoir. A brief scramble up the banking, and I was on the Southern Upland Way.

Twenty years of walking have left the SU Way green and almost unmarked. It has its good bits, which are quite widely spaced apart, and it has its fairly good bits. Above Daer Reservoir it turned off for one of its rather bad bits – 10 miles through trees to Beattock – so I left it and headed down to the Evan Water.

High and out of sight, buzzards were squeaking across the quiet valley. Ahead and below, a faint low rumble told me that the spruce-lined slot contained the main road out of England. The wide dual carriageway was marked, of course, on my map. But I've lived in Nithsdale for two decades now and the map is an old one. The dual carriageway has become a motorway.

Shouldn't matter. There are farms on either side of the valley. So one or other of them must have a bridge leading over to the old road, no?

No. The further farm has simply been abandoned, its access cut by the six lanes plus hard shoulder. Hopping across the carriageway is not just illegal, but

Above Black Hope in the Moffat Hills

also unpleasantly life-threatening. (As against the Crib Goch Ridge, say, which is pleasantly life-threatening.) No over, no across, and the next bridge a mile away through the spruce. But there is also under. The Evan Water gave me a long concrete tunnel, quarter full of water, with a 9-inch concrete walkway leading into the darkness. It doesn't have the glamour of Crib Goch; but grim is a sort of good. Even if it does mean wet feet.

Beautiful grey and pink stonework, topped off with broken slate; nettles everywhere; and the continuous grumble of the motorway. Howcleuch Farm is gone, and the Evan is no longer a place for unwheeled people. Even more gone was the Roman fortlet I passed in a forest clearing, lost under thigh-deep ungrazed grasses. I emerged to hill breezes and 50 miles of grey air on the rim of the Devil's Beef Tub.

Southwards, now, the River Annan ran down green valleys to the Solway. North, bleakly interleaved bogland and moor were the top end of the Tweed. Under my ankles was the hole in the hill where Armstrongs and Eliots (plus the odd Turnbull) hid the Englishmen's stolen cattle when the Englishmen came to get them back.

Armstrongs and Eliots now ride the green ridges on four-wheel motor bikes; which makes things easy for us walkers. A quad-bike path leads comfortably up onto Hart Fell. And the Moffat Hills, unlike some of the Southern Uplands, are real scenery. Deep stream valleys are edged with rotten rocks and sideways-growing rowan. The marshes drain over the edge in the spectacular waterfall called the Grey Mare's Tail. And above the waterfall is small but lovely Loch Skeen, cradled in its bog hollow.

Rotten Bottom lives up to its name in every way except that it's actually at the top; to get to White Coomb you have to sink knee-deep in its green embrace. But the hillwalker, like his friend the broken wall, emerges onto the opposite slope and finds short sheep-nibbled grasses. It was a weekend in late summer, so the hills were busy, and accordingly at this point in the walk two other walkers did pass me, no more than 50 yards away. Then it stopped being busy again.

White Coomb, at 5 o'clock. The hazy day was fading towards grey evening. A few sun-specks fled eastwards towards somewhere with a better climate. But lightweight shoes and short Southern Upland grasses, long summer days and chill evening air, make for fast walking, along the last rounded ridge of the Moffats and down to Meggat Head. During half an hour off the ridge end, two cars passed along the strip of tarmac that divides the ranges.

Looking carefully left and right, I stepped across into the Manor Hills.

Broad Cairn on Deeside; Broad Peak in the Karakoram; the Breithorn above Zermatt; and Broad Law in the Southern Uplands. They are large (especially Broad Peak) but otherwise unexciting. Broad Law does boast a peculiar onion-spiked bandstand; there are also a small and a large radio mast. But grassy paths and fence-following are great for the slightly aching legs, the fading brain. I crossed four hills called things like Water Head and Black Cleuch Hill. The sky turned from grey to black-and-scarlet stripes, with Biggar and Peebles glowing orange around the edge. In the half-light, bog-cotton glowed almost luminous, as I waded through a knee-deep dreamy sea of it.

There are, as I'd hoped, good paths across Dun Rig. The question is, how often to hop across the fence in the hope that the good path may be existing over this particular bit? For there are also bad paths, where you sink knee-deep in the dark, wake up a sudden grouse by treading on its tail; and the trouble with following the fence is the bits of the previous fence that twist around your ankles.

On television there used to be the 'Crystal Maze'. Imagine the opposite: a maze that's soft, black, and floored with fallen fence posts. That's the night-time peat hag on the way down from Dun Rig. But up out of the peat is short

White Coomb, one of three 2500-footers on the walk, with Megget Reservoir

heather, soft like shag-pile; switch off the torch, step anywhere, and gaze with half-asleep eyes at hill shapes and the stars. The night before me, two boys saw the Northern Lights from these hills. But even the Southern Upland darkness was pleasingly dreamy.

I had, however, outwalked my schedule. Hill darkness is one thing: darkness across the impassable fords of Tweed was not so desirable. And if there's one thing better than treading the benighted heather, it's lying down on it and going to sleep. So I stopped in a hollow below the breeze and unrolled my bed. The heather twigs adapting to my weight made soft clickings against the bivvy bag, so that I thought it was raining, but it wasn't. I lay under the stars and slept my way back onto the schedule. And at dawn I came down to the Tweed.

The Tweed, whose source I'd passed 16 hours before, was now alarmingly wide. There was no sign of the 18th-century workmen on their stilts; more seriously, there was no sign of their ramped way down in and up out again. However, the wider the shallower, and 100 metres downstream were ripples and water crowfoot. The difficulty was getting in, down a steep bank of goosegrass and willow herb. And the more serious difficulty was getting out, up a bank of head-high nettles. After that, a comfy rail-bed path led into Innerleithen.

Walking in between the breakers' yards, a warm crusty smell of fresh croissants drifted in the early air. A nasal hallucination, or someone baking deliciously but in private? I wandered into the village in search of a drink – the Manor Hills had had plenty of water to squelch into suddenly, but none in clean streams.

The loos of Innerleithen were locked against the pre-dawn vandal. However, there was a six-in-the-morning newsagent with his light on. He looked up at the man in bush hat and rucksack, wet to the knee and sprinkled all over with goosegrass seeds. 'It'll stay dry,' he suggested mildly, 'but that's the best we can say. 75 pee.'

I wandered down the road and went to sleep on the lawn. My friend's dog found me there at breakfast time. It had been a proper walk, I could tell: it cost in bus tickets more than 9 quid to get back home.

50 MILES IN A DAY

For most of us, 50 miles is a bit of a superhuman effort. I give myself various advantages:

- Lightweight shoes.
- Comfortable ground: the grassy hilltops of the Southern Uplands, mostly with a quad-bike track along the top, are ideal for going a long way without getting totally exhausted.
- Long days of May or August, a full moon, and an OK weather forecast.
- Light rucksack: this is the tricky one. Stay under 12lb (5kg) while including plenty of food and water, and enough gear in case of foul weather, exhaustion, and nightfall, all perhaps happening at once.
- A map that marks fences: paths are hard to see by moonlight, but a fence is dependable.
- A friend at the end is a more enticing destination than a bus stop, a hilltop, or even the sea. Depending on the intimacy of the friend, when I arrive at 4 in the morning, I find the key under the flowerpot or go to sleep in the garden. A really kind friend would drive out to pick up the body if I collapsed near the end of the journey.
- Or, one could relax into the supporting arms of the Long Distance Walkers' Association (see chapter 15).

Chapter 15

A Hundred Miles at Once:
Two Days and Nights over Exmoor

THE EXMOOR HUNDRED

For runners, the challenge that counts is the 26 miles and 300 yards that make up the Marathon. What's the equivalent for walkers?

The aerobic limit is when the body is using oxygen as fast as it can be taken in. The Marathon keeps us at or near this limit until the ready-use fuel store (glycogen in the blood and liver) is used up – and then for 5 or 6 miles beyond. This is what makes the event special for the recreational runner. Walkers who eat can keep going until they get blisters or fall asleep. I can testify only that a walk across Scotland from Oban to Arbroath (220 miles, 50,000ft of climb and a 30lb sack in 10 days) requires less effort than 26.2 miles along the road in 3.25 hours. The day after arriving at Arbroath, I was still walking around. The day after the Marathon, I could only get downstairs if I did it backwards.

It is possible to compare walkers and runners in terms of challenge. The Marathon is the greatest task that a healthy and determined runner has a sporting chance of achieving. The corresponding challenge for walkers is the 100-miler organised by the Long Distance Walkers' Association.

Each year the walk visits a different part of England or Wales. The route will be on paths, tracks and mud; only the occasional linking section will be on tarred road. It will involve at least 12,000ft (3600m) of uphill. That's roughly three times up Ben Nevis, but spread over 100 miles it constitutes undulating rather than mountainous. The time limit is 48 hours. There will be a score of checkpoints, offering food and footcare and friendly encouragement. To ease congestion, any walker remaining in a checkpoint for 2 hours, perhaps having fallen asleep, is deemed to have retired. You may, of course, lapse into slumber between checkpoints – provided you're far enough ahead of the 2mph pace that determines the checkpoint closing times.

Entry for the event is limited to 500; it is normally oversubscribed. Depending on the weather, about 350 of the 500 will finish within the time limit. A special badge is awarded to those achieving their 10th 100-miler. One LDWA member, Roger Cole, has completed every one of the 32 held so far (the 2001 event, in Lakeland, was postponed due to foot-and-mouth disease). And one final odd fact: over the 33 years, the average age of the entrant has risen by

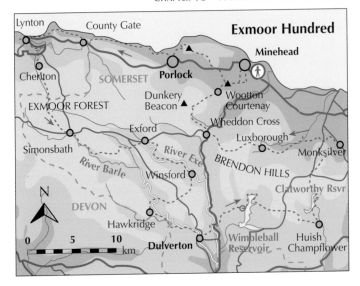

one year for each year of the event. This does suggest that the same 500 people will be walking 100 miles for ever…

This is strange. Walking 100 miles is not fun. I know, because I've done it – five times. Each time at the 50-mile mark, which is the walk's first midnight, I've promised myself never, never, to do this awful thing again.

Which is why I found myself on a Virgin Cross-country passing the back of Bristol late on a lovely May evening. Later in the evening than timetabled, indeed: but an on-train manager called Colin helped me with my connection through to Minehead. And I still got there in time for some sleep on the school-room floor before the start at 10am on Saturday – there's a later start time of 2pm for those who want to up the suffering by doing it faster.

Start: Minehead, 10:00am Saturday

I set off up the first slope at a brisk jog, so as to get photos of the colourful throng. But that was no excuse for continuing at such speed, stomping over the gravelly tracks of Periton Hill and down a long leafy path. Periton is listed as a Marilyn, but on my previous visit I'd absent-mindedly missed the trig point in the trees (you know what a Marilyn is from Chapter 6: 150m of drop all round, has to be bagged). This time I missed the trig because of trying to persuade one of my fellow walkers not to go to expensive, dangerous, dull Everest but to the Alpine 4000s instead. The first checkpoint at 8.5 miles opened at 11.45; I reached it at 11.43. Very silly speed! Especially as I hadn't run anywhere at all for about two years.

Checkpoint 1: Bossington by Porlock, 8.25 miles, 11:43am Saturday

Exmoor is hilly. The hills may be small but they are steep: passing through Porlock we smelt the toasty aroma of scorched brake pads. Exmoor even has a long-distance hillwalking history, consisting of Coleridge, Wordsworth, and Tarka the Otter.

The fictitious Tarka ran from the middle of Dartmoor, along green riverbanks and over the high grassland, before drowning the most annoying of the otterhounds and slipping into the River Exe. (The book, by Henry Williamson, was published in 1927.) Tarka's Trail was to make the easy bit in the middle of our walk. The poet Coleridge, when he had friends he thought ought to enjoy Exmoor, took them a 37-miler along the coast path as far as Lynton. Hazlitt, for one, enjoyed his long day out: 'The light of his [Coleridge's] genius shone into my soul, like the sun's rays glittering in the puddles of the road.' The poet's personal challenge was to make up the energetic first third of our walk.

It was on one of his Lynton walks that Coleridge stopped off at an overnight checkpoint at Ash Farm (just above our Mile 12), popped some laudanum to soften the pain of the blisters, and wrote *Kubla Khan*. Above Culbone Church are the

> *... forests ancient as the hills*
> *Enfolding sunny spots of greenery.*

I was reciting *Kubla Khan* to myself (this early in the walk, brain still working pretty well) but only got to 'five miles meandering with a mazy motion' when someone caught up with me and wanted to talk about socks.

On the Somerset Coast Path, you don't see the sea so much as smell it. The way is on sunken tracks, with salt air seeping through the gorse bushes, then down into a hanging wood. But eventually it emerges to high grassy clifftops, finds itself already in Devon, and descends in zigzags into Lynton.

Checkpoint 3: Lynton, 23.5 miles, 4:02pm Saturday

To say that Lynton is a quarter of the walk is grossly misleading. The first 25 miles are easy: feet intact, legs fresh, plenty of company. The final 25 miles will be at least twice as lengthy as these ones...

Descending to Porlock from Selworthy Beacon

The little villages of Lynton/Lynmouth are faded seaside Victoriana (complete with rack railway for lazy Victorians in high boarding houses) – except that much of it/them was swept away in a flash flood in 1952. You can't tell; Victorian seediness is much the same in any century. We walked the promenade between yellow bedding plants and climbed through steep little streets, as a buzzard drifted gently overhead, and out on the bay a rocket maroon alerted dinghy sailors to the turning of the tide.

Behind Lynton we turned inland along deep wooded rivers, quite like the Jura that's on the edge of the Alps. A folded stream valley led onto the grassy top of Exmoor. The whole crossing of the high ground was on lawn-like grass gone golden under the evening sun.

Checkpoint 5: Simonsbath, 33.5 miles, 7:08pm Saturday

Thirty-three miles – that's no more a third of the walk than 25 was a quarter. So it means little that so far it's been quick and comfortable. Almost 4mph is actually too quick. And as for comfortable – any pain at this stage and the next 66 miles wouldn't bear thinking about.

Not thinking about the 66 miles is easy all along the River Barle, grass paths out of earshot of road, green light through the leaves. The last sunlight

Above Lynmouth, 20 miles into the Hundred

turned the River Barle into polished metal, and the green of the surrounding slopes seemed equally shiny and artificial, as if sprayed on. Tiredness disables the brain, sharpens the senses, and turns evening Exmoor into an opium dream. Then the sun dropped behind the beech trees, and the world turned shadowy grey.

Checkpoint 6: Exford, 41 miles, 9:14pm Saturday

For a non-runner, running all the downhill and some of the flat for the first 41 miles had been surprising, and also not sensible. But easy jogging turns to painful jolting. I realised that walking, even on downhill tarmac, should now start seriously if an eventual end to this walk was to be achieved.

Checkpoint 7: Winsford, 46.5 miles, 11:15pm Saturday

Night is a time for relaxation. However sincere one's speed, the pace slows in the dark; and slowness is sensible anyway at this stage. Meanwhile night navigation is intriguing, as when at midnight we went round a gorse bush and something large made sudden hoofbeat noises just in front of us.

And there are others to chat to and to share the flickering torchlight. Just as Coleridge chatted with his companion Hazlitt on those challenge walks of two centuries before: 'His voice sounded high as we passed through echoing grove, by fairy stream or waterfall, gleaming in the summer moonlight!'

Pale lamps moved through the wood, and at 1am we crossed the medieval Tarr Steps. Torchlight shone on the ancient stones and the water gurgling below.

A steep little climb from the river saw a harrowing scene. Keeping pace with me was a mother with a daughter who looked close to the 18-year entry age for the event. But now, daughter was having to encourage Mummy, who was staggering into the verge and doing quite a lot of vomiting. Fortunately it was in the dark, but the sound effects were harrowing enough. Feeling that bad before the half-way point, Mummy must have had it – happily, a checkpoint just ahead offered a cut-off for her suffering.

Downstream in the dark, leaf-mould odours rose from our footsteps, and the River Barle chuckled alongside. I shared my torchlight with a stranger who'd accidentally left the extra-bright halogen bulb screwed into his torch, with the result that his batteries ran out straight away, and his replacement batteries ran out 45 minutes after that. At the end of 8 miles to Dulverton, he had become a friend and comrade – but his face I never knew.

Breakfast stop: Dulverton, 58 miles, 3.51am Sunday

Shadows, and footfalls fading down a distant corridor: the secondary school at Dulverton had turned into any place where travellers pass in the dark. An airport, say, or a motorway service station when the night coach pulls in and the passengers huddle in a cafeteria that smells of cold frying oil. I sat on a bench sized for infants, to wash and repair my feet; I put on fresh socks from the bag that the walk organisers had carried forward for me.

Compass and map aren't much use on town streets under streetlights. I followed my written route instructions to the old part of the town where, up an outside staircase of soft golden limestone, breakfast had been laid in the town hall. The real runners will have confronted their sausages at midnight or even earlier. Such fast types must not be let get cocky: they'd have spent the next bit of the night climbing a narrow, steep, leafy track across to the River Exe. Six hours behind me, those arriving at Dulverton after 10am would be disqualified: not simply on the grounds that 10am is disgracefully late for breakfast, but also to let the event end at some point.

As I settled my fried breakfast onto an empty table-corner, I spotted the the mother–daughter pair – the daughter now looking less youthful than 12 hours before and easily old enough to be in the event. They were just shouldering their small rucksacks and stepping out into the darkness. Forty miles down the path, they would eventually finish the walk 2 hours ahead of me.

Tarr Steps, which are crossed by torchlight halfway through the Exmoor Hundred

I left breakfast into quite the noisiest dawn chorus: the edges of Exmoor have an awful lot of oak trees to twitter in. I didn't see any deer, and oddly, neither did the runners at the front, but two of the walkers did watch a family of badgers at dawn.

The scenery got less interesting after that – quiet country at the back of the Brendons, country lanes between high hedges. An outbreak of bovine TB had diverted the route onto these roads, although even the original field edges wouldn't have been exciting. But there's not much point in scenery after Mile 65. Two and a half hours, and 8 miles, behind me, Walker 108, one Luis Broz, was just leaving breakfast.

Checkpoint 11: Huish Champflower, 72 miles, 8.20am Sunday

Seventy miles might seem like most of the way, but mentally the final 30 is at least as long as the first 60, and by that reckoning Huish is hardly more than half.

I was suffering more than some. My over-excited first 40 miles meant that I was now plodding these roads without any pleasure. The first of the runners had passed through this little village hall at 1 in the morning: he was now at the final checkpoint, and would be completing his walk at 9am. (Just two out of the 450 would achieve a 24-hour circuit.) Twenty miles behind me, the last walker was crossing Tarr Steps, half-way through the walk. A total of 450 folk spread over 45 miles is only one every 3 minutes. So now it was lonely; every quarter-hour someone who'd got the initial speed correct would arrive from behind and jog gently past.

Along the grassy paths of Clatworthy Reservoir, in the glow of the new day, passed those real runners. Most of them will have been walking. None will have been particularly cheerful. They, too, started too fast, and their legs have been painful for 50 miles. Around the middle of this second day will come the walkers. One or two, who started slow and kept on eating and drinking, may not be completely miserable. Blistered of course, tired, but with any luck no serious injuries in the tendons and ligaments. Just as well; for, after the long flat bit, the hills will rise again as the sun goes down. None will be enjoying the sunset, none appreciating the pretty villages of Monksilver and Wheddon Cross, for the second night is now upon them. After midnight will come the limp and the lame. And as the third day dawns above Dunkery Beacon there pass the saddest few: they have jogged and walked 90 miles but they aren't going to make it back to Minehead in time.

Checkpoint 12: Monksilver, 80.5 miles, 11:33am Sunday

Eighty miles ought to feel like almost over, but even the runners will take 6 hours still to the finish. When you're a mere walker 20 miles is a long day's walk, especially on sore legs. A checkpoint lady is in a feather hat as a deranged Victorian. She had only donned the outfit at daylight, worried the more far-gone walkers might think themselves hallucinating when actually we weren't.

Now we're back in the hills, which have steepened and got higher during Saturday night, even though one of them, Periton Hill, is exactly the same hill that we did at Mile 5. It's become seriously hot, and the next stretch – up the valley side, down the valley side, up the other side, down the other side – has me averaging 2mph and wondering if I'll be in by midnight. Sit down on a tree stump in the shade, drink all my water, and apply sun cream very slowly and thoroughly to cover up my limbs but also to cover up the fact that what I am actually doing is having … a … little … rest.

Checkpoint 14: Wheddon Cross, 92 miles, 4.37pm Sunday

Something leapt out of the nettles in a cloud of feathers, leaving something else dead and half-plucked. A sparrowhawk? The victim had been a pigeon. I wasn't

Nice and flat round Clatworthy Reservoir

paying attention, I was suffering dire thoughts of trickling into the second night and I'd given away my spare torch batteries during the previous one.

But the drinks of water had been effective, the temperature had fallen, and in fact that previous bit had been under-measured on the route description. My speed picked up to a steady plod. Up in the hills again, the surroundings were well worth plodding through. Rivers, beech trees, moorland, with the sun for the second time getting rather horizontal.

> *But Ah! that deep romantic chasm that slanted*
> *Down a green hill athwart a cedern cover…*

Ah, indeed: not to mention eek! and ouch! Exmoor is over-equipped with romantic chasms, and the two stretches of sunken track found at Mile 95 certainly had me 'wailing for my demon lover' not to mention fresh socks, fresh feet indeed, and a slice of fruit cake. Twelve hours behind me, the final walkers would be doing this in the small hours of the third morning. When I spoke to them afterwards they didn't seem to have minded it especially; they'd stopped having emotions many hours before.

Checkpoint 15: Wootton Courtenay, 97.5 miles, 6.47pm

Noticing that the walkers coming through have lapsed into an infantile state, the final checkpoint is decorated with balloons, and serves jelly and custard as well as the hallucinatory fruit cake. Sustaining fare for the final 500ft up the hill we'd started off on. Sustaining enough that, somewhat to my own surprise, I managed the 20-metre side-trip into the trees to bag that trig point. Ahead, evening light was lying across the Bristol Channel. I was joined by Luis Broz, the one who'd left breakfast 2 hours behind me but with the advantage of having got the first day's pace correct. Together we guessed our way down the last stony path, under the last trees, with the white spires of the Minehead Butlins catching the last of the sun. And breaking into a trot through the back streets of Minehead aiming for a finish in under 34 hours.

Finish: Minehead 100 miles, 8.02pm

But there are more back streets than expected and we actually finished at 8.02pm. Badge; certificate – they put my time as 20hrs 02. Which was actually my arrival time, and 14 hours less than I'd actually taken. I should have not told them and framed the thing. Next, supper.

Night is for a sleep and a forgetting on the floor of the maths department. Exmoor had been an easy one, I thought the next morning; the climbs steep but not long, the paths mostly not stony; but above all the weather benign. Sunshine is pleasant to look at, certainly; but much more important is having dry socks and feet not just for 20 miles, not just for 50 miles, but for the whole way round... Yes, having slept, having forgotten, Exmoor had been almost enjoyable, as I watched the last walkers, weighed down by two days and nights of the place, staggering in under the early-morning streetlights.

Strange it felt to be heading home on blister-free feet. 'So you got to Minehead OK,' asked train manager Colin, now heading up the line again again on Virgin Cross-country. And when I explained (censored, leaving out the distance) what I'd been up to: 'Somehow, I didn't think you'd been headed for Butlins.'

SURVIVAL SKILLS: SORE LEGS AND FEELING SICK

Runners on the Marathon go for the first 20 miles on ready-use fuel: glycogen (a sort of sugar) in the bloodstream and liver. When this is used up they 'hit the wall', and thereafter run with less efficiency and more pain using body

Foot care from St John's Ambulance at the end of the Exmoor Hundred

fat as fuel. Cyclists call it 'hunger bonk', because for them 'hitting the wall' is something even more painful caused by slippery roads and braking at the wrong moment.

For Marathon runners it is not worth trying to refuel on the run (ie to eat) as it takes too long for food to turn into glycogen.

For long-distance runners (50 miles up, not mere Marathons), eating is essential. Running on fat is painful, but also those skinny types run out of fat and start burning their own muscles – muscles built over long nasty nights doing hill repetitions under streetlights in the rain.

Digesting food, in order to generate glycogen, itself requires energy. If glycogen reserves drop too low, the body simply closes down the digestion. Food put in is sent back out again – 'can't use this' – and ends up in the hedge bottom. So the aim of the runner must be to run just slowly enough, and eat just enough, that glycogen remains above this level. Until the last 2 hours or so, when he (or she, of course) can forget about eating and use up all the glycogen running.

Sometimes the legs complain before the stomach does. Tiredness-pains in the legs are due to lactic acid build-up: the bloodstream is the exhaust pipe for the muscle engine, and it isn't taking away the waste products fast enough. The solution here is not to stop – the muscles then sieze up – but to slow down. After 5km, the lactic acid is flushed away, and you feel great, and you go back to going too fast.

Before admitting to anything so ordinary as tiredness, a couple of other factors should be considered:

- Hypothermia – the body uses energy to warm itself up. Putting on an extra thermal top could release energy to the stomach and legs.
- Dehydration – digestion requires water to work.
- Potassium deficiency, or other minerals, or salt, may come into it also.

WHEN YOUR STOMACH IS SAYING 'STOP'

1 Drink water, and put on more clothes if necessary.

2 Try a hit of instant glycogen: one of those green drinks, or a home-made mixture of glucose, or a more sophisticated mix of glucose and salt. Glucose converts directly into glycogen, and may generate enough of the stuff to allow digestion to restart in 20 minutes or so.

3 Slow down (else that glucose hit will get used up by the legs, leaving none spare for stomach operation).

4 Eat some proper food (starchy carbohydrate). Glucose is in-and-out like a flash, not satisfactory for long-term operation of the running machine. Complan, or complex-carbohydrate powder, may stay in better than LDWA fruit cake.

5 If proper food won't stay down, the only remedy is to slow drastically to let the body re-start digestion, and not speed up again until some food has been successfully ingested. A total rest of half an hour may even be required.

FIVE HUNDREDS

The Hundred is a particularly difficult event to go slowly enough on. I've not succeeded in five tries:

Cleveland After the first 35 miles run too fast, I found myself all alone, behind the real runners, and in front of everyone else. So there was no urge to overtake, and the night slowdown came soon after. But from 70 miles on, I was driven forward by a large party right behind me threatening to overtake. The later checkpoints offered Complan (powdered food for the very ill), and the Complan kept staying down for long enough. 25.5hrs – my least unsuccessful Hundred as a runner – but I couldn't walk for two days afterwards.

Yorkshire Again, the first 30 miles much too fast – at 12 miles out I was alongside the eventual 17hr winner. Stiff legs at 35 miles made the overdoing-it-ness obvious. I slowed down and managed to keep eating until an elderly bloke just in front misled me into more briskness between 45–50 miles. Eating attempts then led to nausea. At 60 miles (Dent) drastic measures: 45-minute stop, sleep. From then on I could eat, with difficulty, and only threw up once. 25.5hrs

White Peak I used the separate start for runners, so started not the usual 'too fast' but much, much too fast. A fast companion for the first half of the night meant I continued much too fast. At 60 miles, complete collapse. I stopped for 1.5hrs, slept, almost got disqualified under '2 hours in the checkpoint' rule. Walked the rest. 28hrs

Lake District This time I cleverly signed in for the slow walkers' start, with checkpoint openings timed for 3.75mph. I got excited and ran the downhill bits, arriving too early at some checkpoints. Even so, I got to the 70-mile mark still enjoying it. However, it had been raining, and 600m of stony descent from Coledale Hause finished off my feet. So the second day was suffering. 32hrs

Exmoor Too fast for first 50 miles, but realised in time and slowed down. Dry feet all the way helped. Enjoyable (almost). 34hrs

Crossing Ingleborough on the Yorkshire Dales Hundred of 1996

PART V: RIVER DEEP MOUNTAIN HIGH

Chapter 16

The Welsh 3000s:
15 Peaks in One Day

Concept	The fifteen 3000ft (914m) peaks of Wales, with added scrambling
Distance	45km (28 miles)
Ascent	3600m (12,000ft)
Start	Bwlch y Ddeufaen (SH 720 715)
Finish	Pen-y-Pass (SH 648 556)
Maximum altitude	1085m Snowdon
Terrain	Grassy hills, rocky hills, boulderfields and scrambling
Target time	One day
Standard strong walker	15hrs

The Welsh 3000s, with its stunningly simple concept – everything over 3000ft high in Wales – is the finest tough walk south of Scotland. Its three ranges, the Carneddau, the Glyders and Snowdon, are tough in such interestingly different ways. The first recorded crossing was by Eustace Thomas in 1919, the same man as the Derwent Watershed (Chapter 10). However, Victorian hillwalkers probably trod it before him.

The one defect of the 15 hills is that they don't form a convenient circuit, so that return transport needs to be arranged.

The fine, tough walk can be made even finer, and tougher, by scrambling Tryfan's north ridge and the Bristly Ridge; and taken even further by finishing around the rest of the Snowdon Horseshoe.

The route
Foel-fras can be approached from car parks at Bwlch y Ddeufaen (SH 720 715) via Drum; at Llyn Eigiau (SH 732 663) by slopes northeast of Dulyn Reservoir;

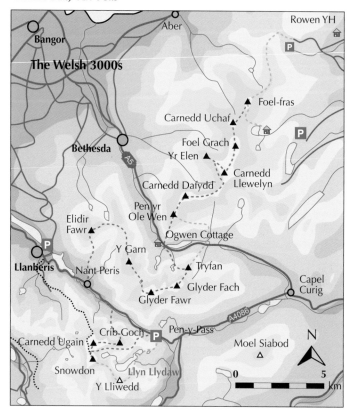

or, for bus travellers in particular, from Bethesda via slopes of Drosgl. Visit **Carnedd Uchaf**, **Foel Grach**, and then **Carnedd Llewelyn** before **Yr Elen**. Contour the southwest slope of Llewelyn, past a valuable *spring*, to **Carnedd Dafydd** and **Pen yr Ole Wen**.

The usual descent from Ole Wen is by its really unpleasant southwest spur to Ogwen Cottage; nicer, and no slower, is the east ridge and Afon Lloer to Glan Dena (SH 668 605). Cross to **Tryfan**'s North Ridge; you could now contour left to find Heather Terrace which leads to the col behind Tryfan's Far South Peak (830m); or scramble straight up the ridge, Grade 1. The final tower is Grade 2 taken direct, with a bouldery gully round right at Grade 1.

WELSH 3000S – SCHEDULE

	Distance mls/km	Ascent ft/m	Time min	ETA
Start: Bwlch y Ddeufaen				0:00
Foel-fras	3.4/5.5	1700/520	120	2:00
Carnedd Uchaf	0.9/1.5	100/30	20	2:20
Foel Grach	0.8/1.2	350/100	25	2:45
Carnedd Llewelyn	1.1/1.7	350/100	35	3:20
Yr Elen	0.8/1.2	200/60	20	3:40
Carnedd Dafydd	2.5/4	600/180	70	4:50
Pen yr Ole Wen	0.9/1.5	250/70	25	5:15
A5 Glan Dana	1.6/2.6		45	6:00
Tryfan	0.8/1.2	2100/620	110	7:50
Glyder Fach	0.9/1.5	900/270	60	8:50
Glyder Fawr	0.9/1.5	350/100	30	9:20
Y Garn	1.4/2.3	800/240	60	10:20
Elidir Fawr	2.3/3.7	700/210	75	11:35
Nant Peris	2.1/3.3		45	12:20
Blaen Nant	1.4/2.3	150/50	40	13:00
Crib Goch	1.4/2.2	2600/770	135	15:15
Carnedd Ugain	0.9/1.5	650/200	55	16:10
Snowdon	0.7/1.1	300/90	25	16:35
Pen-y-Pass	3.0/4.8		75	17:50
TOTALS	**28/44.5**	**12,000/3600**		

Finish over Y Lliwedd

	Distance mls/km	Ascent ft/m	Time min	ETA
Snowdon				16:35
Y Lliwedd	1.1/1.7	500/150	50	17:25
Pen-y-Pass	2.6/4.2		60	18:25

Note Schedule assumes fairly confident scrambling, and some leg strength persisting for the steep slopes down and up at the end. Nervous scramblers, strong descenders and happy boulder-walkers will all find the times inaccurate.

Take screes to left of Bristly Ridge, or Bristly Ridge itself (Grade 1). From **Glyder Fach**, save time by scrambling across Castell y Gwynt, rather than losing height to its left. Paths cross **Glyder Fawr** and **Y Garn**. After **Elidir Fawr** a good path leads down to a footbridge at SH 608 596, and Nant Peris.

From Blaen Nant (SH 622 569) the hollow beside Dinas Mot then a waterfall at SH 622 561 gives access to the north ridge of **Crib Goch**. The route over the Pinnacles and **Carnedd Uchaf** (Crib y Ddysgl) is described in Chapter 2, as are the descents from **Snowdon** to Pen-y-Pass or (easier in the dark but longer) Llanberis.

To finish in style over Y Lliwedd, descend from Snowdon by the southeast ridge, with some steep outcroppy ground below giving clean scrambling (Grade 1). Ascend Y Lliwedd scrambling to left of the path next to the crag tops. From the summit a path drops to the outflow of Llyn Llydaw, and Pen-y-Pass.

FOEL-FRAS TO SNOWDON WITH EXTRA FUN

'I'm phoning' (I admitted with embarrassment, for I really don't approve of that sort of thing) 'from the summit of Snowdon. Is that the North Wales police?' And I told them about the flashing lights and the cries for help from the hillside opposite. The slope of Crib y Ddysgl above the Pig Track is a nasty place to be, with scree dropping over the edge of small outcrops into darkness. Even so, if I were the Mountain Rescue I'd be leaving the light-flashers till dawn – only 3 hours away – and let them walk down on their own. But I'm not the Mountain Rescue; so when folk shout 'Nine nine nine!' I dial.

Though I did try to make it sound boring. 'No, no, not screams for help: what we hear are just shouts. And by the way, us on the summit of Snowdon, please don't come and rescue us. We're very happy up here.'

Normally, having called the Rescue, you lie back in the bivvy bag and say what silly people they must be on Crib y Ddysgl, and how one would never get into such a situation. This little conversation we did not have. Two hours earlier in the night, we had been on that very same nasty hillside...

It had all started, at 8am, on Foel-fras. The fifteen 3000ft summits of Wales make up Wales's best walk. To make it even better, just add scrambling: the long rocky north ridge of Tryfan, and the Bristly Ridge of Glyder Fach. And three strong blokes like us can carry the bivvy gear over a mere 22 miles, can't we?

Well, I'm not so strong as the others, so slow uphill. Glyn isn't used to scrambling, so he's slow on that. And Colin does like to stop for a brew. Over our morning teacups, we eyed up Tryfan across the deep hole of Nant Ffrancon.

Glyn and I had done that North Ridge before, and in bad weather. We went up the North Ridge, in running shoes, so as to save 10 minutes in a five-day

Scramblers on Bristly Ridge

race across Wales. You do funny things when you're running, and come back afterwards and wonder why. But at least Glyn knew he could do it, because he already did. Bristly was another matter. The Bristly Bit began with a pinnacle we climbed right over, which was OK, but on the other side was another pinnacle with two descenders taking awkward steps above a mighty drop. 'Don't worry,' I said as reassuringly as I could, 'those guys are way off route.'

'We are not-so off route,' they replied across the airy chasm. They were; but the moral damage was already done. Below me in the gap, 'I can't do this next bit,' said Glyn decisively.

I thought about the 1000ft of Bristly Ridge we'd already come up, and the awkward step in the start-off gully that was going to be even more awkward if we had to do it again downwards. I remained silent. And the encouraging words 'Well, maybe...' came drifting from below. You go round, not over, that second pinnacle, into a cosy groove on the left.

The ridge remains Bristly but not beastly, with drops on one side but lots to hang on to along the top. It rises, flattens off, and drops a couple of feet to let you step onto the stony plateau of the Glyders. After that, it's up and over the summit boulderpile. But why, Glyn wondered, were we also going up and over the Castell y Gwynt?

I explained about the awkwardness of measuring the drop around the Castle of the Winds, the way it may perhaps have 50ft of drop around it, and how it could then arguably be the 16th Welsh 3000. And even if it isn't, it saves a couple of minutes. And even if it doesn't do that, it's fun.

After Glyder Fawr there's a nasty scree descent to a nice lake, just the spot for another brew-up. As it was 4.30pm, we had time for a leisurely tea break – 4.30pm being about an hour too late to get across Crib Goch in daylight, so we'd be bivvying in the high green hollow of Cwm Glas Mawr.

Accordingly, with the low sun already reddening the screes of Crib Goch, we wandered peaceful and relaxed along the green easy bit at the western end of the Glyders. At 6pm on Elidir Fawr, I explained about how there wasn't enough day to go all the way.

'Come off it,' said Colin. 'We can't possibly take two days over the Welsh 3000s.' Glyn agreed. An hour down to Nant Peris; 2 hours up the side of Snowdon; and that would still leave us an hour of daylight for the crossing of the rocks.

Well, there is a slanty grassy path down the steep side of Elidir Fawr, and with a bit of jogging we did manage to hit the A4086 at 2 minutes past 7. A mile and a half up the road – that was 7.30pm – we tried not to breathe in as we passed through the tempting barbecue smoke of Blaen Nant's campsite. We then went up 550 vertical metres in an hour and a quarter, and even Colin admitted that he did feel slightly tired while we were doing that bit.

At the top was the prospective bivvy site. But it was already occupied. Perched on the small ledge, 2000ft above Llanberis Pass and 1000ft below Crib Goch, was a little row of green tents. 'And those young folk are going to be noisy in the night,' Glyn pointed out. 'Probably they've brought up a guitar.'

Besides, it was only 8.45pm, with the sun still painting the place pink all around us. So we went on over Crib Goch, slowly hand and foot along the crest, wondering what it would be like to be benighted at this particular place, and fairly happy about the fact that we weren't going to be. At 9.30pm we passed onto grassy Bwlch Goch, with pleasant bivvy sites for us to lie inside our bags without sliding off, and watch the sun rise over Llyn Llydaw. But no, there was still a half hour of dim-light time before the night time.

The rocks rose again before us. However, there was no need to get benighted on that rocky rim, as a bypass path strode confidently around the obstruction.

The bypass path of Crib y Ddysgl is well trodden and used by many. When it eventually dwindles to nothing in the middle of a face of scree and outcrops, roughly half-way between the Pig Track and the horizon – well, you have the

North Ridge of Crib Goch, fading light

consolation of knowing that it's dwindled to nothing for lots of other folk before you. We came to a sloping scree platform where it would be just possible to lie down without sliding. But even now it still wasn't properly dark, and anyway there'd be a better place further on.

There wasn't a better place further on. However, the next 2 metres could be seen and didn't seem dangerous, and neither did the 2 metres after that – and by slanting upwards we eventually emerged onto a ridge. A trig pillar loomed, and behind it was the silver-grey sea, and the orange lights of the Welsh seaside from Llandudno to Anglesey.

At the Pigtop Pillar stood a solitary night walker, phoning his wife to find out if she loved him enough to drive to Pen-y-Pass in the dark. At the top of Snowdon, an hour before midnight, there were no young people or guitars. Even so the place was scarcely peaceful, as the generator of the café rackets away throughout the hours of darkness. We managed to get away from that by circling to the back of the cairn and dropping a little towards Bwlch y Saethau. But then came the shouting across the corrie. And after that came the helicopter.

Y Lliwedd from Bwlch y Saethau

We sat in our bags, dangled our legs over the northeast face, and watched the flashing beacons. As a sort of *son et lumière* the sound effect was raucous but the illuminations were impressive. The searchlight picked out bits of Carnedd Ugain, and then the winchman dangled in the shaft of light, picked up a person, dangled again and picked up another. The helicopter whirred and flashed away in the direction of Bangor. Perhaps the two stuck walkers were now being instructed in the mountain distress signal (six flashes or shouts spread over a minute, then a minute of silence). Perhaps they were just saying 'Thanks guys, Pen-y-Pass'll do us nicely', and being told that as they'd been rescued they had to get checked at Bangor Hospital, 30 miles from the car park and 4 hours after the last bus. Or perhaps they'd really needed rescuing: the website would tell us eventually.

A year later, it did. They were two young people from London, benighted rather than hurt, but the man from the Mountain Rescue passed no judgement

192

against them: 'They were not sufficiently experienced to know that they just needed to sit it out.'

After the helicopter, things quietened down. Half a million a year visit Snowdon, but most of them in the daytime. About 2am a party reached the cairn above us: from their conversation they had just achieved the National Three Peaks over 21.5hrs. Another party arrived at dawn, chattered merrily above our bedroom, then went away again – they had climbs to do on Cloggy. We sat up in our bags and watched the sun rise above Crib Goch, while Colin tried to make tea without any water. About 2000ft below mist was creeping out of the south, slopping over the Bwlch y Saethau, and pouring down onto Llyn Llydaw. Y Lliwedd stuck up out of the cloud-sea like a shark's fin in the early morning porridge.

When you've done the 3000s, the Snowdon Horseshoe seems like quite a short walk. And we were two thirds of the way around it already. After 5 night hours relaxing on the gravel, Y Lliwedd at dawn was irresistible.

At the foot of Snowdon's ridge we dipped into that slopping mist. This meant that, as we rose up the ridge of Y Lliwedd, its great north face emerged on our left through wisps of vapour, like a Welsh myth. Meanwhile on our right the Brocken Spectre strode through the air with his halo around his head.

The top of Lliwedd was warming nicely under the new sun. But no water meant still no breakfast. Below us the mist was drifting away and the first figures were appearing on the Miners' Track. It was time to stop walking over high hills, and to taste pleasures of a lower sort.

The Gorphwysfa Cafe at Pen-y-Pass serves breakfast from 8.30am or even earlier. Sore feet descend slowly on scree-covered rocks, so the coffee was well heated-up by the time we got there. The car park of the new day was already almost full. Glyn headed south for some serious trekking through the Rhinogs. Colin headed north to retrieve his car, stranded at a car park near Conwy. For me, if a hill's worth doing it's worth doing twice; so I went back up Snowdon by its Gribin Ridge.

There were more people on top this time.

Chapter 17

The Lakes at Length:
Lakes 3000s and Old County Tops

STUFFING THE DAFFODILS

What's winter for? Supposing you were an ice-axe owner, with several layers of fleece and a really woolly hat; then winter would be for going up Red Pike to Pillar, and breathing the air that comes bright and sharp out of the north; for watching snowy Great Gable going pink in the sunset; and then for trying to spot in the moonlight the bulges of black ice below Black Sail, and not noticing one of them, and falling over painfully on your bottom. But maybe a crampon is a bit of intimidating kit too far – your hat may be woolly but it's not frostproof – and a sofa is really more comfortable than a sudden impact on the stonework of the Wasdale path. In that case, winter is for the fireside, and a copy of this book, and admiring the few photos I've put in here of those foolhardy folk in their spiky shoes. The photos are mildly enticing, and maybe that ice-axe after all – but for comfort, let's make the ice-axe for *next* Christmas...

Couch potato or chilly cramponner, spring is for a quite different sort of loveliness. Spring is for Wordsworth's daffodils along the shore of Ullswater. Spring is for going gently between the green leaves, and lingering in the scent of the hawthorn blossoms as it drifts across Wastwater; for the plover on the moor, and the woodpeckers clattering from end to end of Borrowdale. Spring is for hanging about all day on a single hill, watching the parsley fern uncurl among the stones of Carrock, looking (if you know what it looks like) for the mountain ringlet butterfly among the grass stalks of Brandreth.

But spring gives way to summer. And midsummer's for saying 'Stuff those daffodils.' The sun's up at 4, and stays up till 9. Early is great, before the people, with the air cool and the valleys full of shadow. And late is just as great, with the people gone away again, and the day's heat breathing back out of the rocks. So how about joining up the two: stay up there right through one of the long days of summer, seeing just how far the fells can take you.

It's not a competition, or if it is, it's a competition with the mountain rather than against your fellow humans. If you're a fit walker, it might be the line of the Roman road, from Penrith to Windermere all the way along the top of High Street. That one covers 23 miles (36km) of country, but with only 3600ft (1100m) of ascent. You could attempt the complete circuit of one of the eight valleys. Eskdale is the shortest (19km and 1700m) but not otherwise noticeably

Lakeland: what winter's for, demonstrated on Pillar (evening view to Great Gable)

easy, with Scafell, Scafell Pike, Bowfell and the Crinkle Crags giving rugged up and down all the way. By contrast, the circuit of Buttermere (30km and 2900m) is jolly long, but it has almost-level sections across the Derwent Fells and the High Stile ridge. The ridge to Great Borne looks equally level on the map; but by the time you get there, you'll be counting every contour. You may not even notice the way the sun goes down behind the Isle of Man in shafts of mauve and yellow; because you, in complete contrast, will be going down behind Gavel Fell in black darkness...

If you're a strong fellrunner, or a very strong walker, your midsummer challenge might be a whole section out of Wainwright's *Pictorial Guide*: the northwestern ones, as a circuit from Crummock, are a matter of 50 miles and 18,000ft (80km/5500m). And if you're Joss Naylor out of Wasdale, summer fun means every Wainwright-listed hill there is, one after another, in 7 days 1hr 15min.

If a thing's worth doing, then it's worth doing a whole lot more. People have been overdoing it in the Lakes for a century, with a circuit of Skiddaw, Scafell Pike, Helvellyn and Blencathra recorded in 1870. Thomas Watson and his guide Thomas Wilson, a Borrowdale shepherd, walked through dense cloud, then snow showers on Scafell Pike, and on Blencathra crawled through a gale across the summit plateau.

Today this challenge has been made slightly easier by replacing Blencathra with the more convenient Scafell, for a circuit of the four 3000-footers. With modern footwear and clothing, and modern leisure time to let us strengthen our legs every weekend of the year, the 43 miles and 10,000ft (72km/3100m) are within reach of ambitious fellwalkers. Until recently, 200 tried it every year in an event organised by the Ramblers Association. That event has been dropped due to a loose boulder lurking threateningly on Scafell. This is a shame, as the obstacle can be avoided and the walk itself is superb, showing new aspects of Lakeland as well as of your own physique.

From Keswick's Moot Hall, the day starts before dawn with an ascent of Skiddaw. This makes good sense; Skiddaw's wide paths in the dark uphill are a lot easier than Helvellyn's ones would be, in descent, at the long day's ending. Also, darkness helps you avoid that universal error: starting too fast. The night climb may be practical – more importantly, it's romantic. Between black trees you see the orange sea of streetlights, and the silver sea of Derwent Water under the moon. As you get higher, the air chills, and the view widens to row on row of fells humped beneath the stars. And at the summit, sunrise.

The next bit of the walk is Borrowdale. All of Borrowdale. No grumbling: this is Lakeland's loveliest valley, and the day's first rays are glowing among the oak leaves. The day's next pleasure is meeting the first walkers getting out of their cars at Seathwaite, and you've got 5 hours and one big hill behind you already.

But there's a bigger hill ahead. Up the Corridor Path, and over the Lingmell col, and down to Hollow Stones. Here you can avoid the boulder in Lord's Rake by ascending a little grassy rake just to right of the Shamrock. You miss the excitement of Scafell Crag on the way up; but if you find the small path contouring leftwards from below Foxes Tarn, you compensate with excitement below Scafell East Buttress on the way down.

The crowded cairn on Scafell Pike marks the noontime of the long day. Two hours after England's high point comes the walk's low point. The unavoidable climb onto High Raise is 1000ft (300m) of relentless grass.

By comparison, the 2000ft (600m) up Helvellyn can be less bad. The paths are wide and smooth; the brain, battered into quietude, is able to enjoy the coppery lights of late afternoon reflected in Thirlmere. For the descent the legs

How far do you want to go? Fell-runner on High Snab Bank, practising the 60 miles (and 27,000ft of up) of the Bob Graham Round. Of those who attempt it, about half achieve the 42 summits within the 24-hour time limit.

cheer up a little as the focus of complaint shifts to the toes. Ahead, Skiddaw seems as far away in distance as it is in the remembered optimism of dawn.

By evening, the A691 falls quiet. You could take pleasant paths by St John's and Castlerigg Farm, but nobody ever does. Shadow crawls up the side of Skiddaw: as it reaches the summit, the bars of Keswick stop serving bar meals.

But there's still beer, and the chip shop at the back of the Moot Hall.

A walk can be a lot shorter than the 3000s and still be very long. Earlier in the book I considered the Three Peaks of various counties. Now, in the mountain section, it's time to consider the Three Peaks of Cumbria – Cumbria that was formerly Cumberland, Westmorland, and Lancashire-beyond-the-Sands. The walk of the old county tops – Helvellyn, Scafell Pike and Coniston Old Man – is 7 miles shorter than the Lakes 3000s, but in every other way it's even better. It leaves out that boulder-blocked gully on Scafell, as well as the A591 and the Borrowdale Road. Instead it offers the banks of Duddon, and the ridge to Swirl How. It has wonderful cross-country by Slater's Bridge and among the old mines and oak trees of Little Langdale. And it has Upper Eskdale, the great empty place among England's highest peaks.

There are days for doing it gently, and taking time off for dancing with the daffodils. And there are days for leaving Wordsworth to wander with his lonely cloud and be off to see how far you can get. Except that Wordsworth is right there beside you on that path. Up into the hills at dawn was the poet of Grasmere, and a 30-mile man on the days when he wasn't pottering gently round Rydal Water watching the moss grow. And so was his sister Dorothy, with her skirts tucked up, striding along the high road at 4mph. Coleridge too, in the days before illness and opium; Coleridge thought summer was for walking far and walking fast. In August of 1800 he walked right along the Dodds to Helvellyn by moonlight, and down to Dove Cottage. He woke up the other poet, and they spent the rest of the night in the garden discussing their forthcoming book.

The Dodds in the dark? Now there's a long walk for one of these short summer nights...

THE SIX TRICKS FOR GOING HALF AS FAR AGAIN

1 Treat your feet
Give your feet a treat: a brand new pair of socks. Wax your boots and perhaps also Vaseline your feet. If they're dry for the first 6 hours, then the initial blister is postponed from noon to 6pm.

2 Eat lots
Eat something every hour. Put cereal bars in pockets, or in a bumbag worn back to front, and eat on the move. If you lose your appetite, slow down, drink more, and try a sugary drink to restart the stomach.

3 Drink lots
Don't wait till you feel thirsty, as mild dehydration just feels like tiredness.

4 Start early
How early is early? Set off 2 hours earlier than that. Starting in the dark means starting slowly (see below), and a summit sunrise.

5 Start slow
Enthusiasm and excitement means starting too fast and getting tired at half time. A schedule, counting 100m up as an extra 1km and then reckoning 5kph, can help here. And when you're going faster than the schedule says, this isn't superb fitness and vigour, it's a mistake. Slow down.

6 Don't be afraid of the dark

If you've paid attention to feet and food, walking into the dark needn't be a problem. Plan the ending of the walk on smooth paths without steep descents. A diode torch will last all night. A useful moon, shining through the first part of the night, is one week before full moon through to two days after.

Lakes 3000s brief route and schedule

The hills	Skiddaw (931m), Scafell (964m), Scafell Pike (978m), Helvellyn (950m)
Distance	72km (43 miles)
Ascent	3100m (9200ft)
Start/finish	Keswick (NY 266 234)
Terrain	Paths and roads, but awkward over Scafell and rough over Scafell Pike
Target time	Finish by midnight
Standard strong walker	21.5hrs

This is a richly varied walk. Skiddaw at sunrise, and the beauties of Borrowdale, and then it's into the real mountain country: the Scafells, and Helvellyn, and between them the bonus peak of High Raise, which can't conveniently be avoided. At the end, the A591 loses its traffic quite early in the evening, but even so the walk would be nicer without its final 5 miles.

Note The organised annual challenge walk has been abandoned, partly because of the obstructing boulder in Lord's Rake. However, the boulder is avoided by the alternative route below.

The route

From the Moot Hall, cross Fitz Park to the foot of the track for Skiddaw. Go up and down **Skiddaw**. Return to Keswick.

An alternative route now is to use the Cumbria Way to west of Derwent Water, but this takes half an hour longer than the Borrowdale road. That road is

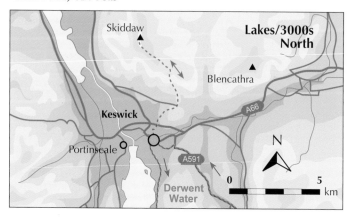

not unpleasant before the day's traffic, and has footpaths alongside. At Grange Bridge (NY 254 174) is a second chance to switch to the Cumbria Way west of the Derwent.

From **Seathwaite**, the bridleway by Stockley Bridge is easier, if less pretty, than the footpath west of Taylorgill Force. At **Sty Head**, take the Corridor Path (described in Chapter 1); but where the path turns up left for Scafell Pike, keep ahead across the top of Piers Gill. Around 50 metres later, as the path bends left,

keep ahead through a tiny col and follow a broken wall up to Lingmell Col. Descend below Pikes Crag to **Hollow Stones**.

The traditional ascent route by Lord's Rake is currently carrying a large boulder, resting on rubble just above the point where the West Wall Traverse turns off. To use either Lords Rake or the West Wall Traverse means passing over, and disturbing, the rubble that supports

Lakes 3000s: the boulder currently blocking Lord's Rake rests on loose rubble

200

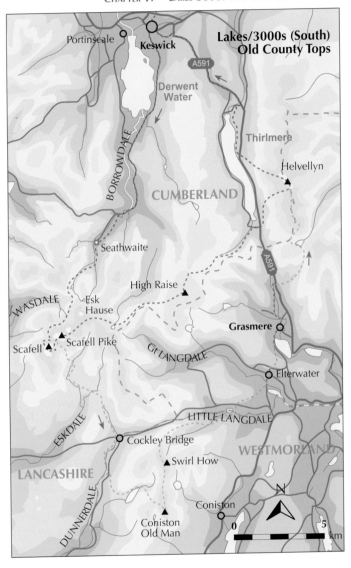

Lakes/3000s (South)
Old County Tops

Lakes 3000s: telephoto views from Esk Hause, looking back down Borrowdale to Skiddaw

the monster rock. The alternative is to take a grassy gap 300 metres further west. Directly below the lowest point of the Shamrock Buttress, from NY 205 071, slant up right, into the gap between the Shamrock and Black Crag. A steep sheep path leads onto the west ridge of **Scafell**.

The descent from Scafell by Broad Stand is a short but exposed rock climb (grade Moderate, or scramble Grade 3). Easier and safer is the route by Foxes Tarn (NY 209 064). This is reached, from the col 200 metres northeast of the summit, by a steep, eroded path southeast. Follow Foxes Tarn's outflow stream down for 100 metres. The easier path continues down a bouldery gully just to the left, but at this point you can also contour out left, on a small cairned path below crags and above very steep ground. This saves 100m of extra descent.

Go up to Mickledore, and cross boulders to **Scafell Pike**. A path, bouldery at first, leads to Esk Hause and Angle Tarn. Fork off left on a smaller bog path to Stake Pass, for the tiring grassy slope to **High Raise**. Drop to Greenup Edge, and head down Wythburn Valley. A small path above the A591 leads to Wythburn Church for the well-used path up **Helvellyn**.

LAKES 3000S – SCHEDULE

	Distance mls/km	Ascent ft/m	Time min	ETA
Start: Keswick				0:00
Skiddaw	4.8/7.6	2800/850	160	2:40
Keswick Moot Hall	4.8/7.6		95	4:15
Grange Bridge	4.5/7.2		90	5:45
Seathwaite	4.1/6.6		85	7:10
Sty Head	2.3/3.7	1150/350	80	8:30
Scafell	3.0/4.8	1900/570	125	10:35
Scafell Pike	1.0/1.6	750/220	60	11:35
Angle Tarn	2.2/3.5	100/30	65	12:40
High Raise	2.8/4.4	850/260	90	14:10
Steel End	3.5/5.6		75	15:25
Helvellyn	2.9/4.6	2250/760	145	17:50
Highpark Wood	2.1/3.3		60	18:50
Bridge End Farm	1.9/3.1		45	19:35
Keswick Moot Hall	5.4/8.6	150/50	125	21:40
TOTALS	**45/72**	**10,300/3100**		

Get down to Highpark car park before nightfall, and you can use the pleasant Thirlmere path to the lake foot. From Bridge End Farm, the path by Low Bridge End, and later by Castlerigg and Spring Woods, eliminates the unpleasantness of the A591, but is 0.5 mile longer; and I don't suppose anyone has ever, at the end of this monster walk, put the scenery in front of their feet – on three occasions I have failed to do so myself. At the edge of **Keswick**, turn left on Manor Brow to the Moot Hall.

Old County Tops brief route and schedule

Concept	The summits of former Cumberland, West-morland and Lancashire
The hills	Helvellyn (950m), Scafell Pike (978m), Coniston Old Man (803m)
Distance	57km (36 miles)
Ascent	2900m (9500ft)
Start/finish	Grasmere (NY 337 074)
Terrain	Good paths, with some open grassland, and boulders over Scafell Pike
Target time	1 day
Standard strong walker	18hrs

To my mind this one is a better walk than the Lakes 3000s: it may miss Scafell but it takes in upper Esk. Its mix of high ridges, tarns and woodland is just right.

Note Recent maps suggest that the highest point of former Lancashire may in fact be Swirl How. Swirl How would make a less satisfying walk, with a horrid steep slope up Grey Friar and no day-end ridgewalk. So I'll specify that when this part of Lakeland was Lancashire, its summit was the Old Man, however it may have been resurveyed since. Pedants should also note that in those days it was 'Scafell Pikes', with a final 's'.

The Route

Grasmere is a good start as you can use pre-dawn hours to ascend Helvellyn on big paths via Grisedale Hause. For better views cross the summits of Dollywaggon and Nethermost Pikes, to **Helvellyn**.

Descend to the car park at **Wythburn Church**, and take a path just above A591 to a road junction signed 'Armboth'. Head up Wythburn Valley to Greenup Edge, and up to **High Raise** – avoiding this summit is more trouble than crossing it. Slant down southwest to Stake Pass. Paths lead to Angle Tarn and Esk Hause, then skirt south of Great End (useful stream here). Boulders impede the crossing of Ill Crag and Broad Crag to **Scafell Pike**.

The straightforward descent into Eskdale is by Mickledore; more adventurous is to descend steep boulders and small outcrops to the col behind Pen (NY 221 067), then bear right, southwards, down steep stony grass. A path to left of

Old County Tops: in Upper Eskdale, view back to Scafell Pike (top left)

the River Esk leads to Scar Lathing, where you head across country to the head of Mosedale.

From **Cockley Beck** the simple, brutal way (used by the fellrunners on the OCT race) is to sweat it straight up Grey Friar. Pleasanter is to follow footpaths to right of River Duddon to stepping stones at NY 239 001. A path under pines leads to open hill and Seathwaite Tarn for Goats Hause and **Coniston Old Man**.

Take the fine ridgewalk north, crossing or skirting Swirl How and Great Carrs (preferably in daylight) to descend Wet Side Edge (smooth grass mostly, with a diminishing path). At the ridge foot, turn down right across Greenburn Beck to a track. This leads down to **Slater Bridge** (NY 312 030), an attractive structure of slab and arch. From the road near Little Langdale village, a track runs northeast to Elterwater. Above the village, paths lead through a little col (NY 336 055) and down through Nicholas Wood to **Grasmere** lake.

Old County Tops: the walk finishes along the ridge from Coniston Old Man to Swirl How

OLD COUNTY TOPS – SCHEDULE

	Distance mls/km	Ascent ft/m	Time min	ETA
Start: Grasmere				06:00
Grisedale Hause	3.1/5.0	1700/500	95	07:35
Helvellyn	2.4/3.8	1250/400	80	08:55
Steel End	2.9/4.6		70	10:05
High Raise	3.5/5.6	1900/550	130	12:15
Angle Tarn	2.8/4.4	200/60	60	13:15
Scafell Pike	2.2/3.5	1500/450	100	14:55
Cockley Beck Bridge	4.8/7.7	150/50	150	17:25
Coniston Old Man	4.8/7.7	2000/600	155	20:00
Slaters Bridge	5.5/8.8	350/100	130	22:10
Elterwater	1.6/2.5	150/50	40	22:50
Grasmere	2.3/3.7	500/150	70	24:00
TOTALS	**36/57**	**9500/2900**		

Note Darkness makes the stony crossing of Swirl How much slower.

Chapter 18

The Cairngorm 4000s:
Five Granite Giants in a Day

The hills	Cairn Gorm (1245m), Ben Macdui (1309m), Cairn Toul (1291m), Angel's Peak (1258m), Braeriach (1296m)
Distance	34.5km (21.5 miles)
Ascent	2300m (7700ft)
Start/finish	Sugar Bowl car park, Glen More (NH 986 074)
Maximum altitude	1309m (4296ft) Ben Macdui
Terrain	Paths, often bouldery, sometimes vanishing on the plateau
Target time	1 day
Standard strong walker	12hrs

Of Scotland's nine summits over 4000ft, five are conveniently grouped in the granite massif of the Cairngorms – the other four, including Ben Nevis, are 50 miles away to the west. The five Cairngorm ones make a circuit that, among the routes in this section, is not especially long or strenuous. But it is especially serious. More than half the distance is above the 4000ft (1200m) level, exposed to wind, rain and possibly also to snow. Shelter is a long way away. But the high plateau has its own beauty, composed of loose boulders, gentle horizons, and granite crags dropping to a green lochan.

Starting with Cairn Gorm gives an initial climb on good paths that can be done before sunrise, and gets the really tricky navigation out of the way at the start, while the brain is fresh. However, it does mean that the only sensible escape, at the Lairig Ghru (see Chapter 12), is passed before the half-way mark. The dreadful thought of reaching the grim boulders of the Chalamain Gap after nightfall should help keep you up to pace. Otherwise, there are the two bothies: Corrour, sometimes squalid and overcrowded, and Garbh Choire, tiny and hard to find under its pile of stones.

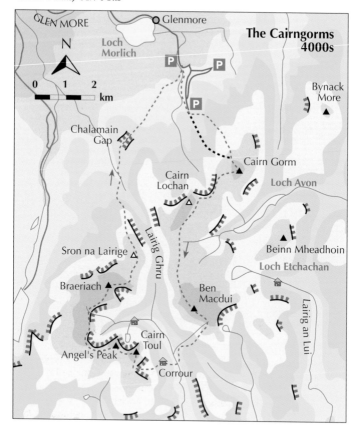

Until the 1997 revision of Munro's Tables, Angel's Peak (Sgor an Lochain Uaine) was not considered as a separate mountain. The remaining four were first combined by members of the Scottish Mountaineering Club in 1909 in a walk that also included two additional hills, Ben Avon and Beinn a' Bhuird. Eustace Thomas (see Chapters 10 and 16) was the first to combine all nine of the Scottish 4000s in a day, in 1924, though he did allow himself a motor car to travel between the two ranges. Fellrunners have now achieved this feat entirely on foot.

Cairn Gorm (left) and the northern corries, from Loch Morlich

The route

Best start is the Sugar Bowl car park, at 450m on the Cairngorm ski road. Cross the road onto a slightly descending path to Allt Mor. Just before a footbridge turn upstream on a good new path to Coire Cas car park.

Immediately above the funicular buildings bear left, under the railway, on a path up the spur to east of the ski area. The path passes the Ptarmigan restaurant to reach **Cairn Gorm** summit. Head southwest on intermittent paths along the rim of the northern corries and past Lochan Buidhe (NH 984 011) to **Ben Macdui**.

Drop southeast, crossing the very top of the Tailor Burn (Allt Clach nan Taillear) and go down the spur to its south – there's an intermittent path among the boulderfields. From the plateau at 800m, rejoin the Tailor Burn to find a small path slanting left into the Lairig Ghru. Turn down-valley on a wide path, and cross a footbridge to **Corrour bothy**.

A built path leads to the col northwest of Devil's Point, and a bouldery one follows the top of eastern crags (or you can divert 200 metres left for grassier ground). The levelling of Stob Coire an t-Saighdeir leads to more boulders up to **Cairn Toul**.

From here to Braeriach, the rim of the Garbh Coire will give tough but beautiful walking. Cross Sgor an Lochain Uaine (nicknamed **Angel's Peak**). Just short of the following col, at NN 948 975, is the only reasonable escape from the plateau: a wide, low cairn at the plateau rim marks the top of a descent northeast on the crest of a gentle spur. But for the final 4000er continue around the corrie rim, to cross the infant River Dee just above its waterfall. Now head uphill northeast, rejoining the corrie rim for the last few steps to **Braeriach** summit.

Follow the corrie rim east, then pick up a good path that skirts to right of Sron na Lairige and descends its northern spur to the floor of Lairig Ghru. After 100 metres following the Allt Druidh downstream, fork up right on a stepped path. This last, cruel ascent leads to the Chalamain Gap, which confronts you with 400 metres (it seems more) of scrambling over huge boulders. No more nasty tricks. A good path, gently downhill, leads to the footbridge below the Sugar Bowl car park.

CAIRNGORMS 4000S – SCHEDULE

	Distance mls/km	Ascent ft/m	Time min	ETA
Start: Sugar Bowl car park				0:00
Cairngorm	2.8/4.5	2600/780	120	2:00
Ben Macdui	3.9/6.2	1000/300	110	3:50
Corrour bothy	2.8/4.5		70	5:00
Cairn Toul	2.3/3.6	2500/760	130	7:10
Braeriach	3.5/5.6	1150/350	125	9:15
Allt Druidh	3.3/5.2	100/30	75	10:30
Sugar Bowl car park	3/1/5.0	400/120	90	12:00
TOTALS	**21.5/34.5**	**7700/2300**		

Note Times can be greatly slowed by high wind on the plateau. While anyone attempting this one should be a happy navigator, there are more route details in my own *Walking the Cairngorms* (Cicerone).

Cairngorms 4000s: not tremendously long, but high and very wild. Plateau edge between Cairn Gorm and Ben Macdui

GETTING THE WIND UP

'Actually, it would quite suit me if we didn't get round these 4000s. My book needs a short chapter on the gentle art of giving up.'

I wasn't serious. We're members of the Long Distance Walkers' Association, we're used to 50 miles and upwards, and we carry a big head torch. We'd recently managed the 36 miles of the Lancashire Three Peaks: this walk would be 14 miles shorter, though with a bit more of up and down. And as we all know, there's no such thing as bad weather, only bad equipment.

So the discussion turned to whether we should divert over the Devil's Point – less than 4000ft, but one the Lancastrian hadn't bagged and an elegant counterpart to Angel's Peak.

Things looked different in the morning, creeping out into the silent youth hostel, wondering what might be going on in the darkness outside the windows. 'Sounds like quite a lot of rain out there,' said my Lancashire companion. But I'd poked my head through the fire door. It wasn't rain out there. It was something more worrying. A brisk autumn breeze was flapping the birch leaves and the pine.

First light saw us weaving between the buildings of the funicular railway's bottom station, and heading up onto the tautologous Aonach Ridge. ('Aonach' is, simply, Gaelic for 'ridge'.) Overhead, cloud-bottoms were stained orange by a lurid sunrise that we couldn't see because of a ridge or Aonach in the way. The ridge crest, when we reached it, was breezy but bearable. Buffetting, that was what we'd been promised by the forecast pinned beside the hostel warden's cage. We were indeed being buffetted. But this was a northern spur, particularly exposed: it'd be less bad on the plateau. We walked in the shelter of a snow-fence, then stopped for breakfast in the doorway of the Ptarmigan restaurant. The ski-tow cables had been taken down for the summer, and anything loose had been blown away or flapped to pieces: so there was not the wind-powered rattle and whine that's the normal soundtrack of the Cairn Gorm ski area.

But there was the wind. The rope handrails that guide us tourists and ski-ers towards the summit were bowed sideways, so that progress was a series of shallow curves, the middle of each arc taking us off the pre-laid pathway. The plateau of Cairn Gorm is the UK's windiest spot. Lowering my foot towards the rounded granite, the wind twisted my rucksack and I had to quickly redirect my step towards a different stone.

Five steps ahead, the Lancastrian thought he heard, through woolly hat and pulled-down hood, a faint cry drift past at 60mph. Awkwardly, he turned through the gale. No Ronald! Oh yes, but there he was, down flat on the ground, legs waving like river weed in the current.

Thankfully we leant against the summit cairn (leaning, in my case, on my unbruised side.) To continue forward still made sense, as a straightforward and scenic escape, by the Goat Track, was half a mile ahead. But as we dropped off the summit dome, the wind got a bit less, and the ground became less stony to be buffetted over. Below the slight shelter of Cairn Lochan we could even stop, and take things out of our rucksacks, and talk. 'Don't mind a bit of rain, and even low cloud,' we agreed. 'But really don't like this wind.' (Four days later, in Glen Etive, it was to be: 'Don't mind a bit of wind and cold – it's this relentless rain I really can't be putting up with.')

Cloud and cold rainwater did descend at this point, but cleared to give a view, between the rolling stony hummocks, to wind-wipped Loch Etchachan and its crags. 'Quite different from Pendle,' said my Lancastrian admiringly. 'Quite different, but every bit as good.' Past little Lochan Buidhe we were back in the open. As we rose towards the top of Macdui so did the wind. We

No regrets? Our escape route took us to Loch Etchachan

scrambled onto Macdui's cairn, clung to the trig point, and wondered how to scramble down again. Across the Lairig Ghru, Cairn Toul and Angel's Peak were going to be another 4 miles of treacherous boulders, all of it up in this wind. We could lie with a broken leg on that wet and windy ridgeline, shivering and listening to the flapping of the survival bag, for 6 or 7 hours or even overnight. Or we could forget about the third, fourth and fifth of the Cairngorm 4000s, and head down westwards instead.

We headed down westwards instead, to the bleak but less buffeted shores of Loch Etchachan.

The gentle art of giving up
The first essential of a challenge is that it should be challenging: if you know in advance that you can do it, then why bother? If you never give up, you're not trying hard enough.

On the other hand, giving up is also a sign of not trying hard enough. Some take this to extremes. On 8 June 1924, George Mallory and Sandy Irvine set off towards the summit of Everest. At 12.50pm they were seen through a break in the clouds, apparently above the Second Step that is the main difficulty, but 5 hours behind schedule. This timing would allow them to return to their tents before nightfall, or to reach the summit: but not both. Everest is an arbitrary lump of snow and limestone high in the earth's atmosphere. Reaching it would gain them some fame, if little wealth.

The goggles found on Mallory's body 70 years later were in his pocket rather than on his eyes, suggesting a descent in the dark. If you turn back, you do so in time to get down in daylight and still alive. This suggests to me that George and Sandy decided to go for the snow-lump and the dirty limestone, rather than the staying alive.

Fifty years later on the same mountain, Mick Burke, trailing behind, met his companions Boardman and Pertemba already descending from the summit. The weather was worsening towards a blizzard. Mick Burke pressed upwards. His companions waited for him at the South Summit in the blizzard, but he did not return.

'Mick Burke... took a calculated risk, *which I suspect many of us would have taken*, when he went for the summit of Everest alone in 1975. He almost certainly reached the summit but was overtaken by a storm and probably fell through the cornice on the way back.' So wrote Bonington, one of the less obsessive of mountaineers, in 1989 (my italics).

Two days earlier Doug Scott and Dougal Haston had gone for it from the top camp, arriving at the summit at 6pm for what Scott described as the best sunset view of his entire life. They bivvied in a snow hole near the summit, 1000m up into the so-called Death Zone, but survived.

American climbers Hornbein and Unsoeld made the same 'summit rather than survival' decision on Everest's West Ridge in 1965. Willi Unsoeld radios base after a rotten rock pitch in the Hornbein Couloir: 'Man, this is a real bear-cat! We are nearing the top of the Yellow Band and it's mighty tough. It's too damned tough to try to go back. It would be too dangerous.... There are no rappel points, Jim, absolutely no rappel points... so it's up and over for us today.' His options are: to look a little harder for the rappel points; or to climb 600m over unknown ground to the summit, on the off chance that the other party members attempting the easier South Col Route will happen to hit the summit at just the same time. Those others would then guide them down the back of the mountain.

Hornbein writes: 'Too much labour, too many sleepless nights, and too many dreams had been invested to bring us this far. We couldn't come back for another try next weekend. To go down now, even if we could have, would be descending to a future marked by one huge question: what might have been?'

Luck gives them good snow and rock above the couloir, but even so they don't reach the summit until 6.15pm. Like Doug Scott 10 years later, they enjoy the sunset and the shadow of Everest stretching away across the world's lower mountains. (But is this a sight, quite literally, 'to die for'?) By pure fluke, their colleagues on the other side have indeed reached the summit earlier in the day. Unsoeld and Hornbein follow footprints down the South Ridge until their torch batteries die. In the dark, Hornbein falls through a cornice. They hear cries for help, and meet two even more exhausted climbers who have come up from the South Col. Together they spend the night in the open with no sleeping bags or bivouac gear. The temperature drops to maybe minus 30°C but the wind happens to be less than lethal.

Hornbein and Unsoeld remain the only folk ever to climb right across Everest: up by one route and down by a different one. Would you like that achievement in your CV? Or would you prefer to have toes? Unsoeld lost all of his.

Bynack More is never less

Turning back from time to time does at least show one to be less obsessive than George Mallory or Willi Unsoeld. This is reassuring for loved ones left at home – and even for us, if we wish to think of ourselves as moderately well-balanced individuals.

Starting from the South Col, you have to reach the summit of Everest by 1pm or else turn back: that is, if you like the idea of staying alive. To be back at Loch Morlich before it gets dark, you need to be crossing the Lairig Ghru before midday. Such calculations, made with untired mind before setting off, make it easier to turn around appropriately. (Not easy enough, as was shown in the Death Storm on Everest in 1996; on summit day the pre-arranged turnaround times were simply ignored, making it inevitable that the descending climbers would run out of oxygen and be benighted).

Two out of the five 4000ers: this is not 'failure', this is 'partial success'. More worthwhile than such wordplay is to select an escape route that itself involves some serious fun. And so from Macdui we turned left instead of right, to reach windswept Loch Etchachan and the area's central Munro, Beinn Mheadhoin. Its tundra is 200m below Macdui, and gave us a more bearable level of buffet. The scramble to its summit rock-tor is a sheltered groove: but the 5 metres of height above the plateau meant a belly-down crawl across its top rock. No standing on this summit, unless we wanted a sharp displacement sideways and a wind-borne descent that wouldn't be as gently floaty as Mary Poppins under her umbrella.

Loch Avon, at the heart of the Cairngorms, seen from Beinn Mheadhoin

Through 20 years of chairlift, it was far too easy to descend to what is, by rights, Scotland's remotest body of water. But there is no exit from the top of the new funicular onto the mountain: this was part of the planning agreement that allowed it to exist at all. So now, paths around Loch Avon are reverting to their wild state. At the loch's end, Bynack More rose into what had become a gentle breeze with moments of sunshine. We took the long way out, by the Pass of Ryvoan and the lovely Lochan Uaine. We'd covered two more miles, and only 500ft less ascent, than the walk of the full 4000s would have been. Under the ancient pines, the evening air was calm, and a few late midges came out to taste the autumn walkers.

Edith Piaf, no, she didn't have any of them at all. Frank Sinatra, he'd had a few (but then again, too few to mention). Me, I end up with regrets over every one of my 'partial successes' unless there's the excuse of a broken leg at least. We would have been just fine across the final 4000s. You can only go by what you know and sadly, the weather forecast hadn't mentioned that the winds would die away in the afternoon and the sun come out. Except that, back beside the warden's cage, the forecast was still up on the wall. Reading it at dawn, I'd decided we could withstand the buffeting, and failed to register where it said 'particularly at first', and 'by the end of the morning mostly 25mph'. (Geoff Monk, who if you read him with due attention gets it right as often as not, is on www.mwis.org.uk.)

Well, the 4000s are a wonderful walk. The one real advantage of not getting round it is the chance to give it another go.

Chapter 19

The Mourne Seven Sevens:
All Northern Ireland's 700m Peaks

BRIEF ROUTE AND SCHEDULE

The hills	Slieves Donard (850m), Commedagh (767m); Slievelamagan (704m), Slieves Binnian (747m), Meelbeg (708m), Meelmore (704m), Bearnagh (739m)
Distance	38km (24 miles)
Ascent	2700m (9100ft)
Start/finish	Newcastle, County Down (J 374 306)
Terrain	Paths, some very steep, and a rough descent off Binnian
Target time	1 day
Standard strong walker	13hrs

In preparation for the Silent Valley Reservoir, the Belfast Water Commissioners spent 18 years (1904–22) building a monumental wall to stop walkers walking on the water supply. Its course is marked on the sketch map with this chapter. Little did they realise that they were creating not a barrier but an encouragement...

Modern methods of water purification mean it's no longer necessary to exclude walkers from the watershed. And the walk around the Mourne Wall, organised by the Youth Hostel Association of Northern Ireland, became Ireland's most popular challenge, attracting 4000 people in a single year. The steep granite ground the wall follows is peculiarly susceptible to erosion, and so in 1984 the organised walk was abandoned.

Its modern replacement, the Seven Sevens, includes the best of the wall walk – or can include, as route choice between the peaks is up to the walker. At the same time it bypasses the steepest, and so most erodable, slopes at the southern end of the circuit. Even so, much steep stuff remains, among the tortopped peaks and heathery reservoirs of Northern Ireland's granite lands.

A start at Silent Valley would make a natural circuit: but in order to roughly match the 32km and 2800m (20 miles/9300ft) of the original wall walk, the route starts instead at Newcastle's Donard Park.

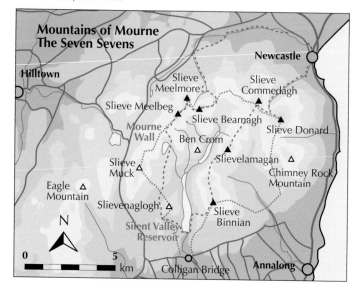

The route

Any route must take in the seven peaks marked with black triangles on the sketch map. Deciding the order in which to do them is part of the challenge. My one offers going that is mostly pleasant and always interesting, but is not the shortest possible. It starts up Glen River for an up-and-down of **Slieve Donard**, then **Slieve Commedagh**, **Slievelamagan** and **Slieve Binnian**, and down to the dam of the Silent Valley Reservoir. Paths (not marked on the 1:50,000 map but obvious on the ground) lead up to the Batt's Road. A classic section of the Mourne Wall leads over Slieves **Meelbeg** and **Meelmore** to **Slieve Bearnagh**.

The scrupulous, or those who just love rough granite, will scramble the tor that's Bearnagh's true summit. This interesting spiral route (Grade 1) starts below the west face. Slant up to the right across a gently angled slab with a drop below. From the slab's top, go up a 2m groove to a gap in the crest.

Now the crest arête up left can be taken direct, not difficult but exposed. More reassuring is to take a pathed ledge running left along the back of the tor. Below the summit, take a body-width crack up right (the right-hand and easier of two cracks) and a continuation crack above, to a gap in the crest to right of the summit. From the gap, make a stomach-traverse (feet dangling to the right) across a boulder, an exposed move that leads onto Bearnagh's summit.

As the song says, they sweep down to the sea. Newcastle, and the Mourne Mountains

From Hare's Gap I descended the Trassey Track to the car park at Clonachullion (J 311 313) and finished through Tollymore Forest Park with its gorges and amusing footbridges.

The annual race has a pre-determined order for the peaks that is different from this. It and the annual challenge walk have a checkpoint at Ben Crom dam rather than the Silent Valley one, shortening the route to 31km and 2600m (19 miles/8700ft).

MOURNE, SEVEN SEVENS – SCHEDULE				
	Distance mls/km	Ascent ft/m	Time min	ETA
Start: Newcastle				0:00
Slieve Donard	3.0/4.8	2800/850	130	2:10
Slieve Commedagh	1.3/2.0	600/180	45	2:55
Slievelamagan	2.2/3.5	1150/340	80	4:15
Slieve Binnian	2.0/3.2	1300/390	80	5:35
Silent Valley dam	1.4/2.3		50	6:25
Slieve Meelmore	4.8/7.7	2000/600	170	9:15
Slieve Bearnagh	1.5/2.4	1100/330	70	10:25
Clonachullion car park	2.8/4.5		60	11:25
Newcastle	4.7/7.5	150/40	100	13:05
TOTALS	**24/38**	**9100/2700**		

Mourne is never less

As everybody knows (because it says so in the song) the Mountains of Mourne sweep down to the sea. What's not always appreciated is quite how quickly and steeply they do this. The 850m summit of Slieve Donard is just 3km (2 miles) from the blue-green waters of Dundrum Bay. Behind Donard lies 15 miles of pointy-topped, rocky-sided, bog-bottomed Irish hill-bagging.

With its palm trees and its esplanade, and the mountains rising out of the back, Newcastle in County Down is a seaside town of the cheerful sand-between-the-toes sort. The houses are painted in a dozen colours, all faded to pastel by the salt air; the awnings are striped; the shops are chip-shops and old-fashioned amusement arcades.

There are few things less cheerful than a really cheerful seaside town in the rain. We sat in the car being indecisive. Before us, the grey sea. Behind, the even greyer mountains. Fifty yards to our left, the blue triangle of Hostelling International.

I am a member of Hostelling International. The others are not, and would have to pay extra. 'And what if you came out of the hostel, in a couple of hours, and saw the sun streaming down?' Peter was the Irish *emigré* who'd got us into these Seven Sevens.

'He would be most surprised,' suggested Alastair, 'given that it's already getting dark.'

'I should simply tell myself,' I explained in a snooty way, 'that I had made the best judgement on the evidence available to me. Anyway, you lot are carrying tents; I'm in my bivvy bag.'

The rain beat on the roof, and the shades of night gathered. And then Peter got out of the car and pulled on his waterproof trousers. So we went. But when, at the top edge of Donard forest, the rain turned to snow: 'Snow, good show!' said Peter. 'I'm going back to that youth hostel,' said I.

Up on the open hill, the lights of Newcastle were seen by the other three in soft focus through a film of snow: 'Just like Christmas!' they told me later. 'Don't worry,' said the Irish guide, 'it's April after all. It won't lie under us through the night.'

He was right about that. Alastair said next day: 'It wasn't lying under us. It was lying on top.' Spindrift whirling in the sheltered back of the Mourne Wall had filled up their tent. Colin had resorted to his earplugs, carried against bothy snorers, to shut out the roar of the storm. 'Ah,' admitted the Irish guide, 'There has been a slight miscalculation on this expedition.'

The following morning, and 2000ft below them as they lay shaking off the snow, I was wandering up through the woods beside the Glen River, enjoying

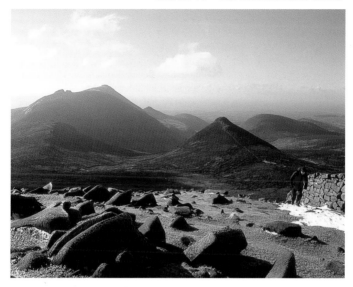

Mourne Wall leads onto Slieve Meelbeg

the way it leaps about in little crinkly waterfalls among the grey boulders. Until I noticed that it wasn't actually doing that at all, but swooshing like washing machines down smooth, yellow slabs. Not having the other three with me meant I could backtrack, and find the line in the riverbed where grey shale gives way to granite, and try to take a picture of it.

In a story like this one, you can leave out several hours and skip straight to the interesting bit. The Glen riverbed, in the space of 6 inches, skips 250 million years.

In both the geological record, and the story of our walk, the interesting bit is the Mourne granite. As the Atlantic Ocean started to open up, a blob of molten rock 15 miles wide floated out of the earth's melted middle into the old grey rocks that were already there. The molten blob cooled and crystallised into granite; rain and wind exposed it; and glaciers carved it into the interesting shapes of today. The steep slopes gathered water, which was eventually dammed below for humans to drink; and in order to stop ignorant walkers from peeing in their own drinks, the water board built a granite wall 2m high all around the skyline.

221

Mourne granite, rough and wrinkly, is rewarding to climb over as it forms the tor tops of the Mourne mountains. Made into the 2m-high Mourne Wall, it formed a very welcome shelter as I plodded up Slieve Donard, with the snow-shower flying over my head.

Alone on a snowy Saturday morning, you're still part of the walking scene. Walkers before leave scraps of litter or, more rewardingly, footprints that guide you through the bog and ease the way up the snowslope. Those of the other three were well-filled in: they had to be an awful long way ahead. (In fact, they'd done Donard up and down in the dark, 12 hours earlier.)

Snowy heather, and rocky drops on the right, and a peaty path that just occasionally led into a speckly-grey swamp of peat and melting slush. The clouds parted, revealing Slieve Bearnagh, which is the most rocky-topped Mourne, in considerable snowy splendour. I deployed my camera and raised it to my eye: and watched Slieve Bearnagh vanish from the viewfinder. Less than a minute later, the same sharp little blizzard arrived on Slievelamagan. I hunched inside my hood, and tried not to get irritated with the wind as it lurched me mid-stride and landed me into one of the slushy boggy bits.

On Slieve Binnian I caught up with the other three. We greeted each other with brief shouts through the gale. Slieve Binnian is the second-most rocky-topped Mourne. The blizzard from behind pressed us against the rough granite: staying on was easy, moving up was rather harder. The top tor of Slieve Binnian was like I imagine the Second Step on Everest (but without the oxygen bottles and frozen mountaineers). The granite flattened, and we crawled to touch the battered iron fence post stabbed into the summit.

Disheartened by their night lying in spindrift, the other three intended a walk-out along Loch Crom and Hare's Gap to a distant sheltered sheepfold – they'd always planned this as a two-day event.

But given that the Seven Sevens has been done in 3hrs 54min, I felt it should now be done in a day. Especially by one who had actually been to sleep the night before. Accordingly, I kept on southwards to the dam at the foot of the Silent Valley. Old tracks made by peat-waggons and quarrymen led through the Mourne moors, past the grim and lonely Lough Shannagh. The snowclouds rolled away, and on nearby tor-topped mountains, knots of hillwalkers began to appear like spring flowers. Behind them, east and south, grey-blue sea was wrinkled like an aluminium blanket. I rejoined the Mourne Wall for the steep climb up Slieve Meelbeg.

And the steep climb up Slieve Meelmore.

And the steep climb up Slieve Bearnagh.

Descending towards Slieve Bearnagh, whose top tor offers the walk's tricky bit

'So did you do it up that summit tor?' they asked me at the sheepfold afterwards.

I didn't. The very gentle slab that you simply walk across; it had high winds, and melty slush, and nobody else about to encourage.

'So you decided the level of risk was unjustifiable?' asked Alastair.

'Simpler than that. I was scared.'

Below Hare's Gap, the million sheep-fields of Mourne County faded into the distance under the evening sun. I made my way down to the sheepfold. It was the wrong sheepfold, and my friends weren't there.

An hour's walk down the Shimna River, my mobile phone summoned me back: my friends had finally arrived. While I'd been enjoying sunshine and winds on the high ridges, they'd been passing slowly up the Crom Reservoir, and stopping to dry out the sleeping bags, and deciding to have supper while they were unpacked. Worse, Colin had diverted up to Slieve Bearnagh, and done that summit tor.

But the other two hadn't. So the next day we went back over the last four of the Seven Sevens. Meelmore and Commedagh, the Mourne pointy ones, are well worth doing two days in a row. And this time, I did get up Slieve Bearnagh.

223

Chapter 20

Tranter's Walk:
18 Munros around Glen Nevis

THE FREEDOM TO FALL

> I [God] made him just and right
> Sufficient to have stood, though free to fall...
> Milton *Paradise Lost* Book III 1667

It was a perfectly routine rescue. Walking down Glen Nevis in the dark in March, we saw two lights above the Steall Falls. 'Can't get down there,' we said to each other; and sure enough, the lights started to flash an SOS. I trotted down to the campsite, requested a ride to the phone box, and called the Rescue. It turned out that 18 people had been behind the two torches; one had fallen a few feet and was slightly injured. The helicopter came for them in the early hours.

Two torches among 18? Dearie me. And obviously they hadn't studied their escape routes in advance. Very stupid, shouldn't be allowed onto the hill, should be made to pay for the helicopter; lucky for them there were a couple of real hillwalkers passing by.

Well, let's look at those real hillwalkers down below. Ice-axes, crampons, torches – but what's that on their feet? Running shoes? And what are they doing in Glen Nevis in the dark anyway? Thirteen Munros? Hmmm... (Actually, I'd just been jolly sensible. I'd just insisted on not doing a further four Munros, and the Devil's Ridge, by starlight. And I'm still regretting that bit of sensibleness.)

Flashback to Striding Edge, late February. Lots of snow, trampled down to a sort of artificial névé. Proper hillwalker, crampons, ice-axe, has just finished a tricky little descent, meets two idiots with no pointy metal bits whatever. 'Best go back,' he tells them. 'Front-pointing you know: can't be done without crampons. Fall off, as like as not.'

I was one of those idiots. The other was someone I met on the way up. We didn't go back. It wasn't as good as the 13 Lochaber Munros; it wasn't as silly, either. But it was good. Believe me, it was chop off the top of the head, spoon out the brains and fling them to the winds stuff. But the sensible young man did spoil it a bit, until we decided he was probably just slightly scared himself after the front-pointing.

Steall Falls: not a descent route off the Mamores

Striding Edge in wonderful winter conditions. An ice-axe is advisable, but is its absence actually immoral?

A friend of mine was ordered off the Aonach Eagach Ridge for being improperly dressed. She was wearing – with the sun warming the rocks and the sky a lovely shade of blue – jeans. And as the years go by, more and more people are telling us what we must do and what we mustn't out on the hill.

Always carry a map and compass. Phone the avalanche helpline. Don't wear trainers. Leave word with some responsible person. Don't chatter on your mobile phone. A tent is essential. Never travel unaccompanied. Walkers should carry insurance and a survival shelter. Crampons and ice-axe whenever you see snow. Learn first aid, and carry a triangular bandage. Don't throw stones, don't build cairns, leave banana skins but not orange peel, do not disclose the grid reference of the bothy.

Considered as advice, much of this is sound. Considered as Rules of Hillwalking, all of it is wrong. Hillwalking isn't a sport, and it doesn't have rules. Decide for yourself where to go, and how to get there, and what to take. Decide badly, and end up shivering in a bivvy bag on the Eskdale side of Scafell Pike. Decide even worse, and end up dead.

The quote at the top is from Milton. Determinism, and Free Will. Call out the Mountain Rescue because you got lost and didn't fancy waiting in the dark until the sun comes – and the MR may give you a dirty look or worse. But call the MR because you've been a damn silly fool, and the MR may well be oddly sympathetic. We've all been, on occasion, the Fool on the Hill. The members of the MR Team have probably been it. I myself have been it. This is called self-reliance. This is called freedom. There's not a lot of it about, and we need it.

TRANTER'S WALK BRIEF ROUTE AND SCHEDULE

The hills	18 Munros (3000-footers): Ben Nevis (1344m); Carn Mor Dearg (1223m), the Aonachs (1236m), the Grey Corries (1177m), the Mamores (1130m)
Distance	59km (37 miles)
Ascent	6200m (21,000ft)
Start/finish	Glen Nevis youth hostel (NN 128 718)
Terrain	High exposed rocky ridges
Target time	24hrs
Standard strong walker	25hrs

I have implied that the best tough walk in Wales is the Welsh 3000s (see Chapter 16), and the best one in England is the Old County Tops (see Chapter 17). Better, and tougher, than either is Tranter's Walk over Ben Nevis, the Grey Corries and the Mamores. It crosses no roads, but 18 Munro summits. Those summits are made of three different sorts of stones: volcanic lavas on Ben Nevis, granite on Carn Mor Dearg, and quartzite on the Grey Corries and some of the Mamores. Thus the high ridges change their character as the day unfolds. Much of that ridgework is on bare rock, with actual scrambling (Grade 1) on the Carn Mor Dearg Arête, An Garbhanach and the Devil's Ridge to Carn a' Mhaim. It is a route for walkers – just. Its founder, Philip Tranter (son of the historical novelist Nigel Tranter) achieved it in lightweight boots of Spanish leather in 1964. He walked it, Mamores-first, taking 23 hours despite falling asleep for 2 hours on Aonach Beag.

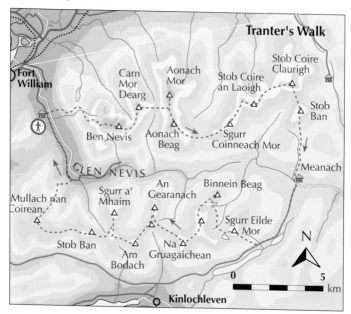

Even so, you could divide it into two at Meanach bothy, and it would just become two jolly demanding daywalks. My own circuit of the 'walk' was in running shoes. My winter attempt failed when it got dark on An Gearanach and I didn't fancy reversing the scrambling move by torchlight. The winter walk has been achieved, in bad snow and weather, in 30 hours by Glyn Jones; he was awarded the Fell Running Association's Long-distance Trophy for the achievement.

As walks go, they don't come tougher than Tranter.

The route

Clockwise is the better direction, to do the 1200m climb to Ben Nevis in the dark, get the really long uphills in early, and also to cross the highest and most serious ground while still fairly fresh.

The tough and experienced walker contemplating this one is a skilled map-reader and doesn't need a written description. Here are a few hints anyway. The very steep nose down from Stob Coire Bhealaich (NN 207 708) can if necessary be avoided by a gully 400 metres to the south. From Stob Ban at the end of the

An Garbhanach of the Mamores, during an attempt on the winter Tranter

Grey Corries, a stream running south, the head of Allt nam Fang, has grassy banks through the heather.

Meanach bothy is north of the river opposite Luibeilt. The Abhainn Rath river here isn't always crossable. The quickest way up Sgurr Eilde Mor is to jog along the track to the head of Loch Eilde Mor. Descend Binnein Beag south-west, on runnable scree. Binnein Mor is easiest by the grassy northern corrie to the paired lochans, then southwest onto the North Ridge. The key to the descent of the final hill, Mullach nan Coirean, is a stile at NN 132 681, though the forest path below is difficult in the dark.

TRANTER'S WALK – SCHEDULE

	Distance mls/km	Ascent ft/m	Time min	ETA
Start: Glen Nevis				0:00
Ben Nevis	4.0/6.4	4400/1300	180	3:00
Carn Mor Dearg	1.2/1.9	550/150	70	4:10
Aonach Beag	2.6/4.2	1800/550	110	6:00
Stob Coire Claurigh	5.2/8.3	3000/900	200	9:20
Luibeilt	4.1/6.6	600/200	95	10:55
Section	**17.1/27.4**	**10,350/3100**		
Sgurr Eilde Mor	2.9/4.6	2200/650	130	13:05
Binnein Mor	3.1/5.0	2600/800	145	15:30
An Gearanach	3.1/5.0	1400/400	115	17:25
Sgurr a' Mhaim	3.0/4.8	2200/650	135	19:40
Mullach nan Coirean	4.1/6.6	2200/650	155	22:15
Glen Nevis	3.6/5.8		95	23:50
Section	**19.8/31.7**	**10,600/3200**		
TOTAL	**37/59**	**21,000/6300**	**1430**	

Note Schedule is 5 percent faster than 'standard strong walker' so as to achieve 24hrs. Slowdown is built in from Luibeilt. Standard-walker time for the full-day walk to Luibeilt is 12hrs; the second half, for the standard walker starting fresh, is 13hrs.

An Garbhanach on a summer evening

Chapter 21

Start/Finish

Whan that Aprille with his shoures soote [showers sweet]
The droughte of March hath perced to the roote...
And smale fowles maken melodye...
Than longen folk to goon on pilgrimages.
Opening words of Chaucer's *Canterbury Tales* c1380

The very first written work recognised as being in English records a multi-day trek between London and Canterbury (53 miles/85km). The evening gathering at the favourite pub; the happy gaggle of walkers; the lofty conversations on theology and folklore at the back and the lower-toned middle field with its unsuitable jokes – it's a typical LDWA challenge, lacking only the rucksacks with the dangling plastic mugs.

A few years before that, the very last written work of Anglo-Saxon is a long-distance trail out of Somerset, via the dangerous wastes of Wirral, to somewhere in the Peak District. It was undertaken – mostly off-road and in winter conditions – by Sir Gawain, on his way to a head-chopping contest with the Green Knight. Unlike King Arthur, today's employers won't allow us two months off to explore Offa's Dyke Path.

Five weeks before finishing this book, I took a walk in winter conditions around the Old County Tops. From Scafell Pike I looked south to the Welsh coast; below, in Little Narrowcove, the tiny stream had created an effect of icy organ-pipes, with the tower of Pen impending like the grim god looking down into the cathedral. Out on the Great Moss, the icy top of Scafell Pike lay reflected in the River Esk; the afternoon light was smeared like honey across the screes.

Three hours later, the ridge of Coniston Old Man, and a fingernail of new moon hanging in the west. Directly below it, the triangle of Harter Fell rises out of the sea of darkness like the shark rising to gobble up the girl swimmer in the poster for the film *Jaws*. Snow is grey under torchlight, and the empty space behind the cairn of Swirl How is a pit of darkness. This is navigating the way it ought to be, no little grey screen of the GPS but the pole star glittering over Wet Side Edge; and then as the ridge bends the less romantic lights of Tilberthwaite and Little Langdale.

Quest or challenge walk, peak-bagging or pilgrimage; it's all peculiarly pointless. Even so, it's more natural than watching team sports on an electric

Heading down off High Raise, Scafell Pike ahead, on the winter circuit of the Old County Tops

box. It has something in it of hunting, gathering and war, and may even be as fundamental to the human condition as football hooliganism or shopping.

A well-formed challenge walk isn't just a distance, a climb and a time. It's a sort of story – appealing directly to the imagination, and with further knowledge, unfolding further. We can trace our game of 'doing it in the hills' back to a 9-day Lakeland backpack of the poet Coleridge in August 1803; and over two centuries our walks have written themselves histories and biographies. Ingleborough and the other two, with their biscuit-tin prettiness combining so uncomfortably with gritstone bogs and the limestone just-plain-weirdness of Great Douk – is not this the life story of that special little realm that is Yorkshire? The Derwent Watershed is a memento of the primitive booted bog-bashers, the tough (and didn't they know it) men of the Pennines between the two World Wars. Through the Lairig Ghru has passed the whole history of Scotland.

'Old men should be explorers,' says Tennyson. Old women as well, of course. Our legs get slightly slower, our knees less bendy; but at the same time

233

Evening on Ill Bell, with Windermere (eastern Lake District)

our gear gets lighter, our navigation more cunning. With the passing of the years, helpful factories devise LCD torches, and lightweight shoes that are also slightly waterproof. But more than all this, we can enlarge our imaginations. Instead of going further and faster, do it overnight, with that new LCD torch; or do it in winter. Tune in to the cultural resonances, and do it more romantic. The Three Peaks by Public Transport wasn't just more intriguing and environmental than the Three Peaks Straight. It was also quite a bit easier...

Every pair of legs has, at the other end of it, a thinking brain. Let fly the imagination; then bend down and lace up the boots.

Information and Internet

Maps

Harveys 1:25,000 Superwalker (available for most of the routes here, www.harveymaps.co.uk), Ordnance Survey 1:25,000 Explorer, and OS 1:50,000 Landranger are all good maps. My recommended map depends on whether 1:25,000 detail is useful, and otherwise on which gives convenient coverage.

Public transport

Journey planners covering the UK are on www.traveline.org.uk or 0870 200 2233.

Accommodation

Youth Hostel Association 01629 592700 www.yha.org.uk
Scottish Youth Hostel Association 08701 55 32 55 www.syha.org.uk
Campsites www.UKCampsite.co.uk
Independent hostels www.hostel-scotland.co.uk, www.independenthostelguide.co.uk (UK including Northern Ireland)

2 The National Three Peaks

Best maps: Harveys Three Peaks Challenge Map Set, comprising Ben Nevis (with summit at 1:12,500); Lakeland West; and Snowdonia: Snowdon.
The Institute of Fundraising (publishes the code of practice 'Outdoor Fundraising in the UK')
Park Place, 12 Lawn Lane, London SW8 1UD
020 7840 1000 www.institute-of-fundraising.org.uk
The Nevis Partnership, Units 6 & 7, Lochaber Rural Complex, Torlundy, Fort William PH33 6SW www.nevispartnership.co.uk
Lake District National Park Authority
Murley Moss, Oxenholme Rd, Kendal LA9 7RL
01539 724555 www.lake-district.gov.uk
Snowdonia National Park Authority
Penrhyndeudraeth, Gwynedd LL48 6LF
01766 770274 www.eryri-npa.co.uk
Wooden Spoon Vauxhall Four Peaks Challenge www.woodenspoon.com
01889 582889.

Railway Children www.railwaychildren.org.uk
Point your search engine at 'Three Peaks' 'Ben Nevis' for a dozen personal accounts.

4 The Yorkshire Three Peaks
Best map: Explorer OL2 Yorkshire Dales.
Yorkshire Three Peaks Club was founded in 1965, and is still run, by the proprietors of Pen-y-ghent Café, Horton in Ribblesdale, Settle BD24 0HE. The Three Peaks fell race has been run since 1955, and currently takes place on a Saturday at the end of April: www.threepeaksrace.org.uk

5 The Lancashire Three Peaks
Best map: OS Explorers OL41 Bowland and 287 West Pennine Moors.
Public transport: For the tired, bus B10, two-hourly through the day, links Newton and Whitewell with Clitheroe (trains to Whalley).
Accommodation: The camping barn on the route at Greengore has closed, but there are others at Chipping and Downham – book through YHA above.

Borrowdale Bus on the 'Three Peaks by Public Transport' challenge

6 The Somerset and other Three Peaks
Best map: OS Explorer OL9 Exmoor.
South Wales Three Peaks Trial is held in late March
www.cardiffoutdoorgroup.org.uk
The Marilyns
Listed in *Relative Hills of Britain* Alan Dawson (Cicerone ISBN 978 1 85284 068 6)

8 The Dartmoor Ten Tors
Best map: OS Explorer OL28 Dartmoor.
Live firing information www.dartmoor-ranges.co.uk
Exeter University's Ten Tors site www.events.ex.ac.uk/tentors/

Public transport (escape for independent walkers): Occasional buses
Postbridge to Tavistock link to Okehampton
Supplies: There are two small post office shops at Postbridge and Princetown.
Accommodation: The Two Bridges Hotel has an appropriately named but
rather upmarket Tors Restaurant; cheaper accommodation can be found in
Princetown.

9 The Lyke Wake Walk
Best maps: OS Explorers OL26 and OL27 North Yorks Moors West and East.
Accommodation: Osmotherley youth hostel is open July–Aug, flexible opening
March–October 0845 371 9035 osmotherley@yha.org.uk
To return, take a bus 80/89 (hourly) Osmotherley to Stokesley (Abbott & Sons,
01677 424987). Take another to Middlesborough or Guisborough, then Arriva
93 (www.arrivabus.co.uk) along A171 towards Scarborough. Alight at The
Ranch NZ 941 004, and take a bridleway east to the track to Beacon Howe.
www.yorkshiretravel.net
New Lyke Wake Club www.lykewake.org

10 The Derwent Watershed
Best map: OS Explorer OL1 Dark Peak.
Much of the route is on access land opened under the Countryside and Rights
of Way Act. However, there are widespread restrictions on dogs, and some
on humans too during grouse shooting from 12 August–12 December. The
Pennine Way is a right of way.
Access restrictions maps: www.countrysideaccess.gov.uk or via
www.openaccess.gov.uk

Information: Upper Derwent Information Centre 01433 650953.
High Peak Marathon race www.highpeakmarathon.org.uk

11 The Across Wales Walk

Best maps: OS Explorers 213 Aberystwyth and 214 Llanidloes.
Across Wales Walk, September: www.acrosswaleswalk.co.uk; the event is
usually booked up soon after entries open in May.
Across Wales charity walk, Glandyfi (south of Machynlleth) via Staylittle and
Llandinam to Kerry, late June: www.newtown-rotary.org.uk

12 The Lairig Ghru

Best maps: OS Explorers 404 Braemar and 403 Cairn Gorm; if starting at Linn
of Dee, 404 isn't needed.
Accommodation: Youth hostels at Braemar (large and comfortable), Cairngorm
Lodge at Glenmore village, and Aviemore (Inverey hostel has closed). Braemar
and Aviemore also have independent hostels, hotels etc.
Public transport: Buses to Braemar only from Aberdeen. Aviemore has trains
and Citylink coaches to the south. Best return Aviemore to Braemar is train via
Inverness to Aberdeen, then bus. www.travelinescotland.com

15 LDWA Hundred

The LDWA's annual Hundred, in a different place each year, is on the late May
bank holiday weekend. Priority goes to LDWA members. Entry conditions include
completion of a 50-mile walk in the preceding year. See 'Other events' below.

16 The Welsh 3000s

Best map: OS Explorer OL17 Snowdon
Accommodation: Youth hostel at Pen-y-Pass (busy), also Rowen, Idwal
Cottage and Llanberis (small, seasonal); bothy at Dulyn reservoir SH 706 664.
Public transport: Snowdon Sherpa bus S6 links Pen-y-Pass with Bethesda
www.traveline-cymru.org.uk, or www.gwynedd.gov.uk (search site for
Snowdon Sherpa) Bws Gwynedd 01286 679535.
More information: the 2010 edition of *Welsh Three Thousand Foot Challenges*
by Roy Clayton and myself (Grey Stone Books ISBN 978 1 902017 02 0) has a
full, detailed route description of both the 'normal way', starting at Snowdon,
and the southbound route including scrambling on Glyders and Tryfan. Some
(not much) detail of the scrambles is in *Scrambles in Snowdonia* by Steve
Ashton (Cicerone ISBN 978 1 85284 088 4).

*Ridge north of Y Garn
on the Welsh 3000s*

17 The Lakes 3000s

Best map: The whole route is on OS Landranger 90 (Penrith), but add OS Explorer OL6 South West Lakeland, or Harvey's Lakeland West, for Scafell detail.

Public transport: Buses from Borrowdale return to Keswick to 8pm in summer. The last bus across Dunmail Raise is at 5.40pm, earlier than most walkers weary enough to want it will get there.

Further information: *Lakeland Mountain Challenges*, by Roy Clayton and myself, has a detailed route description including off-road alternatives (Grey Stone Books ISBN 978 0 9515996 8 6 (new edition forthcoming 2011)).

17 The Old County Tops

Best maps: Descent from Scafell Pike is helped by large-scale map, as for the Lakes 3000s above. Explorer OL6 with Harveys Lakeland Central is the only way to cover the route at 1:25,000 scale in just two maps.

Accommodation and food: Between Elterwater and Grasmere four youth hostels are right on the route. A very early Grasmere start allows a bar meal at a fine inn, the Three Shires, Little Langdale.

Further information: *Lakeland Mountain Challenges*, as for Lakes 3000s above, has a detailed route description.

In Wythburn Valley, heading west from Helvellyn on a winter circuit of the Lakeland Old County Tops

18 The Cairngorm 4000s

Best map: Harveys Cairn Gorm has more accurate path detail than OS Explorer 403 Cairn Gorm.

Accommodation: Start/finish at Cairngorm Lodge youth hostel in Glenmore village adds 4km and 120m (2.5 miles/400ft, 1hr). From Heron's field use Allt Mor path, not road, to Sugar Bowl. See also 'Lairig Ghru' above.

Further information: While anyone attempting this one should be a happy navigator, there are more route details in my own *Walking the Cairngorms* (Cicerone ISBN 978 1 85284 452 3).

19 The Mourne Seven Sevens

Best map: OSNI 1:25,000 Mourne Country.

The official Seven Sevens, held in early August, is a challenge walk (Spartan Red Sox Walking Club www.spartanredsox.org.uk) and a race (www.nimra.org.uk).

Public transport: Plenty of cheap flights to Belfast. Ulsterbus takes 1.5hrs to Newcastle www.translink.co.uk 028 90 66 66 30.

20 Tranter's Walk

Best map: Harveys Ben Nevis.
Accommodation: Glen Nevis youth hostel, or the equally convenient bunkhouse at Ben Nevis Inn www.ben-nevis-inn.co.uk; the bothy at Meanach is a simple unlocked shelter with no facilities, www.mountainbothies.org.uk

Other events

Long Distance Walkers' Association: Its members' magazine *Strider* lists dozens of challenge walks every four months; some are also on www.ldwa.org.uk
Membership: 7 Shetland Way, Radcliffe, Manchester M26 4UH.
Williamson Across Ross (Ullapool to Alness, late May) organised for Children First, Inverness by Natural High Guiding, Cannich, by Beauly IV4 7LY www.naturalhighguiding.co.uk

Aonach Mor, just one of the 18 big hills on Tranter's Walk

Appendix 2

Walks Summary

2 The National Three Peaks Challenge: Ben Nevis, Scafell Pike and Snowdon within 24 hours

The hills	Ben Nevis (1344m), Scafell Pike (978m), Snowdon (1085m)
Distance	44km (27.5 miles)
Ascent	2900m (9800ft)
Terrain	Paths, mostly reconstructed: possible navigation difficulties
Target time	14hrs (+10hrs driving)
Standard strong walker	13.5hrs

4 The Yorkshire Three Peaks: Pen-y-ghent, Whernside, Ingleborough

The hills	Pen-y-ghent (694m), Whernside (736m), Ingleborough (724m)
Distance	33km (23 miles)
Ascent	1400m (4600ft)
Start/finish	Horton in Ribblesdale (SD 808 725)
Terrain	Paths well made and boggy, tracks and lanes
Target time	12hrs
Standard strong walker	10.5hrs

5 The Lancashire Three Peaks: Longridge Fell, Easington Fell, Pendle

The hills	Longridge Fell (350m), Easington Fell (396m), Pendle Hill (557m)
Concept	A rival to the Yorkshire Three Peaks
Distance	58km (36 miles)
Ascent	1600m (5400ft)
Start/finish	Whalley (SD 733 362)

Terrain	Field paths, tracks and lanes, open hilltops
Target time	18hrs
Standard strong walker	15.5hrs

6 The Three Peaks of Somerset: Dunkery Beacon, Periton Hill, Selworthy Beacon

The hills	Dunkery Beacon (591m), Periton Hill (297m), Selworthy Beacon (308m)
Distance	25km (15.5 miles)
Ascent	900m/3000ft
Start/finish	Porlock (SS 886 466)
Terrain	Field paths, tracks and lanes, open hilltops
Standard stong walker	7hrs

8 The Dartmoor Ten Tors: 50 miles of moorland over two days

The hills	Ten tors chosen from a list of 18
Distance	58km (35–55 miles)
Ascent	About 2000m (6000–7000ft)
Start/finish	Okehampton Camp (SX 587 925)
Maximum altitude	584m Kitty Tor
Terrain	Open moorland, largely pathless
Target time	34hrs including night stop

Descending Snowdon – on the Ten Tors expedition.
The Dartmoor Snowdon is a small peak southeast of Two Bridges.

9 The Lyke Wake Walk

Concept	A full crossing of the North York Moors
Distance	62km (39 miles) to Osmotherley
Ascent	1500m (5000ft)
Start	Ravenscar Beacon (NZ 970 012)
Finish	Osmotherley (SE 461 981)
Maximum altitude	454m Round Hill
Terrain	Paths, often boggy in eastern half, rebuilt and smooth in west
Target time	24hrs
Standard strong walker	16hrs

10 The Derwent Watershed: 39 miles in the Dark Peak

Concept	Around the Derwent Reservoirs
Distance	63km (39 miles)
Ascent	1700m (5600ft)
Start/finish	Car park near Edale station (SK 124 853) or other points on the circuit
Maximum altitude	636m Kinder Scout
Terrain	Two thirds on good paths, one third on swampy bog
Target time	24hrs
Standard strong walker	18hrs

Pennine Way, north of the Snake Pass on the Derwent Watershed route

Across Wales Walk: field paths in the west

11 The Across Wales Walk: from the English border to the sea over Plynlimon

Concept	English border to the sea over Plynlimon
Distance	72km (46 miles)
Ascent	1700m (5600ft)
Start	Anchor, Shropshire (SO 174 855)
Finish	Clarach Bay (SN 585 841) near Aberystwyth
Maximum altitude	752m Plynlimon
Terrain	Quiet roads, field paths, and a crossing of Plynlimon
Target time	18hrs
Standard strong walker	18.75hrs

12 The Lairig Ghru: The great through-route of the Cairngorms

Distance	45km/28 miles (full version)
Ascent	700m/2400ft
Start	Braemar (NO 151 914)
Finish	Aviemore (NH 896 123)
Maximum altitude	835m
Terrain	Paths, mostly good, through very remote country
Target time	1 day
Standard stong walker	11.25hrs

A walk is a story; the final ford of the Tweed adds suspense (Southern Uplands)

14 Southern Uplands: Fifty from your Front Door

Concept	Visit a friend 50 miles away
Distance	80km/50 miles (or your usual maximum + 50 percent)
Ascent	1500m/5000ft if you live somewhere hilly
Start	Your front door at dawn
Finish	A suitably distant friend
Terrain	Off-road
Target time	1 day
Standard stong walker	20hrs

16 The Welsh 3000s: 15 peaks in one day

Concept	The fifteen 3000ft (914m) peaks of Wales, with added scrambling
Distance	45km (28 miles)
Ascent	3600m (12,000ft)
Start	Bwlch y Ddeufaen (SH 720 715)
Finish	Pen-y-Pass (SH 485 56
Maximum altitude	1085m Snowdon
Terrain	Grassy hills, rocky hills, boulderfields and scrambling
Target time	One day
Standard strong walker	15hrs

17 The Lakes 3000s

The hills	Skiddaw (931m), Scafell (964m), Scafell Pike (978m), Helvellyn (950m)
Distance	72km (43 miles)
Ascent	3100m (9200ft)
Start/finish	Keswick (NY 266 234)
Terrain	Paths and roads, but awkward over Scafell and rough over Scafell Pike
Target time	Finish by midnight
Standard strong walker	21.5hrs

The Old County Tops

Concept	The summits of former Cumberland, Westmorland and Lancashire
The hills	Helvellyn (950m), Scafell Pike (978m), Coniston Old Man (803m)
Distance	57km (36 miles)
Ascent	2900m (9500ft)
Start/finish	Grasmere (NY 337 074)
Terrain	Good paths, with some open grassland, and boulders over Scafell Pike
Target time	1 day
Standard strong walker	18hrs

Lakes 3000s: a non-standard route that adds 20 minutes avoids road and takes in the wrong side of Derwent Water

The River Dee flowing at 4000ft, on the plateau before Braeriach (Cairngorm 4000s)

18 The Cairngorm 4000s: five granite giants in a day

The hills	Cairn Gorm (1245m), Ben Macdui (1309m), Cairn Toul (1291m), Angel's Peak (1258m), Braeriach (1296m)
Distance	34.5km (21.5 miles)
Ascent	2300m (7700ft)
Start/finish	Sugar Bowl car park, Glen More (NH 986 074)
Maximum altitude	1309m (4296ft) Ben Macdui
Terrain	Paths, often bouldery, sometimes vanishing on the plateau
Target time	1 day
Standard strong walker	12hrs

19 The Mourne Seven Sevens: All Northern Ireland's 7000m peaks

The hills	Slieves Donard (850m), Commedagh (767m); Slievelamagan (704m), Slieves Binnian (747m), Meelbeg (708m), Meelmore (704m), Bearnagh (739m)

Distance	38km (24 miles)
Ascent	2700m (9100ft)
Start/finish	Newcastle, County Down (J 374 306)
Terrain	Paths, some very steep, and a rough descent off Binnian
Target time	1 day
Standard strong walker	13hrs

20 Tranter's Walk: 18 Munros around Glen Nevis

The hills	18 Munros (3000-footers): Ben Nevis (1344m); Carn Mor Dearg (1223m), the Aonachs (1236m), the Grey Corries (1177m), the Mamores (1130m)
Distance	59km (37 miles)
Ascent	6200m (21,000ft)
Start/finish	Glen Nevis youth hostel (NN 128 718)
Terrain	High exposed rocky ridges
Target time	24hrs
Standard strong walker	25hrs

Ben Nevis the nice way: the Carn Mor Dearg Arête could add excitement to your recce day (Tranter's Walk)

INDEX

LISTING OF CICERONE GUIDES

For full and up-to-date information on our ever-expanding list of guides, please visit our website:
www.cicerone.co.uk.

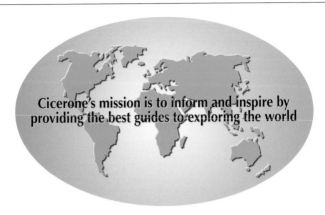

Cicerone's mission is to inform and inspire by providing the best guides to exploring the world

Since its foundation 40 years ago, Cicerone has specialised in publishing guidebooks and has built a reputation for quality and reliability. It now publishes nearly 300 guides to the major destinations for outdoor enthusiasts, including Europe, UK and the rest of the world.

Written by leading and committed specialists, Cicerone guides are recognised as the most authoritative. They are full of information, maps and illustrations so that the user can plan and complete a successful and safe trip or expedition – be it a long face climb, a walk over Lakeland fells, an alpine cycling tour, a Himalayan trek or a ramble in the countryside.

With a thorough introduction to assist planning, clear diagrams, maps and colour photographs to illustrate the terrain and route, and accurate and detailed text, Cicerone guides are designed for ease of use and access to the information.

If the facts on the ground change, or there is any aspect of a guide that you think we can improve, we are always delighted to hear from you.

Cicerone Press
2 Police Square Milnthorpe Cumbria LA7 7PY
Tel: 015395 62069 Fax: 015395 63417
info@cicerone.co.uk www.cicerone.co.uk